AF593638

THE SAILING AUSTRALIANS

THE SAILING AUSTRALIANS

TEXT: **BOB ROSS**

PHOTOGRAPHS: **MALCOLM GRAY**

LONDON:
ROBERT HALE & COMPANY

ADELAIDE:
RIGBY LIMITED

LONDON: ROBERT HALE & COMPANY
ADELAIDE: RIGBY LIMITED

First published in Great Britain 1974

Robert Hale & Company
63 Old Brompton Road
London SW7 3JU
ISBN 0 7091 4455 5
Printed in Hong Kong

CONTENTS

PREFACE

ONE WINTER'S DAY, Malcolm Gray and I were leaning on the bar of an Adelaide beach-front pub. We had been out sailing on St Vincent Gulf, testing a little cruising yacht for *Modern Boating* magazine. To the tune of the wind whistling dismally through the saloon bar shutters, Malcolm was expounding, with his usual enthusiasm, his idea of a book of pictures capturing the spirit of Australian yachting. He was dressed, as is his habit in summer and winter, in a pair of shorts and a tee shirt, trying to prove that the biting chill of the winter wind was only a state of mind that sailors could overcome with the power of thought.

I thawed out sufficiently after the third rum to really listen to what he was saying, and agreed to supply the words as Malcolm viewed the sailing scene, coast-to-coast through his salt-laden camera lens.

I don't know of anyone better qualified than Malcolm for the difficult task of capturing the emotions of sailing, from heart-thumping spinnaker rides on a wild day to drifting, with concentration on sail trim when it's quiet. He's an art teacher as well as a photographer and a sailor through and through. His camera shutter clicks to instinct as the subject boat jumps the wave or rolls crazily to windward. His inspiration has been St Vincent Gulf where the yachts thrash around on the big sou'west summer sea breezes, their sails backlit by the afternoon sun, clear green waters stirred almost constantly into steep whitecaps.

A Saturday afternoon for Malcolm means wading chest high through the small breakers tumbling on to the Adelaide beach at Largs or Glenelg, camera bag held over head, to join a bucking patrol boat; bouncing around after the yachts; trying, and failing, to keep the corrosive salt spray off his precious cameras. A camera rarely lasts out two seasons.

He'll never give up when he senses a picture possibility. During the world Flying Dutchman championship in Adelaide, on a day when the wind blew well over thirty knots and only a handful finished, he dragged me out some hours before the race in a sixteen-foot cruising sloop with a one-and-a-half horse-power British Seagull outboard puttering on the transom. We dawdled out to the windward mark and waited. Malcolm reasoned that the sea breeze would come in so strongly that the motor patrol boats would never make that windward mark once the race began. And he was right. From our cockleshell vantage point, he snapped great pictures of Rodney Pattison's *Superdocious* bursting through the waves, and was the only photographer to do so that day. He was all concentration as he steadied himself, and the long 400 mm lens, against the mad rolling action of our boat. Then he promptly collapsed, laughing with gleeful achievement on the cockpit floor, once he had his shot. It didn't matter that he was drenched with spray, bumped and bruised. He was high on photographic champagne that day and I had to argue to restrain him from hoisting full sail for a daredevil ride home afterwards.

So he packed his camera bag and went all over Australia, from Perth in the west to Brisbane in the east, to depict the sailors in action. He winkled them out from their haunts ashore; from the clubs, boatsheds, and waterfront pubs, as well as chasing them over the water. And his camera probed a dimension of yachting never really seen before, even by many of its devotees. It probed out the character of yachting.

5111

THE SCENE

THE NATURE OF THE Australian yachtsman is shaped by the winds that fan the 12,446-mile coastline of this island continent. In the southern States, the yachtsman is under the constant threat of a dangerous, icy blast from the earth-circling Roaring Forties. In the far north, he has to keep a weather eye for tropical cyclones. In between, there's the risk of a "buster" from both systems. But most summer weekends you'll find him sailing happily in firm, steady sea breezes, generated by the heat of the land mass. In summer, the only place thousands of Australians want to be is the water, either in or on it. At the weekend, they pour from the sweltering workaday cities, with their bikinis, boards, shorts, and thongs, to the beaches. And about 150,000 have graduated beyond this elementary communion with the sea to sail boats.

The sea breeze, sou'west in the west and south of the continent, or nor'east on the east coast, blows steady and true, usually from ten to a brisk fifteen and often to a more hair-raising twenty knots. So the Australian yachtsman is at his best in moderate to strong winds where muscles on the sheets, nerve with the spinnaker, skilled hands, and determination from skipper and crew are needed. He's not as good as the Europeans and Americans when it comes to light, drifting breezes where the twitching nose and the patient hand on the helm seek out the drafts of air that hardly seem to be there at all. He doesn't get the practice for it and hasn't the patience. But when the wind gets up and there's a hard slog to windward to be tackled, or a wild downwind ride under spinnaker, the Australian yachtsman is among the world's best.

The Australians didn't take on the world at yachting until after the second World War. Boats had been sailed and raced since the foundation of the colony but in the pre-war, pre-jet days, there was little thought of

FACING PAGE: An Australian Moth, perfectly controlled with full-length battens, shows off her hollow scow bottom

The Cherub pack converging on the gybe mark during an Australian championship in Adelaide

international competition. Gentlemen went yachting in yachts, predominantly of English design, with clubs having "Royal" charters. The rest went sailing in open boats like the loosely-restricted 12, 16, and 18 foot skiffs, or in locally-designed class boats like the VJ, VS, and Moth. The old distinction between yachting, as a sport practised by gentlemen in peaked caps and whites, and sailing, for scruffs in football jerseys, lingers on; even in an age where skiff hands move freely into the Olympic class yachts, ocean racers, and even America's Cup challengers sponsored by the Royals and other "posh" clubs.

But, helped by a keen administration anxious to weld the whole amorphous mass of the sport into a unified whole, yachting has probably become more emancipated in Australia than anywhere else. One of our best America's Cup crewmen is a truck driver. It will be an event when there is a truck driver in the famous-family lineup on an American Twelve.

International competition has done more than anything else to slash the social barriers from Australian yachting in recent years. Not surprisingly the deeds abroad of the Sturrocks, Northams, Hardys, Forbes, and Cuneos have helped many a youngster persuade his dad that he should go sailing.

Before and during the war, the only overseas sources of inspiration we youngsters had were the Manfred Curry and Uffa Fox books, and the occasional dog-eared copy of *Yachting* or some other English or American magazine. Then the English naval officer and designer, Captain John Illingworth, showed us how to ocean race by cleaning up the very first Sydney-Hobart fleet after persuading them to race. Three years later, Jock Sturrock and Len Fenton took a Star to sail in the British Olympics, and by 1956 Australia was able to field a full team to meet the world's best yachtsmen at the Melbourne Olympics. Sturrock won a bronze medal, and from then on the Olympic classes headed the outgoing modern mood of Australian yachting which other classes were also to take up. They quickly realised they had to compete against the world's best in off-Games years to have a hope of staying in the running when the Olympics came around. So, in these days, a steady stream of Olympic hopefuls find their way to Europe during the Australian off-season. Class associations help them raise the fares, and the cost of freighting their boats, by means of an interminable round of raffles, barbecues, dances, and gambling nights. The competitors knock heavily on the doors of business houses, airlines, and shipping companies for help. Except in the form of a grant to the Olympic team as a whole, there's no government assistance; but in Canada and some European countries, yachtsmen of proven ability are subsidised to compete in international events. Our yachtsmen raise their own funds the hard way, and the price of experience is high. The round-trip sailing expedition for a 20-foot Flying Dutchman two-man crew, will cost between $4,000 and $5,000 in fares, boat freight, and living expenses. They make personal sacrifices, selling their cars, mortgaging their houses, and taking second jobs just for the opportunity of competing against the world's best.

And it's becoming harder to keep up with the competition. In the late 1950s and early 1960s, Australian sailors, especially dinghy sailors, enjoyed a golden period. Accustomed to making their own fittings, or improving on the stock equipment they bought, they set the pace internationally with better boats and better rigs. Rolly Tasker—narrowly beaten at the 1956 Olympics by New Zealander, Peter Mander, who, like Tasker, made his own sails and fittings—won a world championship in the Flying Dutchman Class in 1958 and was runner-up in 1960. At this time, other international dinghy classes were catching on in Australia. A keen group of 505 class sailors in Adelaide sponsored a trip by Bryan Price and Chris Hough to the world championship at Larchmont, New York in 1963, and they won against sixty-two competitors from ten nations. They sailed a fibreglass hull, finished in wood by a talented young boat-builder, Dave Binks, with more than fifteen pieces of equipment they had designed themselves. A year later, another Adelaide skipper, John Parrington, with Chris Hough as crew, won the world championship at Cork in Ireland, again in a boat sponsored by the St Vincent Gulf 505 Association. On that trip, they secured the 1966 world championship for Adelaide. Jim Hardy, later famous as America's Cup skipper on *Gretel II*, with Max Whitnall as crew, won that championship from the mighty Dane, Paul Elvstrom, and many other European champions.

Australia won its first gold medal, in the 5.5 metre class at the 1964 Olympics, with a crafty oldster, Bill Northam, at the helm. A crew from near-neighbour New Zealand, Helmer Pedersen and Earl Wells, won the gold medal in the Flying Dutchman class at the same Olympics, only to be beaten by the Melbourne crew, Ian Twentyman and Ray Reynolds, in the Interdominion championship on Port Phillip Bay on the way home.

At that time, the down-under sailors seemed right at the top of the pile. Their techniques and equipment were copied by northern hemisphere sailors and Australian sailmakers and boat-fitting manufacturers built up strong export business. But the wheel turned. Yachting in Europe shook off its post-war malaise and the Europeans, with their intensive programme of top international racing throughout the summer, took over as the innovators. The British stopped being simply good sports but losers, and became winners. They were led first by John Oakeley and David Hunt, world Flying Dutchman champions in 1967, and then by Rodney Pattisson and Iain Macdonald-Smith, continuous world champions and Olympic champions until 1970 when, after winning the worlds in Adelaide, they split their combination. The FDs, fastest and most sophisticated monohull centreboard sailing craft afloat, pretty well set the pace for development in the other international dinghy classes. This has tended to make the Australians conscious of their problems of isolation from Europe and North America and, through the great distances they must travel between their own cities, from each other. But it's made those involved in international classes even more determined to jet to Europe.

This constant effort to climb the expensive miles to the northern hemisphere rewarded the Australians handsomely in the 1972 Olympic Games yachting regatta at Kiel, Germany. Dave Forbes with John Anderson as crew won the gold medal in the Star Class; John Cuneo with Tom Anderson (John Anderson's twin brother) and John Shaw were gold medal winners in the Dragon Class. Australia was the most successful sailing nation at the Games. The Australians were at the crest of the wave again.

Determination is the characteristic trait of the Australian yachtsman. Belonging to a sparsely-settled country on the other side of the world from the accepted centres of power, he is spurred with an aggressive desire to show the world he's as good as they are. This means that any Australian yachting crew making the great and costly effort of competing in the northern hemisphere is dedicated to winning. It was this approach that won the Admiral's Cup for Australia in 1967. The Australians went into the international offshore teams racing series, at their second attempt, completely organised. They practised together in home waters, then in difficult tides around the Isle of Wight where the Cup races are sailed, swapped information and ideas, and worked and planned as a

A Lightweight Sharpie picks her way across a leaden sea

team. They attacked the long races with the non-stop mental concentration and the physical effort of a short harbour race. The British, left floundering astern, and accustomed to treating the Admiral's Cup as just another jolly event within their great annual holiday picnic, Cowes Week, said the Australians took it all too seriously for the sake of sportsmanship. But by the time the next Admiral's Cup came around in 1969, the British had adopted the Australian approach.

A high-flying trapeze man works to keep a Lightweight Sharpie motoring to windward—without much assistance from the mainsheet hand

The America's Cup challenges were also fired by the national "show them we're as good" syndrome. Australians just won't accept that although America has held this most prized of all yachting trophies since 1851, it cannot be won from America. Through three challenges since 1962, we've shown ourselves more blindly determined than anyone, since Sir Thomas Lipton for Britain challenged five times between 1899 and 1930, to win this unwinnable pot. Unlike Sir Tommy, we're not particularly gracious losers. We'll accept a beating but won't swallow our tongues over anything we regard as unfair. So in both the 1967 and 1970 challenges, we disputed the measurement procedures before the racing and in 1970 sparked off a controversy—only history can erase the personal bitterness—over a protest decision by the New York Yacht Club, sitting as prosecutor, judge and jury, which disqualified *Gretel II* from the second race after she had finished first.

John Gilder, twice world champion in the 420 class

Another group of Australian sailors who won't take "No" for an answer are the catamaran sailors. Led by the Melbourne father-son design team of Charlie and Lindsay Cunningham, after three unsuccessful sorties, they won the international Catamaran Challenge Trophy (popularly known as the Little America's Cup) in Denmark in 1970. The winning crew, Bruce Proctor and Graham Candy, sailed *Quest III*. This was designed to a hull shape used by the Cunninghams over the three previous challenges.

Less spectacular classes have skirmished overseas and won world titles, sometimes to the surprise of their most ardent supporters back home. In 1968 Roger Byrne and Bill Binks won the world Jollyboat championship in America. Their club, Port Melbourne, was the only one in Australia sponsoring the eighteen-foot Jollyboat, and their Jollyboat Owners' Association, with 100 members, raised $2,500 to send the crew away. In 1969, young David ("Shorty") McKay, in a boat he built and mostly designed himself, won the world Moth Class championship in America. As the eleven-foot one-man Moths have long been a favourite with Australian youngsters, with about 900 of them on the water, Shorty's win was less unexpected. The following year, he successfully defended the trophy on Port Phillip Bay, Melbourne. That same year, Syd Lodge and John Bolton, of Perth, won the world championship in the Hornet Class. The Hornet is an English-designed sixteen-footer that is sailed in Perth and Melbourne but nowhere else in Australia. In 1968 Toni Redstone, sailing a borrowed boat with a borrowed crew, won the world Thunderbird Class championship at San Diego. Two years later, the Sydney fleet hosted the world championship for this twenty-six-foot class of plywood cruiser-racer and a local, Tony Parkes' *Moonraker II*, won it.

A team of three Australian 5.5 metre yachts went to Scandinavia in 1969 where one of them, *Pam*, skippered by Gordon Ingate, took off the Scandinavian Gold Cup in Norway. They enjoyed less success in the world championship which followed, in Sweden, but gained the right for Sydney to stage the world championship the following year. On the lumpy waters off Broken Bay, Dave Forbes, the 1968 Star Class Olympian steered a Sydney boat, Kevin McCann's *Carabella*, to a win over top competitors from Sweden, Norway, USA, and the Bahamas.

Later in 1970 an Adelaide crew, John Gilder and Doug Giles, after training heroically all winter on icy St Vincent Gulf, won the world championship for 420s (a fibreglass dinghy class, thirteen feet nine inches long, originating in France) at Tel Aviv.

Achieving a rare double, especially for this 19,000-strong class of boat, they won the world championship a second time, at Cherbourg, in 1971, where they faced a fleet of sixty from fourteen nations. Another Adelaide crew, Peter and Steven Sievewright, was runner-up. With a third

Australian crew, Greg Mellody and Sam Ross of Melbourne (seventh in the world championship), the Australians won a teams race series which preceded the world championship.

Gilder moved through well-worn paths in his early sailing career. From being a hopeful thirteen-year-old, sitting on the jetty at Royal Freshwater Bay Yacht Club, waiting for someone to be short of a crew on a fresh day, he gained a permanent berth in a Cadet Dinghy and then became a Cadet skipper.

He sailed in the Stonehaven Cup before moving on to Sharpies and sailing some races with Jack Cassidy in the 16-foot skiffs.

Then he went overseas for a time, sailing a Graduate for a season in England before moving to Canada where he was responsible for a brief surge of interest in the Australian Quickcat catamaran class. He built one to sail himself and, as a result, some fifty others were built there.

Eventually, he built a B-Lion cat. His catamaran sailing for the first time made him aware of the forces acting on a boat as it sails. Because of their speed, the effect of the apparent wind, which the speed of the boat itself creates, is magnified in cats.

Moving back to Australia and to Adelaide, he decided on the 420 as his next boat. He was starting a new job, in a new city, and did not have a great deal of time to put into sailing. The low-maintenance fibreglass 420, with its strict one-design rules and the promise of international competition, appealed to him.

Gilder and Giles turned up for the Tel Aviv world championship well prepared but without any idea of how 420s from other countries were rigged or sailed.

Gilder recalls: "We took delivery of our boat, one of 100 brand new boats supplied for the series by the Israeli Government, and hoisted our sails. A lot of the other competitors gathered around and laughed at them. But that afternoon, we joined in a tune-up race organised by the Israeli team. I missed the start by two minutes, mistaking the start gun for the prep gun. But we were second around the first mark, passed the leader down the first reaching leg and went away to win by four or five minutes. They didn't invite us to race with the team again. And we started to receive some very handsome offers for those 'crook' sails." The sails were just right for the quite lumpy sea conditions for which the European rigs were unsuitable. The Australians had more boat speed than anyone else and they could afford to use cautious tactics, playing the middle of the course going to windward.

They won their second world championship after a series of niggling disputes with the French measurer who didn't know his job, couldn't speak English, and didn't have the right equipment. Their boat was weighed five times in four days.

The 420 world championship was held in Adelaide in 1973 and again an Australian crew won. Finnish-born Anders Wangel, a professor of medicine at the University of Adelaide with Gilder's former crew Doug Giles, had a comfortable victory from crews representing eleven nations.

John Gilder concentrates on the wave pattern to gain maximum downwind drive while sailing his 420 in the Gulf of St Vincent

John Gilder was runner-up, and Australians swept the major placings with the best visitor, Jean Chaussade of France, back in tenth place.

Wangel's thirteen-year-old son Chris, with his mother as crew, was eighth. Young Chris almost won the Australian championship which preceded the world titles, after only four weeks in the 420 class. John Gilder won this championship by .3 of a point from Chris Wangel, with Anders Wangel third.

While the heroes of the sport have battled on the international scene, sailing has broadened and deepened its hold at home. The wonderful thing about this sport, or pastime if you approach it that way, is that you can follow it from the time you can walk, through a whole lifetime. You may take it as lightly or as seriously as you like. And, no matter how proficient you become, there's always something new to be learned or experienced. Some Australians embrace sailing when they are very young and not just as "crew" on parents' boats but as sailors in their own right. One six-year-old flew across the continent, from Sydney to

The Cherub class *Jazzer* with Jamie Wilmot at the helm, competing in the Australian championships in Perth

Perth, for an Australian championship in the eight-foot-seven-inch Manly Junior Class with his fifteen-year-old skipper. He stayed with a Perth family and, on returning home, proudly showed his parents a trophy won for being the youngest forward hand. And young Robert Wilmot, of Sydney, began crewing in Manly Juniors when he was four.

The Wilmots are a phenomenon of Australian junior sailing. There always seems to be a new one bobbing up in the results. Five of the six children are progressing through Manly Junior, Flying Ant, Cherub, Javelin, and Flying Dutchman classes. The eldest, Jamie, is a sailor of great promise although of slight stature because of a childhood illness. At eighteen years, weighing little more than seven stone, he began sailing a Flying Dutchman with, fortunately, a very large crew in Jim Cook, then aged nineteen. They began winning races right away, to the astonishment of some of the class's veterans, and in the 1972-73 season the pair were New South Wales champions. Jamie has won State and Australian titles in the Flying Ant Class, and State titles in the Cherub and Javelin classes. He presents a big grin from beneath a straw thatch of hair to the old lags of the class who try and "psycho" him before a big race, then tackles them on the water with complete confidence. His pretty teenaged sister, Jeanine, has won many races in the Flying Ants, Cherubs, and Javelins. She has won the world and Australian women's Cherub championships and the Interdominion Javelin championship. Her little sisters, Mandy and Rowena, sail a Cherub and a Flying Ant and Robert, the youngest, won the Australian Flying Ant title when he was nine. Their parents, Mr and Mrs Bob Wilmot, both sail too although they seem to spend most of their spare time at regattas, pushing youngsters' boats in and out of the water, and they help other people's children as well as their own.

The Manly Junior, an eight-foot-seven-inch, snub-nosed pram-type dinghy carrying mainsail, jib, and spinnaker is the strongest trainee class in Australia with more than 1,500 boats registered. Next in popularity is the eight-foot Sabot, with more than 1,200 registered. Many clubs run special instruction classes for boys and girls in these classes and, human nature being what it is, the youngsters are soon at it, racing as hard as anyone. After one Manly Junior championship in Sydney, the organisers were dismayed to receive fifteen protests alleging breaches of the racing rules. Some were lodged "because Dad said I should" but the majority were from youngsters who knew the rule book backwards. As with most junior sport, there is a loading of over-protective parents. Two brothers filled first and second placings at an important championship. The father roasted one son for not winning by more and the other for being beaten.

But it's thanks to the parents that the junior sailing classes are booming. A generation ago, most children could only begin sailing by pleading their way into a crew. These days, more parents can afford to put their children straight into sailing, with boats of their own. And sailing has become adopted by a number of schools as an official summer sport.

From the ruck of these trainee classes, the Australian youngsters can move into such good junior classes as the Moth, Flying Ant, Cherub, VJ, International Cadet, Thorpe 12, and Swinger.

The Moth, a one-man boat, has been the joy of young Australian yachtsmen since Len Morris, of Melbourne, first designed in 1928 its simple boxy scow shape, eleven feet long with eighty square feet of sail. Forty years later, with the Australian numbers reaching 1,000 boats, the Australian restrictions became the basis for new rules to make the Moth truly international. The Australian Moth has remained a scow, tremendously fast in our strong breezes, while in Europe and America the trend has been to a skiff-type hull which is superior in light winds. Because the restrictions are loose enough for exponents to pull designs around to suit themselves, the class has appealed to the experimenter and has led to some interesting refinements in hull shape and rig. But hulls have evolved mainly to the streamlined, moulded, concave-bottom type introduced by Peter Cole.

The Cherub, a restricted twelve-foot dinghy, was designed by a New Zealander, John Spencer, who was one of the first to realise the potential of lightweight plywood construction in big yachts as well as small dinghies. He designed a smaller version, the ten-foot-six-inch Flying Ant, and the bigger fourteen-foot Javelin, on the same lines.

The VJ, designed in 1931 by Rohu and Sparrow, is an eleven-foot-six-inch craft that the crew of two sit on, rather than in. It is fully enclosed and is kept upright with the help of swinging planks which enable the crew to extend their bodies right out over the water. Because it is simple to build, cheap, and fast, it won over thousands of Australian youngsters and at the height of its popularity claimed more than 3,000 boats. It still has a strong following, including yachtsmen in their thirties who claim they just haven't found a better boat to sail.

The pronounced dropout rate from junior classes, around the age of eighteen, has sailing club administrators worried. There are several reasons: pressure of school examinations, the lure of surfboard riding, and the secondhand motor car. But after a few years, the dropouts drift back and take on such exciting machines as the Lightweight Sharpie, a lean, light plywood version of the old European Twelve Square Metre Sharpie, Skate, Gwen 12, Rainbow, the 12, 16 or 18 foot skiffs, fourteen foot Javelin or restricted fourteen foot Dinghy, 505, Flying Dutchman, or the catamarans. The cats, which have shaken off old prejudices to become accepted by all sailors, have a progression of their own from trainer classes like the Arafura Cadet to the hot B and C class racing machines.

The high-performance dinghy scene is fragmented again, to the single-handed classes: Olympic Finn, OK Dinghy, and most recently, the Contender, just about the ultimate in one-man sailing speed designed by an Australian, Bob Miller. Bringing the concept of steering from the trapeze to singlehanded sailing, this long, flat sixteen-footer, reminiscent of the Flying Dutchman, won selection as an international class at trials conducted by the International Yacht Racing Union, against designs submitted from all over the world, in Holland, in 1968.

Many yachtsmen become too old for the high-performance dinghy classes—although some of the hardy ones never do. Roger Gale, of Sydney, was one of these and he was sailing Finns well into his fifties and winning races in twenty-knot breezes. The Australian racing yachtsman moves into such international one-design keelboat classes as the Dragon, Soling, Tempest, Star, or the non-Olympic plywood Diamonds.

The racing yachtsman may go into offshore racing or sail in one of the rapidly growing small cruiser-racer classes like the Endeavour 24, Thunderbird, Bluebird, or Hood 23. These small yachts, designed not only to be fast enough for racing but also to offer enough accommodation for an overnight race or weekend's cruising, are quickly winning popularity with the incentive of low-maintenance fibreglass hulls, a variety of new designs, more distance racing, and more organised class racing. The growing cost of buying and maintaining bigger yachts is helping, too. The Junior Offshore Group in Sydney, which administers the small offshore yacht of less than twenty-four foot waterline, has a steady increase in numbers of twenty per cent each year and had a record entry of seventy yachts for its annual interclub JOG Challenge Trophy races in 1973.

Big yachts are still being built, and raced hard by owners intent on winning a place in the Admiral's Cup team or taking out the Sydney-Hobart race. The millionaire yacht owners have turned almost entirely to ocean racing. The days of the beautifully-lined big metre yachts that used to grace our harbour waters are over. Congestion of small-boat traffic on our too-few sheltered waterways and soaring costs have slowly killed off big-yacht harbour racing although a handful of Eight-Metre yachts still battle out first division on Sydney Harbour and race

TOP: A Lightweight Sharpie gets out of control, with rudder right out of the water. BOTTOM: The boat has screwed up, but the crew has spilt wind from the spinnaker and the desperate-looking skipper has some rudder, and regains control

Cherub crews leap for the weather gunwale and survival, as spinnakers get away and boats stagger after the gybe mark

for line honours supremacy in Perth. The America's Cup keeps the Twelve Metres alive although they are raced only when crews are training for an America's Cup challenge. So the money scene has shifted very much to ocean racers. And with a new forty-eight footer costing up to $150,000 to launch, it's amazing that new, big offshore yachts continue to slide into the waters in such numbers.

Outside the natural cradle to the grave progression followed by many yachtsmen, a strong subsidiary movement to sailing has developed in small, modestly-canvassed and inexpensive "family" dinghies. First of this breed to take hold in Australia was the Heron, an eleven-foot-three-inch plywood boat designed by Jack Holt of England. There are about 3,000 of them sailing in Australia. Close behind in number is the Mirror Dinghy, with an estimated 2,500 boats, also designed by Holt as a project for the mass-circulation newspaper, the *London Daily Mirror*. It is possible to knock the Mirror Dinghy up at home from a pre-cut plywood kit, rig it, and launch it for less than $300. Following in the same strain are the bigger Holt designs, Enterprise, Lazy Es and GP14s, all with a good following in Australia, and some locally-designed ones like the moulded skiff type Flying 11 and the sheet-plywood Frisco. The fibreglass manufacturers, inspired by the popularity of the plywood family boats, have given us the 420, Corsair, Vagabond, Gipsy, and Sparrow. Frank Bethwaite, by taking a good Javelin hull, modifying it slightly and re-drawing the rig to eliminate trapeze power, gave us the most sophisticated family dinghy class of all, the Northbridge Senior 14, where the tuning-minded can fiddle to their heart's content without over-exerting their ageing tissues.

The common concept of all these boats is that they can be sailed and raced by father-and-son, husband-and-wife crews. They have opened the way to hundreds of middle-aged Australians, without previous sailing experience, into the sport. In them are to be found a number of dropouts from the more deadly-serious classes, who are finding new enjoyment by sailing with their families. Well, that's the beautiful theory. In practice, the beastly competitive urges turn many of these civilised people into sailing demons. Fathers reduce sons and wives to tears by yelling insults at them in the heat of a race, old friends fall out over protests, amateur builders labour to produce rule-beating hulls. But the scene as a whole is peaceful enough to soothe such frictions fairly quickly; son goes off and sails with someone else's dad, wives take over their own boats, the protest-happy ones get theirs as everyone learns the rules. Championships and regattas in these classes are usually jolly family affairs with steaks sizzling on barbecues after the racing and, if the regatta is in the country, there is camping by the boats with singing and socialising around the campfires at night. While they don't cost much, boats like the Heron give sailing pleasure to the broadest range of people. I once saw a Heron on a trailer behind a Bentley at St Kilda in Melbourne. Looked strange to me, but not to the surgeon who was keenly anticipating an afternoon of hard, wet slogging around a Port Phillip Bay course.

The scow-like Rainbow is a simple, popular Australian design. This one rolls her way downhill

An extension of the family dinghy concept is the trailer-sailer, a small yacht with a cabin, a couple of bunks, and a retractable metal centreplate which allows it to be hauled out of the water on to a trailer and taken home behind the family car after a day's sailing. The type was pioneered by Richard Hartley, the prolific New Zealand designer of boats that are suitable for amateur construction. In the late 1960s, the fibreglass manufacturers, inspired by Hartley's TS 16, first introduced to Australia in 1963 by the Mona Vale boatbuilders, H. and J. Griffin, suddenly saw its possibilities. The trailer-sailer was particularly suited to areas like St Vincent Gulf and Port Phillip Bay where moorings are hard to come by. By 1970, seventeen different types of trailer-sailer, from sixteen to twenty feet long, were on the Australian market.

FACING PAGE: Gwen 12 in perfect balance. Designed by Charlie Cunningham, the fast, seaworthy twelve-foot class remains popular with sailing Australians. THIS PAGE: *Judy*, an Adelaide Trailer-Sailer

The streamlined shape of the typical Australian scow-type Moth was evolved by the ingenuity of generations of young Australian sailors from the original Len Morris design

A major weakness of Australian sailing is that the number of classes, somewhere between sixty and seventy, spreads the talent thinly. And with great distances separating the major centres, it's difficult for the top competitors to meet more than once a year, when Australian championships are held. This can mean trailing a boat thousands of miles; from Brisbane to Perth, it is 3,315 miles by road, one way, and from Sydney to Perth, 2,668. But each summer, they pack up and do it. In Europe, they could have gone from London to Moscow and halfway back again for the same time it takes them to span the Australian continent, enjoying a yacht race at any one of a dozen regattas along the way. But, in this great empty country, there's little choice.

Sailors from different Australian locations are conditioned by their home-water conditions. Thus the Perth sailors, blown along most summer afternoons on the protected waters of the Swan River by a hard sea breeze, popularly known as the "Fremantle Doctor," excel in high winds but sometimes suffer from mast breakages and other equipment failures in the steep seas of Port Phillip Bay, or St Vincent Gulf. By getting to terms with these steep, short waves, the sailors from Melbourne and Adelaide are quite at home in lumpy waters. Everyone should experience the heart-catching shoots, dropping ten or fifteen feet down the face of a St Vincent Gulf wave, just once in their sailing lives. Hobart and Sydney sailors are attuned by both the high land surrounding their courses and the tides, to be good in shifty breezes and currents. The Queenslanders who work out on the short, choppy waters of Moreton Bay, where there is a wide range of breezes, are good all-rounders.

Besides the coastal locations, the inland waterways are claiming a growing number of sailors who go as far inland as the Menindee Lakes near Broken Hill, 735 miles from the sea, and as far up as the Snowy Mountain lakes, 3,000 feet above sea level. Country sailing calls for specialised skills. A Sydney friend, Kevin Shephard, recalls an inland regatta in Gwen 12s on Lake Keepit, 300 miles inland. A local farmer, who turned up with a boat rigged with fencing wire, but a highly-polished centreboard which gave him away as a sailor who knew what he was about, offered advice from under his broad-brimmed hat: "Stay away from them blackberry bushes, there's never any wind over there." The race began in a calm. Shephard and his crew, peering through their polaroids for the faintest catspaws of wind on the surface of the lake, were outstripped by the farmer who headed for the blackberry-bush shoreline and won by half an hour.

"Where did you pick that puff from?" they asked.

"I saw it coming down the gully," the farmer said.

"Come off it, how could you see wind before it reached the water?"

"By the cows turning around. They always face into the wind when they're eating grass."

"Really!" the Sydney sailors exclaimed.

"But don't be fooled by the horses. They always face the other way round, their tails to the wind." Shephard concluded: "That's the great thing about sailing. There's always something new to learn."

Bob Miller

"I've always been a dreamer and always shall be."

Bob Miller repairs a sail aboard *Apollo* after a Sydney-Hobart race

Bob Miller's story just about spans the whole sailing scene of the post-second World War generation. It's not typical, because there is only one Miller, so his story is larger than life for everyone except him. But all yachtsmen who were children at the war's end will identify elements of their own experiences within it.

At the age of thirty-six, in 1973, Miller had become Australian champion in the Soling Class, probably the toughest Australian championship of any to win. With partner, Craig Whitworth, he headed one of the country's biggest sail lofts (with allied boat fittings, spar-making, and design activities) and he had designed one internationally-recognised class, the Contender, and a string of successful ocean-racing yachts. He was also finishing the design of the 1974 America's Cup challenger, *Australis*. Not bad for an ex-apprentice fitter and turner who had to make it the hard way, in sailing and in business.

Bob Miller is a great natural talent. Perhaps it is just as well he is unfettered by too much formal education, for his free-running creative instincts just won't accept any proposition because someone else has said it is so. Winning sail shapes and hull shapes have flowed from his mind, sometimes weird as well as wonderful, and there have been failures as well as successes. But he's learned and succeeded by trying out all his ideas the hard way, in the great test tank of yacht racing competition.

"I've always been a dreamer, and I always shall be," is not an unexpected Miller confession.

His business partner, Craig Whitworth, who was formerly his sailing partner, is his opposite. A year younger, Craig is completely practical. He takes the Miller ideas and puts them to work, earning money for their company. Without Whitworth to anchor him firmly to the ground of reality, the Miller story might not have been a success story. Whitworth has a great deal of affection and respect for his partner: "Bob is one of the few really original thinkers I know. He can be involved in a problem, even right away from yachts, tune in on a separate conversation about it, and make one comment that will sum up the whole thing very clearly. But he has to have the environment that leaves him free to create, and there's where I come in."

Although Miller is a dreamer, he's no introvert but one of the great characters of the sport and everyone has a favourite Miller story. My own is about the time when he was reserve for the Australian Olympic team in Acapulco. He hired a very bad Mexican mariachi band to play in the posh Caletta Hotel, where the Olympic yachtsmen were staying.

"I picked them up at the bull fights on a special night they had for the very poor people," Miller said. "Their instruments were battered and they were bad, so bad they were good." Miller led the ragged band through the dining room of the Caletta, conducted them through a few numbers, and turned a dull evening into a riot. The tuba player was shut up at last by a heap of coins tossed into his instrument.

Enthusiasm for sailing bubbles constantly from Miller, punctuated by a good deal of arm-waving and eye-blinking. The latter is the result of a fall from a yacht mast in his youth. An interview with him is an emotional as well as an intellectual experience.

"I get mad ideas every day of my life," he told me, "and if I don't do some of them I go stale, I get sick to death of being alive."

Bob Miller is alive and well and, as I write this, engrossed in designing an America's Cup challenger for Alan Bond of Perth which at the same time would mean fulfilment of a life-time ambition.

Miller's first sailing memories are of model yachts at Newcastle, the industrial city 100 miles north of Sydney.

"There was a pool at the beach where the kids raced their toy boats. I hounded my grandmother until she bought me one. It had an iron keel and was solid oregon but used to fall over when the sail got wet. One of the boats had been made by a father and I thought if this other kid's father could make a boat, I could make one. I read some books by a famous old model designer called Daniels at the library and, with razor blades, a bunch of pins, and a tube of glue, made my own boat out of balsa.

"And I learned. I made a box-like sharpie out of sheet balsa but didn't put any rocker in the keel. It was bigger and lighter than my other boat, and had good sails but it wouldn't go. So I cut the sides and put a kink in the bottom and suddenly it sailed like a rocket. I realised then how important it was to have a boat designed correctly.

"Then my boats used to kill the other kids' boats, and I never played with them any more," Bob Miller said.

Apollo, heavily reefed during the 1969 Sydney-Hobart race

When he was about nine years old, Bob used to cross the Hunter River on a ferry to watch the VJs sail from the local club.

"I was too shy to push myself in, so I just watched. Being near them was a good thing for me. And one day a fellow took me out for a sail. I forget his name but he was a real nut. He was yelling at me all the way, 'avast' and 'belay' and everything else. But I was as happy as Larry because I went out on a boat.

"A kid called Eddie Harvey and I used to go down to the wharves, fishing, where the fishermen used to leave their boats. And we'd pinch their rowing boats, take out a broom and flour bag and blow around the harbour, then put the boat back. We'd get caught now and then and abused, but it seemed worth it. Or we'd go down to Lake Macquarie, hire a six-metre canoe for a couple of hours, paddle around the corner from the boatshed and then push up our own sail.

"I sailed 16-foot skiffs on the Hunter for a time. There was a move by the old skiffies to restore the boats that had been sailing before the war and I joined this old skiff called *Adele,* so old you could see through it. I spent a couple of years chucking lumps of water over the side.

"The first real yacht I ever saw called into Newcastle on a cruise from Sydney to Port Stephens. The crew let me look over her while they filled the water tanks. I begged them to take me with them, but they wouldn't and I followed the yacht with my bike, right out to the end of the breakwater. Then there was a race from Sydney to Newcastle, won by *Wings,* the thirty square metre. So I whizzed home, got out my balsa, and made models of thirty square metres. Then I made a really wonderful Daniels model, a Marblehead Class sloop that was so fast, I couldn't run around the pool at the beach before it bashed into the other end.

"So I used to catch the old train that ran once a day to Belmont to sail the model on Lake Macquarie. I built more models and eventually had half a dozen of them, with other kids racing them, and I'd be trying things on them all the time. I began to read up books with pictures of beautiful old boats in them and make balsa-planked models of the old cutters like *Shamrock*, with big bowsprits, topsails, and yards.

"Then I picked up a ride on a Vee Ess at Belmont one day. The owner was in the Merchant Navy, away a lot of the time, and I used to sail it when he wasn't there. It was old and heavy and I used to come last, but I was happy. In the end he gave me this old boat, which was called *Rendezvous*. I kept it for a few years and then decided to build myself a little yacht.

"By this time I was an apprentice fitter and turner with the railways. I'd tried to get a job as a boatbuilder with every yard in Newcastle; places that built lifeboats, rowing shells, sailing boats, and even the State Dockyard. But I couldn't get a job as an apprentice boatbuilder as I didn't have my intermediate certificate from school.

"I built this twenty-foot yacht in a backyard, under the inspiration of Uffa Fox. I used to read all his books because they were the only ones around at the time with pictures of recent yachts in them. I didn't have any money, so I couldn't put anything in it to make it strong. There were no frames and when anyone warned me it would fall to pieces I used to say it couldn't because it was 'all scientifically worked out.' And when I cast the lead, it exploded and went all over the yard. But it turned out to be pretty fast and in light weather I could beat the thirty square metre yachts on the lake, although I spent about as much time repairing it as sailing it.

"While I was beginning to believe that this boat was really good, the Stars came up from Sydney for an Easter regatta and I just couldn't burn them off. They were too fast and had too much sail, although I could beat them when it was blowing. Joe Adams, one of the Star blokes, was a bit impressed with my boat and asked me down to Sydney to sail in the Stars. I bought an old motor bike, just to ride the 100 miles to Sydney and Joe drove me around in his old Armstrong Siddeley. I was only about sixteen and the place filled me with wonder. I'd never seen so many magnificent yachts. I used to think the yachts at Lake Macquarie were beautiful but they were shoddy alongside some of those I saw that day.

"We went and saw the Stars, hanging up out of the water at Pittwater and met Ted Kaufman who was doing up his Star. He had some minor problems. His runners kept washing aft when they were freed off so that week I made some clips so that when you pushed the runner forward, it would automatically clip out of the way. I presented them to him next time I came to Sydney, and he invited me to sail with him. For a time I used to ride backwards and forwards to Sydney to sail with Ted, but in the end I had myself transferred in the railways to Sydney and went to live with Joe at Punchbowl. Ted won an Australian championship in Sydney, but we were beaten when we went down to Melbourne in 1956 for the Olympic trials.

"In the meantime, I met up with Carl Ryves. His father had built him a Star called *Pineapple*, a big heavy box with dirty old cotton sails, and I sometimes used to go over to Hunter's Hill and sail with Carl. Then I built a catamaran at Carl's place. I had a mad idea about cats being marvellous boats. Well, some of them are, but the one I built was a bloody awful thing, although Carl and I used to sail it all over the Harbour, racing ferries and anything else we could get near. Then Carl built his Flying Dutchman, one of the first ones in Sydney, and I used to sail with him occasionally when his regular crew was away. By then, I had left the railways and gone to work for Peter Cole, the sailmaker. Peter was my hero because he had been a great Vee Ess sailor, winning a lot of championships while I had my old Vee Ess. I sailed with Peter for a couple of years on a little ply yacht called *Avenger*.

"Norman Wright came down from Brisbane for the first Australian Flying Dutchman championship and persuaded me to go back with him and start sailmaking. Although the Brisbane scene wasn't as good as Norm had made it out to be, Norm was good for me because he would never put the kibosh on any idea I ever had, no matter how mad it was. He would always encourage me, taking the possibilities of an idea to the extreme all the time. While I was measuring up a forty-five footer for a new sail, I fell from the mast and hurt myself badly. I was in hospital for three months while my smashed back mended. Norm made me a drawing board I could use in bed, brought yachting magazines for me, and I virtually designed my first 18-footer, *Taipan,* while I was laid up in hospital.

"Norm, who had been world champion in the 18-footers, was always talking about them and his enthusiasm was infectious. But his Flying Dutchman could beat the Brisbane River 18s on the wind and I suggested we make it like a Dutchman, for three blokes with two on trapezes. And Norm said: 'Oh that's a terrific idea.' Although he might have thought it wouldn't work, he didn't say so. But he did persuade me to make a model before I built it, to look at and help assess the building problems [a practice Miller has followed with every subsequent design].

"I was obsessed with lightness, down to making the keel out of five sixteenths of an inch plywood and the frames out of three sixteenths of an inch plywood. The stringers sat on top of the plywood and the frames didn't touch the bottom of the boat. The best bit of timber in the thing was a grown ti-tree knee stem, from the same piece of wood Norm had built the stem of his last 18-footer, *Jenny.* He insisted I have something that was old-fashioned in the boat. Norm made me a mast out of Bunyah pine, and it was very light.

"Our first race came. I had a genoa, but borrowed Norm's Flying Dutchman mainsail, which was ridiculously small. And I remember, as plain as day, how all the other boats shot away from us, left me for last, and eventually the rudder gudgeon or something broke. They all laughed and poked off at me. I really got mad and that week with the help of Norm, who told me then that I had everything too light, strengthened the whole boat. He had let me find out for myself first. I made a mainsail and next weekend we just took off and led the fleet home by a full reach of the river, so far ahead you couldn't see another boat.

"I did very well that year on the Brisbane River. It was like Danish furniture that boat, and with hardly any fittings on it, although it was beautifully simple to work. But it had weaknesses which became apparent when we took it to New Zealand for the world championship. The Sydney experts were saying before we went that the boat was no good and the newspaper headlines were 'Revolutionary boat from Queensland kills 18-footer class' and all this garbage. And I thought, 'wait until I get you on the water, you bastards.'

"It's blowing hard in Auckland and they have a meeting just before the first race and say I've got to cut the deck off my boat. The rules said it had to be a half-decked boat, which I took to mean a boat with some deck on it but which they said meant exactly half the area of the boat could be decked and no more. Well, the deck was the only thing holding that boat together but Brin Wilson, the boatbuilder, loaned me his shed and I hacked the deck out. They all had lee cloths on their boats

ABOVE AND BELOW: A cherub competition in South Australia, conducted by the Henley Sailing Club

TINA OF MELBOURNE VIC.

LEFT: End of a race. Barry Scott, skipper of *Tina* of Melbourne, spreads out sails and waterproof gear to dry and wonders whether it's all been worthwhile. TOP: Cherubs racing in big seas during an Australian championship in Adelaide. BOTTOM: The crew goes for the spinnaker hoist in a tight mark-rounding situation during a Cherub race

Constitution Dock, haven for the battle-weary Sydney-Hobart fleet, is in the heart of Hobart. By day and night, hundreds of people stroll the quayside for a look at the yachts and the yachtsmen

TOP: The Royal Queensland Yacht Squadron's futuristic clubhouse at Manly, Brisbane. BOTTOM: End of a yachtsman's day

TOP: The Cherub, designed by John Spencer, a New Zealander, has become a status symbol among Australian teenagers. They have taken the twelve-foot speed machine to their hearts. BOTTOM: Sailing is no longer a "he-man" sport. Such girls as South Australia's Brenda Gameau, who sails in the Moth class, show championship skills and physical endurance

TOP: A crowded ferry follows an 18-footer race in Sydney. Up to 5,000 people follow the 18-footers on a good afternoon. Betting is illegal, but tolerated, and some bookies hire their own ferries for selected customers. BOTTOM: The "keg out the back" is still a feature of some of the less-wealthy small boat clubs

which had the same effect as much more deck than I had on my boat. So I covered the bow compartment with a lee cloth. But they made me take it off while the local boats and the Sydney boats had canvas right up to their masts. The Sydney crowd, not the New Zealanders, instigated all this and it really got me down. But we went out. It was blowing hard and in the big ebb tide on Auckland Harbour, every wave would half fill the boat with water. By a miracle, we didn't capsize and came third. We won one race in a medium wind, when the waves weren't so much of a problem, and in another the jib halyard broke and the mast fell down. I was too green and getting into trouble all the time on the course. My spinnakers were lousy, we could have carried bigger ones, but I hadn't the experience with 18-footers to know. So I went home with my tail between my legs but vowing that next time I'd make a super boat that would just wipe them all out.

"This new boat, *Venom*, was streamlined and very 'Manfred Curry' in style. I was so anxious to build it, I just drew the lines out full size on the sail loft floor and started to build from that, without drawing plans. Because I hadn't planned it properly, the boat took me forever to build. In the end I got sick of it and Norm finished it off.

"We won our first race on the river by miles. Craig Whitworth was sailing for'ard hand for me that year, with Norm Wright on the sheet. I met up with Craig through making the sails for his Gwen 12, and we became good friends. Although he hadn't started sailing seriously until he was about eighteen, he caught on very fast and was a smart and enthusiastic sailor.

"I'd tried to solve our spinnaker problem of the previous season by making a big Sharpie type spinnaker out of three-quarter ounce cloth. I made some really terrific spinnakers for the Sharpies at that time, round like the French Herbulot, but cut so that you could carry them really shy. This one was masthead, and double luff with a very simple method of gybing with rope snotters on the braces instead of clips.

"The world championship was held on the Brisbane River that year (1961) and the Sydney boats looked faster and better than ours with big sails of good quality. Where I had gone to New Zealand overconfident the year before, I was almost beaten before I started this time.

"We were waiting for the start of the first heat, all sitting in the bottom of the boat relaxing, when a puff came along and capsized us. She filled with water and sank, with about ten minutes to go to the starting gun. The other boats were all milling around and I didn't know what to do but Craig tied the spinnaker braces together and swam for the shore. And there he is, swimming away, and Normy and I are swimming, trying to tow the boat to the bank, and the current's washing us down river. Eventually, Craig begins floundering, and sinks, so we have to pull him back to the boat. So Normy and I get on the rope and swim, and finally we make the mud and bail the boat out.

"By now, the others had gone, out of sight around a bend in the river. It was blowing like hell, and we caught up to third place. But, after all that, they disqualified us for getting outside assistance because Craig had jumped ashore and grabbed a bucket from a guy to bail out the boat.

"So the next heat came, over the southeast course which included a tight reach and a square run around a bend in the river following the first windward beat. I didn't get a very good start, but we passed all the others except Lennie Heffernan. We came out on this shy reach, both of us going like the hammers of hell and we were keeping up with Lennie under our little flat spinnaker. We'd never used the big new spinnaker before, and as we reached the bend in the river I thought, boy, this is the time. So down with our little spinnaker and up with the big one. Boom. It filled and we were off, and I thought, we're through him. But Heffernan did the same thing; pulled down his flat spinnaker, hoisted a giant one, and hauled a ringtail up the leech of the main as well. But we went away from him just the same and ended up winning that championship.

"I took the boat down to Sydney one weekend for a race. Carl Ryves crewed for me, and some bloke who had never sailed before, but we beat them by twenty minutes or something. But the people on the ferry threw bottles and beer cans at me and said, 'Take the cheater back to Queensland' and all that sort of thing. I gave the 18s away after that. I'd proven my point and I didn't love sailing them. They were rotten to

Bob Miller and audience in Hobart

sail at that time because they treated you like racehorses; 'come up so-and-so' on the starting line to get all the boats away together, and so on.

"About this time, Craig Whitworth was offered the Royal Queensland Yacht Squadron's Flying Dutchman, *A.S. Huybers*. This was a German-built boat that Norm Wright had sailed in the 1960 Olympic trials. Craig was on the tiller, because it was his boat and I was bigger and therefore better for the trapeze.

"The boat was a bit run down and we restored it like a vintage car, spending a whole winter on it and making the blocks and other lightweight fittings you couldn't buy. In 1962, after we won the Australian championship and first Interdominion Flying Dutchman championship held on the Harbour, we decided to stay in Sydney and open up a sailmaking business." So that was Bob Miller's story.

Craig Whitworth, who had been working as a salesman for his father, a manufacturer's representative, takes up the tale: "We were at the presentation of trophies at the Royal Sydney Yacht Squadron when the idea of a sailmaking partnership in Sydney first occurred to me, and I had a yarn with Bob on the lawn outside. He said 'right oh' and a short time later we packed up our Volkswagens and headed for Sydney, with no idea of where or how we were going to start, and only a couple of hundred dollars between us. We searched everywhere for a loft and were at the really desperate stage when an agent told us of an old dance hall at Spit Junction. They wanted twenty dollars a week rent. It was more than we could afford and the hall was miles bigger than what we wanted. But we saw the landlord and offered him half price. He gave it to us and we were in business."

Miller and Whitworth did little sailing in the next two years while establishing the loft but when they did resume, they formed the best Flying Dutchman combination in the country, winning the Australian championship three times, plus an Interdominion and numerous State championships. They were as close a team afloat as they were ashore. Whitworth is a cool, calculating helmsman who leaves nothing to chance in preparing a boat and who has an all-consuming desire to win. He believes all his success in sailing has been due to the hours he has put beforehand into his boat and equipment, and to his determination to succeed on the water.

Miller, the natural, was an ideal trapeze man; lithe and as agile as a cat on the gunwale, moving restlessly to keep the boat on her best sailing lines, lightning fast in sheeting home the big overlapping genoa through a tack and in handling the spinnaker.

They pioneered a new style of thin aluminium mast for the FDs which later became popular with a number of other dinghy classes both in Australia and overseas.

The two men went to Europe in 1967 to watch Carl Ryves sail the *Contender* in the second International Yacht Racing Union single-handed dinghy trials. And they sailed themselves in the world 505 titles at La Baule (without success because their boat was a dud) and in the world FD championship at Montreal, also without success because they couldn't master the extremely light winds that characterised the series.

About that time, the design side of the Miller personality was emerging strongly. Encouraged by his success with the 18-footers, he did a few dinghy designs and even while he was working with Norm Wright was always drawing yachts which no one would build. Then Ted Kaufman came to him for help in designing his new forty-foot ocean racer, *Mercedes III*. Ted had firm ideas about how the profile of the boat should look, and that part of it was all his. Miller drew the lines and designed the keel. "The beautiful thing about that boat is its keel," Miller said. "It's a bit big, but beautifully streamlined and that was my bit."

Mercedes III, the first of a line of famous yachts built by Cec Quilkey of cold-moulded thin oregon skins, was a sensation; hardly ever beaten in her first season and top performer in the victorious 1967 Admiral's Cup team.

The *Contender* began as a "boxy sort of a boat" Miller built on the verandah of his house in 1967. Encouraged by Whitworth and a journalist friend, Lou d'Alpuget, who helped talk the manufacturer of Contender sailcloth, Silk and Textile Printers, into helping with the fares, Miller built a rounded version of the hard-chine hull. This, Carl Ryves sailed in the IYRU trials at La Baule, France. These trials were inconclusive because of the unreliable winds. Miller said: "We saw all the boats there and decided ours was the fastest in any sort of breeze but it didn't look seamanlike enough to be picked. So for the next trials I made the same basic shape, a little bit higher."

Craig Whitworth took *Contender* back to Europe in 1968 to win the trials at Medemblik in Holland. Then he and Miller followed through to set up the class rules and take all the other administrative steps necessary to eventually gain for the *Contender* official status from the IYRU as an international class.

Miller has since designed an eleven-foot fibreglass trainer on the same lines as the *Contender* called the *Swinger*. And he has a number of big yachts behind him now, including the fifty-eight foot light displacement ocean racer, *Apollo*, for Alan Bond. In 1969 when Miller and Whitworth moved from the old dance hall to new 12,000 square foot premises at Brookvale, a design office was added for Miller.

After a number of good boats, Miller in 1972 finally drew the lines of the yacht that established his reputation among the world's foremost designers. He murmured as she slid into the water: "That's the best one I have designed so far." The forty-five-foot yacht, *Ginkgo*, for Gary Bogard, soon justified his confidence. She won her first major offshore outing, the 350-mile Montague Island race, and then four of the five Admiral's Cup trials, beating the latest products of the world's most successful design office, Sparkman and Stephens of New York.

The design was intuitive—not tank tested—and original; relatively longer, narrower, and lighter than the fashionable Sparkman and Stephens boats.

Miller says: "I tried for a boat that will be at least equal to the others on the wind in shorter races and very fast downwind. After all, in most long ocean races you crack sheets whenever you can to gain distance towards the next wind change rather than point high."

It was *Ginkgo*'s spartan deck layout and accommodation plan that drew the inevitable fire from the "knockers" when she was launched. The deckline was flush and clean, broken only by a small cockpit for the winch-winding hands just aft of the mast, a cockpit for the helmsman right aft, a small square hatch between them to the main companionway below, and a large hatch forward of the mast for handling sails.

Miller had sailed on a similarly spartan racing machine in the Hobart race of 1971, the former United States' Twelve Metre *American Eagle,* converted to an ocean racer by Ted Turner. Miller explained: "Sailing on *American Eagle* last year showed me that the crew can stay on deck wringing wet and, provided they dress for it, it doesn't affect them. Once you have a little cabin to shelter behind, the crew tend to hide in the cabin and not do anything. On the *Eagle,* everyone on watch worked all the time. A fellow stood at the coffee grinder and he trimmed the genoa or the spinnaker continuously. On most ocean racers, people trim the sails and then go and jump in a box and hide. Or one guy might go around and trim while the others mag down the back of the boat, distracting the helmsmen."

The flush deck does more than give *Ginkgo* a streamlined appearance and keep her crew on the move. It allows the air flow to sweep smoothly around the bottom of the sails, unimpeded by superstructure.

Below, Miller designed one vast communal saloon cabin, strictly for racing only. To pass forward to the fo'c'sle, which is given over to sail stowage, and the toilet, the crewman drops on all fours and crawls through an enlarged "mousehole."

Miller himself sailed on *Ginkgo* in the 1972-73 season, with a crew of cronies from his earlier sailing days, to ensure his theories were properly translated into practice. His own driving force and the skill of the crew had much to do with *Ginkgo*'s success. *Apollo II,* an aluminium version of the same design, was built for Alan Bond to give Miller and the builders, Halvorsen, Morson, and Gowland, experience in aluminium. For the first time, aluminium construction was to be allowed in Twelve Metre yachts for the 1974 America's Cup challenge. *Apollo II,* under a good crew including Jim Hardy (*Gretel II*'s skipper in the 1970 America's Cup), Dave Forbes, Olympic gold medallist in the Star Class, and John Bertrand, Olympic Finn class representative (both with Hardy on *Gretel II*), was next best to *Ginkgo* in the Admiral's Cup trials. Third yacht in the team for England was Syd Fischer's four-year-old Sparkman and Stephens' champion *Ragamuffin,* its crown as Australia's champion ocean racer relinquished at last to *Ginkgo*.

Soon after the shift to the new Brookvale loft in 1969, Miller broke up his crewing partnership with Craig Whitworth. Craig kept on successfully for a time in the Flying Dutchman class, with Max Whitnall as crew, before moving into the new Olympic Tempest class. Miller, meantime, bought a share in a Soling with Ken Berkeley. "I'd had enough of being crew," Miller said, "and I was starting to tell the captain how to sail the boat. When you do that, it's time you were sailing one yourself again, so I went into the Solings."

He and Berkeley, with Dennis O'Neil who was former owner of the Admiral's Cup yacht *Koomooloo,* as crew clicked as a combination to win both the Australian championship and pre-Olympic trials in the 1970-71 season; the Australian championship and Olympic trials in the 1971-72 season. When Miller began sailing Solings, few believed his volatile temperament would allow him to be successful through the high-pressure grind of a championship series. He is still struggling with the demands on patience of light weather sailing, but in moderate to fresh winds Miller's ability to tune a rig and his aggressive sailing nature make him hard to beat.

Subconsciously, Miller is working on his designs all the time. A number of his boats have begun as doodles he has scratched while talking on the telephone. He once drew the lines of a successful 16-footer on an evening newspaper while drinking beer with friends in a pub—he is far more interested in boats than in beer-drinking.

He says: "I don't find designing hard, I like it. I like getting the germ of an idea and getting the thing under way. But I don't like working out all the detail and fiddly bits."

Miller doesn't feel he is held back as a designer by his lack of formal education. "I think it is an advantage," he says, "as you are not inhibited. I was lousy at maths at school. I hated school. I look at a lot of books but I never read them through, although if I see something in them that interests me, I'll read that. I don't even know what the metacentric shelf is. I know it's something about when the boat heels over, the buoyancy in the ends doesn't change. But I've never read an article about it as it bores me to tears."

Miller soaks up design ideas by sailing aboard the boats of other designers as well as his own. "The greatest teacher is to sail on a boat, analysing the characteristics its hull shape gives the boat. This way, you learn from every one you sail on, just as if you had designed them yourself."

He's deeply aware that the isolation of Australia from the northern hemisphere sailing scene is telling against our designers as well as our yachtsmen: "It's no good having an inspiration in this country unless you have the money to back it up yourself, because no one has the money to spend on an experimental design. We just haven't got the number of customers for our own design ideas to be proven and because people aren't rich enough to gamble, they go to the overseas Establishment designers like Olin Stephens. We're still a nation of copiers. What browns me off is that one day some fellow is going to win the America's Cup for Australia, and it will be someone like myself. And that guy will be saying to himself, 'I could have won that years ago if I had been given the opportunity.'"

Miller's pipe dream is a villa in Spain, a sail-loft which Australians can use as a base to sail in the European regattas, with a fleet of boats and beaten-up old cars and trailers ready and waiting for them. "The yacht racing scene is not here," he says. "It's fun but it's not the same as in Europe. If you want to be a super-competitor you feel it is all so futile. In Europe, if you are beaten say in the Dutch championship, you get another chance a week or two later in some other championship. But in Australia, once the national championship is over, you go down like a flat balloon until the following year."

But his real dream is to win the America's Cup: "I want to design the boat, be responsible for it being built, make the sails and the mast for it; not necessarily be helmsman but do everything else, just like a dictator. Dictatorships are lousy for running countries but they are the only way to achieve certain things. Germany had no good roads before Hitler and a Twelve Metre is a similar thing; you have to have one person in control of it from start to finish. And that person should be the captain of the boat or the designer who, if he can really sail well, will make instant decisions from experience."

The Sydney-Hobart race fleet at rest in Constitution Dock, Hobart

Bacardi, Sydney Harbour 18-footer, screams towards the finishing line at Clark Island

THE SKIFFIES

THE SKIPPER HISSED to the trapeze man: "Put your hand into his jib!"

The trapeze man pushed his hand into the jib of the boat just to windward. His own boat was fighting to keep her nose ahead and clear of the blanketing zone of the other's sails. The hand in the jib was meant to slow the other boat by spoiling the airflow around the sail.

"It's not working," said the skipper. "Push your head and shoulders in!"

The trapeze hand, a good crewman, did as he was told. There was a thud, he fell unconscious into the bottom of the boat. An alert hand in the other boat had belted the lump out of the jib with the spinnaker pole stump.

This happened in a 16-foot skiff State championship a couple of seasons ago and while the behaviour of both parties was less than gentlemanly, skiff sailing today is a long way removed from its roaring days of fifty years ago. Then the weapon would have more likely been a whisky demijohn, and the interference more likely to have been cutting away at the rigging of the other boat with a knife.

Skiff sailing began as a sport for the battlers of old Sydney town who couldn't afford the pleasures of yachting as practised by the gentlemen.

These days, the old discriminations have all but disappeared. The skiff sailor is just as likely to be a doctor, an accountant, or an architect. And, apart from the odd incident mentioned above, which is liable to happen in any big fleet of small sailing boats, they're really respectable citizens.

But skiff sailing is still a lively aspect of the sport.

For more than eighty years, the open sailing skiffs, treading a watery tightrope with gunwale only inches clear of the water rushing past, a cloud of sail overhead threatening to drive them under, have thrilled tourists and Sydneysiders alike. When the nor'easter comes in black on a Sunday, it's hard to resist dropping the lawnmower and rushing down to Bradley's Head or Point Piper to watch the 18s planing at speeds of up to twenty knots around courses which seem fiendishly designed to lure the skiffies into carrying bigger spinnakers than they really should. The inevitable capsizes are more serious than in other dinghy classes for the skiffs carry only enough buoyancy to float the boat and crew; not enough for them to be righted and sailed on again.

Developed from the waterman's clinker rowing skiffs which used to ply the landlocked Harbour last century, the skiffs, now divided into 18, 16, or 12 foot classes, seem an anachronism within the modern yachting scene. There's certainly nothing like them anywhere else in the world.

But today, they're more popular than at any other time during their history; mainly because the very loose restrictions on their hulls and rig have permitted all the latest ideas to be tried. They still take a lot of raw strength and courage to sail successfully but also provide an excellent proving ground for the experimenter in hull shape and rig.

And in what other boat, outside of the catamaran, can you expect rides of twenty knots under sail!

Forerunner of today's skiff classes was the 22-footer, adopted by the Sydney Flying Squadron when it was formed in 1890. They'd carry crews of up to twenty men, sitting in each other's laps on the weather gunwale under a spread of canvas of more than 3,000 square feet. *The Yachtsman's Guide to Sydney Harbour,* published in 1898, says that a crewman's experience in one of these boats "consists of hanging desperately out over the moulding, clutching a lifeline, with another man's head in his stomach. He can see nothing but a plunging sail above and a green, foaming abyss beneath. As the boat quivers and slashes along under the colossal sail pressure, a blinding flood of water comes tearing along the close-packed crew and he wonders for five seconds whether he is still above water or whether he should strike out manfully for the shore.

"This is a mighty fine sport but a wee thing damp. See *Irex* smashing to windward against a black nor'easter, there is nothing more beautiful in this world; but see her mainsheet hand five seconds too late in the jibe around Bradley's and you will get a fine view of that famous boat's bottom which is beautiful, but better where it belongs."

The remarks about *Irex* and her tardy sheet hand could be applied just as readily to *Travelodge, KB, Nock and Kirby,* or any number of today's 18-footers; except that they're up on top of the water, breaking the displacement barrier and planing to windward, three of the four crewmen (or in the three-handed boats everyone, including the skipper) balancing from the gunwale on trapeze wires, hurling every last ounce of their body weight against the tremendous forces imposed by the big sail area. Downwind, under a spinnaker of more than 1,000 square feet

This example of teamwork in a modern Sydney Harbour 18-foot skiff is a far cry from the great old sail carriers with their crews of up to sixteen hands virtually sitting in one another's laps. The crew of *Travelodge* has her under perfect trim under shy spinnaker. With another knot or two in the breeze, skipper Bobby Holmes who is hooked on to the trapeze wire, will hop out on to the gunwale as well

with a twenty-foot pole to be handled, the jibe around Bradley's is just as tricky as it was for the lamented *Irex*.

The modern 18-footer, although a much smaller boat in beam and every other respect than the great sail carriers of the old days, still has more sail than she should and remains a tremendous handling challenge. The earliest 18s, around the turn of the century, were nine feet in beam against the six feet of the modern boats, and carried main booms of up to thirty-two feet in length and bowsprits extending twenty feet over the bow. They were gaff rigged and had total sail areas of around 3,000 square feet, more than an America's Cup Twelve Metre carries down-wind. The extra sails included spinnakers set on booms up to forty-five feet long and assembled in sections, ballooners, topsails, ringtails, (extending the leech of mainsails), and watersails (set below the main-boom). This great spread of sail was kept upright by the weight of sixteen hands and the baler boy was one of the important hands aboard. The crew, some of them "shanghaied" on Saturday morning from waterfront pubs, sat double and treble banked in the waist of the boat. One or two men sat on the spinnaker pole when running.

These boats, which were still basically clinker rowing dinghies with sails, were killed by the seven-foot beam, *Aberdare,* the "Galloping Ghost" they called her, from Queensland, which thrashed in 1933 the big-beam Sydney Flying Squadron boats. *Aberdare* was timed over a measured mile on the Brisbane River at twenty-three knots. The Queenslanders had developed the seven-foot beam boats because they reckoned the old-timers were too heavy. The Flying Squadron barred them and this led to the formation of the N.S.W. 18-Footer Sailing League as a breakaway group, sailing seven-foot beam boats, in 1935. The new boats, of three eighths of an inch cedar planking, crewed by seven or eight men, eventually became completely accepted in Sydney until the late 1940s when Queensland again had a smaller boat built, this time of six-foot beam, and challenged the Sydney boats. After a good deal of argument, the six-foot beam boats were adopted by the Sydney Clubs in 1951.

The technique of building boats by gluing together plywood veneers over a mould, enabling much lighter boats than the old cedar-planked hulls with their 7,000 or so nails, was adopted officially in 1955. By then, the tall masts of the Bermudian rig had already replaced the gaff rig. Pacing these changes, crew numbers dropped to six for the earliest six-foot beam boats, to five, and then four, and finally three (for the first time, in Bob Miller's *Taipan,* 1960). In the 1952 world championship, the Australians first learned the art of trapezing from the crew of the boat sailed by New Zealander, Peter Mander, who won the championship that year with *Intrigue.* Now, even the four-handers sail with everyone on the wire, including the skipper when he's needed. He's still able to steer the boat with a long tiller extension.

The world championship, for the J. J. Giltinan Trophy, has never lived up to the ambitions of its title. But it has settled into a good yearly contest between the best 18s in Australia and New Zealand with occasional participation by boats from Fiji and more recently from the West Coast of America. When it was instituted in 1937, with a trophy presented by the then secretary of the N.S.W. 18-Footer Sailing League, James J. Giltinan, invitations were sent all around the world. Among those who replied indicating interest were the rival America's Cup skippers, Harold Vanderbilt of America and Tommy Sopwith of England. It was said that the unsettled atmosphere of Europe stopped them from competing when the championship was first held the following year. The championship has been dominated by the Sydney boats although the New Zealanders have won it six times, and the Queenslanders twice on their own Brisbane River.

There are still hopes of making the championship truly international. The Californian interest in them was sparked initially by Fred Ottis, an American yachtsman who married a Sydney girl. During the courtship, he became fascinated with the 18s. With the help of Alf Beashel, secretary of the League, the Californians bought four Sydney skiffs and, in 1969, three Sydney skiffs went to America to compete against the Californians in the Californian International Sea Festival, at Long Beach. A Californian crew headed by accomplished small-boat sailors, Roger Welsh and George Twist, competed in the 1970, 1971, and 1973 J. J. Giltinan Trophy races. But unfortunately the Queensland and New Zealand delegates combined to defeat a New South Wales move to have the 1972 world championship held in California. It was Brisbane's turn and they stuck out for it. Die-hard attitudes such as this have reacted against the progress of the skiffs right through their history.

That surface just isn't good enough until you can see to shave in it

Attempts are being made to found a racing fleet of 18s in England where Chris Eyre has been trying to interest British firms in sponsoring boats.

But Sydney remains the home of 18-foot skiff sailing. The cost of the boats and their liability to swamp in rough water have prevented development anywhere else in Australia but on the Brisbane River, and even there the class has been struggling to survive in recent years. However, the Sydney fleet of fifty is in a very healthy state. Many are sponsored by business houses and in return bear company names, such as *Gordon's Gin, Heuga Carpets, Corrigan's Express, Vogue Ties, Ansett Airlines, HyMix Concrete,* and *Century Battery,* with brand names and trademarks on their sails.

Betting on the 18s is a harmless-enough vice that spices the day for the crowds of up to 3,000 that might follow an important race. Betting is barred on the official spectator ferries organised by the clubs, but some bookmakers pick up those in the know with their own betting launches from various points around Sydney Harbour. The police used to raid the launches occasionally, but the bookies were often too slippery for them. One former bookmaker to the 18s is known all over Sydney as Dick the Diver, because of an epic swim he once made, with the betting slips in his mouth, to escape a police raid.

While there is prize money from the two poker-machine-equipped, licensed clubs, League and Squadron, no one is making any real money, above the cost of building and racing a boat, out of this sport. For a Sunday club race, the prizes are eighty dollars for first, thirty-eight dollars for second. Then there are eighteen, twelve, six, and two four dollar prizes. Everyone gets two dollars to start and two dollars to finish after eighth place. The club will pay the freight on the boat to go to Auckland and the fares of the crew, if it wins selection for a world championship. The prize money for the world championship winner is $100.

But against this, the boat will have cost up to $7,000 if it is a four-hander down to perhaps $4,000 for a three-hander. "Eighty-five per cent of the fleet is sponsored and that is really the only thing that's keeping the sport going," says Alf Beashel.

Building the hull, from cedar veneers for a total weight of less than 200 pounds, represents only one sixth of the cost. The rest is in the sails, mast, and rigging. Although flexible aluminium masts have given the skiff rigs more versatility to meet different breezes, the top four-handers still have three complete rigs for light-medium, medium-strong, and very strong winds. *Willie B* startled everyone when she appeared for the 1967-68 season with a thirty-six foot high mast. On this was set a 285-square-foot mainsail and 130-square-foot jib. The "intermediate" gear was 230-square-foot mainsail and 100-square-foot jib and the "small" gear, 175-square-foot mainsail and 65-square-foot jib.

A selection of up to five spinnakers is needed. The 1970 world champion, *Thomas Cameron,* carried four: 1,100-square-foot, 800-square-foot, and 500-square-foot parachutes, and a 240-square-foot flat-cut. The three-handers, lighter boats needing less sail, still carry two masts, two mainsails, and four jibs.

The struggle for supremacy between the three-handers and four-handers has been the main debating point around the boatsheds and clubs in recent seasons. The three-handers are extremely fast but extremely demanding with one less pair of hands in the boat. With their lighter weight in boat and crew, they'll jump out on top and plane to windward sooner in medium winds than the four-hander. But in light winds, the four-handers with their bigger sail areas still hold the edge and in fresh winds, with their greater manpower, they can handle spinnakers better. Dave Porter's *Aussie,* the outstanding three-hander of the 1970-71 season and probably the fastest skiff afloat, suffered from capsizes which robbed her of her chances in the big championships. Although she had an excellent crew, trained through the two-man, 12-foot skiffs, there were times when the boat was just too much for them. The three-handers finally triumphed when Denis Lehaney's *Nock and Kirby* won the Australian championship in 1972.

Bobby Holmes, by far the most successful skipper of the modern era of 18-foot sailing, favours the four-hander—partly because he weighs only ten-stone wringing wet, but also because he graduated to the 18s from the four-man 16-foot skiffs. In 1973, Holmes, thirty-three, won the J. J. Giltinan Trophy for the fifth time. Only two others, Ken Beashel and Peter Mander, had even managed to win it twice. He was sailing a new boat called *Travelodge,* designed by the young Aucklander Bruce Farr who created a record of his own by designing the first four boats. After *Travelodge* came *KB* (Dave Porter), *Smirnoff* (Don Lidgard, New Zealand), and *Travelodge International* (Roger Welsh, USA).

Holmes previously won the trophy in 1965, 1966, 1969, and 1971, all in previous "editions" of *Travelodge.* His boats have been fully sponsored by the Travelodge motel chain which pioneered a new hard-nosed approach to sponsorship. Sponsorships of 18-footers had usually been with companies subsidising dollar-for-dollar money spent by the owner. But Travelodge's chairman and managing director, Alan Greenway, had different ideas when he went looking for an 18-footer to sponsor in 1964. He sat in the front of his Darling Point home, overlooking Sydney Harbour, Sunday after Sunday, clocking the 18s with a stopwatch. He settled on *Schemer,* skippered by Holmes, as the best performer and most-reliably-sailed boat. So Travelodge bought *Schemer* from its owner Bennie Walsh, renamed it *Travelodge,* and signed on Bob Holmes to skipper it and provide a crew. Unlike most sponsors, Greenway was not content just to have his company's name on the sail of an 18 as a floating billboard. He was determined that the money invested in the 18-footer should show a direct return, in results.

That approach, which had fully financed Holmes through four different *Travelodge* skiffs by 1973, paid its dividend. Greenway said: "If you are putting up a billboard, you select the best location for it. If Bob Holmes was not a good skipper and did not keep on winning, we would get another skipper or get right out of 18-footer sailing. Winning is important."

For Holmes, the arrangement has been ideal. Running the boat is left entirely to him, although Alan Greenway takes a keen interest, down to timing leading boats around each mark and presenting Holmes with a relative performance graph at the end of the race. Holmes is so involved in his yacht-broking business and with his family of three children that only the encouragement of this dream sponsorship keeps him in the sport at all.

He felt, after his 1973 win, that he should probably retire from 18-foot sailing and concentrate on his work. But he will not: "They're hard boats to give up because they get a grip on you. After you have been sailing all sorts of yachts, good ones and bad, on demonstrations for customers all week and you get out on that 18 on a Sunday . . . it's a bit like stepping into a Formula One racing car after driving a cab."

"The modern 18s go really fast to windward and point high," Holmes says, "and the competition is so keen you have just got to go for that biggest possible spinnaker all the time [*Travelodge*'s biggest is 1300 square feet, as big as that carried on a forty-five-foot ocean racer]. There's only one way to learn how to handle big spinnakers; put them up and see what happens. We broke a mast early in the season. It was a bit stupid but we cracked the number three spinnaker, about 550 square feet, in forty knots of wind. The boat was really going and then we hit a sea and the mast just went, boom, straight over the bow."

Holmes and crew, his brother Bill, Barry Norbis, and Phil Croll—work hard for their wins. They're in the gymnasium twice a week and spend every spare daylight hour during the summer preparing and maintaining their boat, and practising. They have to, to stay ahead of the rising standard of competition. Dave Porter in *KB*, a three-hander fully sponsored by Tooths Brewery, was their hottest opponent in the 1972-73 season. In one test race, to select the New South Wales team for the Australian championship, *Travelodge* and *KB* were never more than fifteen seconds apart around the fourteen-mile course. *KB* won.

Alf Beashel, secretary of the New South Wales' 18-footer Sailing League, and the foremost authority on the 18s, said of Holmes: "He's successful because he takes in everything that is happening around him, all the time. His mind runs ahead in anticipation of the next situation and his tactics are always correct. Because he sailed in 16-foot skiffs before the 18s, his reflexes are very sharp. He's got the knack of carrying big spinnakers because he can lift the boat out of danger with speed. Often it's only the speed of the boat that's stopping it from capsizing."

While the 18s attract the spectators and the publicity, the strongest class within the skiff movement is the 16s. In the 1970-71 season, the registered number of 16s in New South Wales exceeded 300 for the first time. There are smaller fleets in Western Australia and Queensland.

Although their restrictions, like those of the 18s, offer wide variation in hull shape and sail plan, the top boats have evolved to fairly similar ideas and racing at championship level is very close. Restricted to a total 220 square feet of working sail and a maximum spinnaker size of 140 square feet, the 16s can still beat the 18s in some conditions.

They carry a crew of four, although there are moves to allow three-man crews. But the administrators are reluctant to change rules that were first framed in the 1900s. These have allowed the class to develop through individual ideas on hull shape, rig, and division of sail area between main and jib, to a very fast dinghy, able to hold its own with any of the modern international designs.

The class was founded in 1901 by a small group of enthusiasts at Balmain, Sydney. It spread to Queensland and by 1908 enough boats

Homeward run for 16-foot skiffs from the wide reaches of Botany Bay, with *Honest John* in the lead. The 18-footers get the publicity, but the 16-foot skiffs are the most popular with sailors. More than 300 race in New South Wales alone

TOP: This is what modern 18-footer sailing is all about: three men on trapeze wires, and boat and rig so powerful and efficient that it planes all round the course in a fresh breeze, even to windward. BOTTOM: The big spinnakers of 18-footers are the crew's despair and spectators' delight. Sometimes there's not enough wind to fill the sail and the boat can sail straight through its middle. RIGHT: Ted Heath and his crew sort out their sails and congratulatory telegrams at the end of the 1969 Sydney–Hobart race, and Trygve Halvorsen, five times winner of the race (white sweater) shares their elation

The Royal South Australian Yacht Squadron's handicap fleet races from Outer Harbor. Many of South Australia's big yacht fleet are members of the Squadron

TOP: The seas off Sydney Heads often are lumpy and leaden, confused by the backwash from the ocean swell breaking on the cliffs. This Southern Cross Cup competitor was stood on her nose by a "greenie." BOTTOM: A Perth yacht tugs at her stern wave during a solid spinnaker ride during the Cockburn Sound regatta

One of South Australia's keenest offshore yachtsman, Joska Grubic, has built a series of steel yachts, each bigger than its predecessor. This is *Adria,* a forty-five-footer, on the Gulf of St Vincent

were racing there for the first Australian championship to be sailed in Brisbane. This was won by H. Roderick of New South Wales, sailing *Minoru*.

After the first World War the class spread to Western Australia. An attempt to introduce it to Port Phillip Bay after the second World War lived just long enough for an Australian championship to be held there in the 1949-50 season. But during the fifties, the skiffs disappeared from these unfriendly waters. It was just too rough for such open boats.

Hull shapes changed from the round-bilge boat, dictated by the fore-and-aft clinker and then carvel planking of pre-second World War days to hard-chine, after plywood became accepted for boatbuilding. The next development was a combination of fine-entry round bilge forward and a firming to hard-chine aft. This is the most popular hull form of the present time.

The rig has settled into an efficient, modern, high-aspect sail plan with 165 square feet in the main and 55 square feet in the jib being the common choice in apportioning the total 220-square-foot sail area allowed.

A boat capable of winning an important championship will cost between $2,000 and $2,500 and have a constant outlay on new sails. Most of the top boats have three suits of working sails covering up to eighteen knots, eighteen to twenty-five knots, and over twenty-five knot wind ranges plus three big spinnakers, two small spinnakers, a reaching jib, and probably three masts.

In New South Wales, the class is backed by some very strong licensed clubs, all with poker machines crashing away Las Vegas style, and this means some of the skiffies get their sailing cheaply. It's usual for a boat winning through zone and State and eliminations to receive from the club a grant of from $500 to $800, if it means travelling to Perth from Sydney, to compete in a national championship. This would cover the cost of boat freight, train fares, and even leave over some beer money. The Belmont Club, on Lake Macquarie in New South Wales, puts on a "champion of champions" race at the beginning of each season and top boats from all over the country are invited to compete for a cash prize of $500. One prominent crew was able to make enough in a season it began by winning the Belmont $500, with other prize money, to finance a brand new skiff for the following season. But such stories are rare. For the championship aspirant, the game is still a very costly one.

The plodder, who doesn't hope to win a championship, can still enjoy very cheap handicap racing. His boat is housed inside the club, rent free; the average handicap race carries a first prize of twenty-five dollars, and minor prizes of fifteen, ten and five dollars. And he's on three dollars starting and three dollars finishing money. Backing his sailing he has all the social amenities of a licensed club, including first-class but cheap restaurant meals and entertainment, often by top overseas performers. All that's lacking from this rosy picture is any real incentive to improve sailing performance. The clubs are vast: Drummoyne has a member-

FACING PAGE: A 16-footer on a screaming run across the Swan River, Perth. Note the mast bent under pressure from the spinnaker

ship of nearly 3,500, George's River more than 2,500, and Belmont 2,000. A good many of the members are purely social, enjoying the facilities of a typical Sydney poker-machine-financed club. But this means the sailors belonging to them enjoy amenities no other yacht clubs can afford.

Despite the popularity of the skiffs in New South Wales, there have been strong recent moves for a change from four-man to three-man boats. Jack Cassidy from Western Australia, where the fleet of twenty or so is struggling to survive through the cost of boats and the difficulty of getting good crews, has been a main proponent. Ken Beashel, of Sydney, and Nev Buckley, of Brisbane, have been working on preparing designs to Cassidy's ideas. Supporters of the four-hand restriction say it helps put more people on the water. They explain that many of these are youngsters whose size and agility are suited to 16s and that the four-hand restriction encourages team work in a crew. Those who believe the three-handers must come, point out that the trapeze has virtually meant the end of a big man in a 16-foot skiff crew. The six-footer and fourteen-stoner, once much in demand, finds the boat too small for him and a lad three stone lighter, balancing from the gunwale on a trapeze wire, can exert the same swinging power.

The other great controversy of recent years has been whether or not to adopt the International Yacht Racing Union rules instead of the antiquated skiff racing rules. The old rules make for mayhem on starting lines since there are no general recalls for early starters provided and the rules are vague on some right-of-way situations. On a motion by Western Australia, the IYRU rules were adopted as the Australian skiff rules in 1970, although the skiffs did retain some of their own rules as well. Then, in New South Wales, the decision was reversed and racing in that State continued under the old rules. The IRYU rules were adopted again in a modified fashion in 1972 with the sort of compromise decision that reflects the constant conflict between the new and the old in the skiff classes.

The smallest breed of skiff and liveliest of all is the 12-footer; it is peculiar to six clubs in Sydney and to an outpost on the Brisbane River. But this boat is gaining numbers, mainly through introduction of fibreglass hulls that are not allowed in the other skiff classes. The fibreglass hull has brought the cost within reach of the younger sailors. About 60 of the 150 skiffs sailing with the Sydney clubs are fibreglass. They are restricted to an overall length of between eleven feet eleven inches and twelve feet, with a maximum beam of five feet and any amount of sail you care to cram on, although the combination of 120 square feet in the main and 60 feet in the jib seems to be about the most successful. But big 500-square-foot running spinnakers are carried with one massive 800-square-footer making an occasional and usually disastrous appearance. They cost less than $1,000, ready to sail, but give their money's worth in action. One 12-footer was clocked at better than twenty miles per hour during a sustained one-mile planing burst on the Brisbane River in a championship at Easter, 1971.

They've changed, too, since the old days. In the 1920s, 12-foot skiffs racing at Greenwich, Lane Cove, the Spit, and Vaucluse carried more than 300 square feet in their working sails, plus spinnaker and balloon jib, and were sailed by four or five hands. Bowsprits protruded eight feet from the stem and booms extended six feet or more over the transom. Just after the second World War, the boats were sailed by three hands, but still with gaff rig. Around 1950, Ken Minter rigged *Joan* with trapeze and now all skiffs are sailed by two hands, with one or both on trapeze.

In the mid-fifties, the 12-foot skiffs permitted buoyancy to be carried so that the boats could be righted after a capsize.

The first Interdominion championship, for the Silasec Trophy, was held with the New Zealanders in 1956 and continues annually, alternating between Auckland and Sydney.

Dennis Dignam launched the first fibreglass skiff, *Venture*, in 1968, and these fibreglass hulls, costing just over $305 against a wooden moulded boat's $550, have kept him busy building ever since.

While the class is mainly stocked with teenagers, there are some greyhairs. Dennis was one and at forty-two he was content crewing for his fifteen-year-old son Darryl who is a former national champion in the Sabot class.

Ken Beashel

"Send her."

WHEN BEASHO TOLD ME, in his description of how he had won a Soling Class race, that he had run up the mast to free a jammed spinnaker, I was not surprised.

Ken Beashel, third-generation sailor, boatbuilder, designer, is that sort of a guy. I've watched him run out along 12 metre mainbooms and set a spinnaker on a 5.5 metre he happened to be steering. I'm sure if he thought running across the water behind it would somehow make a boat go faster, Beasho could do it.

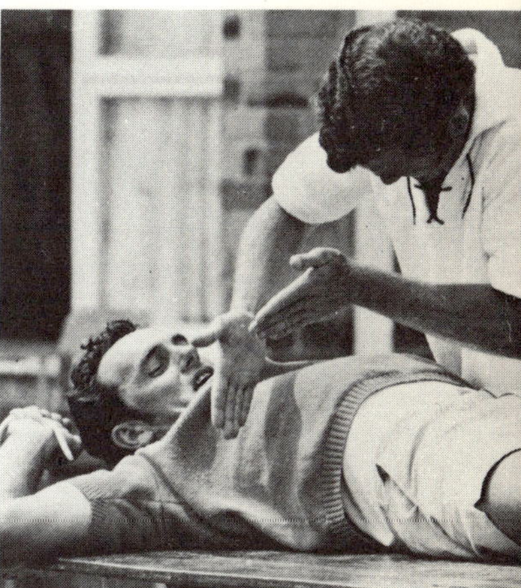

A massage for Ken Beashel during an interval in the 16-foot skiff championships at Perth

The mast-climbing came towards the end of a race in the 1971 Pre-Olympic trials on Port Phillip Bay. Beashel was steering the Soling *Silver Mist* that was owned by his friend, Lindsay Allsop. He had a handy lead at the end of the square run and only the beat to the finish to go. The internal halyard jammed as the spinnaker was being lowered. So they reached the mark with the spinnaker half up, half down, with the prospect of losing the race to one of the pack surfing down on them from astern. Beasho passed the tiller to crewman, Kendall Barrie-Cotter, snapped a few instructions to Allsop, and went for the mast. The crew had to keep the boat heeled at just the right angle in the fresh breeze to allow Beashel to walk up the mast, unclip the spinnaker from the halyard (a job requiring two hands), regain the boat, and sail on. They lost only half of their fifty-yard lead during the whole operation.

Although at thirty-four, Ken Beashel had forsaken his beloved 16-foot skiffs to sail in the Olympic Soling class, he was still a skiffie at his nerve ends, a quick thinker, and a rapid mover in a boat.

He says: "I've found out, since I've been out of the skiffs and sailing slower boats, that you have much more time to think. In skiffs, you have very little time to think and make a decision. And it's the guy that makes the right decision at the right time that wins. You've just got to be aggressive."

Ken Beashel has twice won the "world" 18-foot skiff championship and he has won the Australian 16-foot skiff championship once. He regards this second achievement as the most important one. When Ken talks of a skiff, he means a 16-foot skiff, nothing else. And although his main ambition now is to win a world championship in an international class, like the Soling, the skiff is still his favourite boat.

Ken Beashel leads an enviable life that has been built around his love of sailing. He owns a small boatbuilding yard at Elvina Bay and, with his understanding wife, Barbara, and their three children, he lives on the hillside above the bay in a house that commands a view right down beautiful Pittwater. He devotes most of his spare time to sailing. His favourite "rig" around the home and the yard is a clean white singlet, shorts, and no shoes. His three favourite words are "Let's go sailing" and when he's sailing a fast-planing skiff, his war-cry to the crew is: "Send her."

He has an instinct for knowing which hull shapes are fast and he knows how to tune a rig to perfection in a very short time. For years, it was something of a standing joke that any new skiff Beasho launched for himself would always be late. It would be rigged for the first time on the beach the morning before an important race, and then probably go out and win, or go close to winning.

Legend has it that he was a bit of a wild man ashore in his time; it's said he once wandered out to collect an important trophy at a prize-giving, putting out one hand while munching a meat pie from the other.

And there was the time, when rammed by an Air Force "crash" launch during an 18-foot world championship in Auckland, that Beasho swarmed up the launch's stem like a buccaneer and took a swipe at the coxswain.

Nowadays, Beasho is a gentleman, respected and liked by sailing competitors and business acquaintances. His ability to "send" any type of boat has become well recognised in the sport, and he's in demand to sail aboard ocean racers and other big yachts.

First of the sailing Beashels was Ken's grandfather, Dick Beashel, who owned both 18-foot and 16-foot skiffs when they began racing as a class in Sydney in the early 1900s.

"Those old timers," Ken said, "knew a lot more about sailing than they're given credit for. Back in 1915, they were up with bendy spars; they used to bend their gaffs up to thirteen inches to set their sails, and they had things like headboards in spinnakers, headboards in jibs, and even clew-boards in jibs, which have only just come back into vogue in the modern classes.

"And they knew about wind and weather. My grandfather could predict perfectly, to the quarter hour, the prevailing wind for the day. Without aids like the trapeze, they had to know more precisely what the wind would do so they could select the appropriate-sized sails for the day.

A 16-foot skiff race at Brisbane. The skiff rig, under restrictions laid down early this century, has developed into a modern, highly-efficient form. The through battens, which add stability and control to the mainsail especially in the upper roach area, are popular in New Zealand and Australia but less favoured elsewhere

"On the 18-footers, they used to have up to sixteen men in the crew, and that number took some recruiting. My grandfather used to put on a five-gallon keg every Friday night. Those who turned up would be shangaied to sail in the Squadron race next day." Ken further said of his grandfather: "He lived only for sailing and was a great seaman."

Ken Beashel has a healthy respect for the administrators who framed the 16-foot skiff rules in 1908: "They had a lot of brains, or were just plain lucky. They selected hull measurements and a sail plan that have remained popular right to the present day because they still meet modern concepts of sailing. Even with the trapeze, the sail plan is still right for the hull."

Ken's father, Alf, a good sailor but not a champion, has devoted his life to the administration of the sport and is at present secretary of the N.S.W. 18-Footer Sailing League. As a child, Ken used to go down to the League club at Double Bay, Sydney, with his father and out on the pickup launch. When he was ten he sailed with his father before gaining a berth on a 12-footer.

"Then I crewed on the 16s as well and for about three years was sailing in the 16s on Saturday, 12-footers on Sunday morning, and in an 18 on Sunday afternoon. I never really liked crewing in the 18s because it was such hard, bullocking work. But gee, they had their moments.

"I'll never forget one day watching Cliffie Monkhouse running almost out of control through the tight-packed bunch of moored boats in Double Bay. We used to finish on the first line of moorings and in a particularly close downwind finish before a fresh breeze one day, he was caught with the lot up—peakhead spinnaker and ringtail, unable to touch anything because the boat was nearly out of control, carting through all those moored boats.

"But Cliffie handled her brilliantly, the crew pulled up the centreboard and she tore right up the beach," he remembered.

Ken Beashel built his first boat, a cadet dinghy, to race with the Double Bay 12-footer club.

"And then the VSs came into their own and I sailed some races with Peter Cole, who was champion at the time, in his *Avenger Too*. I set myself up to build one, but before I started gave it up. 'I'm not going to build a chine box,' I told myself, and built a planked skiff instead."

Ken was fifteen then and has since built dozens of boats; many, for himself, at home. "I've built a boat in every room of the house," he once told me. "Even the bathroom."

As soon as he was able to leave school, Ken took up an apprenticeship with a boatbuilder; with Pritchards first and then with Georgie Riddell. He worked on such big yachts as the ten-metre *Even*.

His own ideas on dinghy hull shapes were firming. He built up a good crew and in the 1961-62 season they won the Australian 16-foot skiff championship at Brisbane. Then next season, Beashel and his crew, Hughie Cook, Ronnie Powell, and Bob Hagley went into the 18s and won the world championship in Auckland in *Schemer*. This was a boat designed by Len Heffernan.

"We had gone bad in skiffs the year after our win in Brisbane," Beashel said. "I bought out a bomb design that wasn't any good, and someone came along and asked us to sail an 18. I felt I owed it to Dad to try, and the 18s were beginning to go modern then, and weren't such a bad boat to sail. *Schemer* was about the first in Sydney to have a proper overlapping headsail and she used to speed.

"As skipper, I'd sit on the sheet. You'd wind that headsail on, down through the block, and suddenly it'd pop the mainsail out of the way and the whole boat would slip into gear and take off. You'd have to hang on with your spare hand on the wind, the acceleration was that sudden."

Schemer was a superior boat in the mainly fresh breeze series in Auckland and she won comfortably; she would have won by more had it not been for the famous encounter with the crash boat. This is how Beashel recalls it:

"Three-quarters of the race was over and we were flying, set for another win. An Air Force crash boat was following us closely with TV cameras on top. We reached the layline to the next mark and I wanted to tack. I waved the boat back. Although they were close, I knew there were a few sailing guys on the boat who were intelligent enough to know we were on the layline. The boat kept coming and I thought 'fair enough,' they might want a close-up, and tacked. We were no sooner settled on the new tack when they rammed us amidships, putting their stem right through the mainsail.

"I found out later they had reversed when I signalled, but the weight of the boat kept the craft moving ahead.

"I went through our sails and up the stem of the launch and had a few words with the bloke who was at the helm. I jobbed him, actually. In the heat of the moment, I thought there was every possibility that one of my crew could be caught under the boat. I had some idea of handling operations from their boat rather than ours.

"Only for the fact that my crew were all good sailors, it might have

The real joy of 16-foot skiff sailing is the shy reach under the "flattie," with trapeze men poised on the gunwale. These skiffs are racing on Moreton Bay, Queensland

A fourteen-foot dinghy, the Australian "experimenter's" class, spreads plenty of sail downwind

been more serious. The crew had no warning at all of what was coming up. But they got themselves out of it."

Beashel won the world 18-footer championship for the second time in Auckland in 1968 with *Daily Telegraph*, a boat he designed himself and which was sponsored by Sir Frank Packer. One of its unusual features was a little trimming fin for'ard of the mast.

"I'm convinced a lot of dinghies would be better off for having one," Beashel said. "It meant you never had to alter the fore and aft position of your centreboard. It came into its own in fresh winds when the boat became overburdened going to windward. You just dropped the little forward board. This counteracted the tendency for the big headsail to pull the bow away as you threw the mainsail to keep the boat on its feet. It beats me why others haven't tried it. It's one of the simplest ways of balancing your boat.

"I honestly don't think that boat was any faster than *Schemer*. But it was more adaptable and better for the competition we had to race against. With *Schemer,* we were racing mainly against three-handers and could beat them easily. But with the *Telegraph*, we were up against top four-handers and, although I'm against it in principle, we had to put more sail on to be in the paddock with them."

Beashel designed in 1965 a 16 called *Elvina Bay*. She won the State championship and, although beaten by Ken Minter's *Joan* for the Australian championship that season, boats of the same design continued to excel for the next five seasons. Trevor Beardsmore's *Minx*, off the *Elvina Bay* mould, won the Australian championship in both the 1969-70 and 1970-71 seasons.

Although he is out of them now, Ken Beashel says the 16 is still his favourite boat: "Over the years they have given me as good tactical racing as I've ever had.

"I remember one race, when Ron Gray beat us for the Australian title in Perth; we tacked thirty-two times in half a mile.

"And I've had races with Jimmy O'Rourke at Middle Harbour that are among the best I have ever sailed; tacking in his water, he tacking in mine, with only inches to spare. He'd be trying to put his bumpkin through my back and I'd be trying to do the same thing to him. Bitter-enemy sailing, you might say, but you learned awfully quickly.

"The 16s are easy to tack and get moving after a tack. And for an off-the-wind ride, I don't think anything can beat a skiff. To the spectators, the 18s look better because they carry more sail. But when the seas are running and it's blowing hard, I'd sooner be in a skiff any day. I've sailed on Moreton Bay, where all the other dinghy classes have been blown over and swamped; but the skiffs were still out there, handling spinnakers.

"To be a good skiff sailor, you've got to be able to handle the crew, if you are a skipper, ashore as well as on the water; and if you are a crewman, you've got to get along with the rest and work together at all times. You've got to be more aggressive than in other classes. I'll put it this way: we won our first State title with a win in a race in which only four of us finished on Botany Bay. It was really blowing; the Dragons were racing and couldn't even make the first mark. We went into the wing mark, said we're gybing, and we gybed. The other boats weren't game to take the risk. They 'grannied' (tacked around) and we grabbed ourselves a three-minute lead. The boats are just that fast."

I asked Ken whether the reputation for "bushranging"—beating the gun on starting lines and other illegal tactics—that supposedly goes on in big skiff fleets was justified. Ken's reply on reputation: "No, not in top-line racing. I can honestly say that all the blokes I have sailed against, in the big championships, have always played it as fair as anybody else I have sailed against, in any other class.

"In general skiff racing, 'bushranging' does exist and this is partly why I got out. The things that happened in some of those starts drove me up the wall. Having 150 starters does draw in the public but it is not good at all for those racing. I believe the fleets should be divided up into championship and handicap divisions. As it is, the skiff championship races are great, but handicap racing on a big scale may be holding back the class."

Ken is also an advocate of the change to a three-man 16: "The skiffs as they are don't appeal to the youngsters coming up from the big two-man boats like the Cherubs, Gwen 12s, and even the VJs which have a lot of room for the crew to move around; not like a four-man 16. The kids themselves seem to be bigger with each generation. They find themselves in a boat that's not a great deal longer and with much less room for the crew. And the really big man finds it hard to get a berth in a four-man skiff crew. I believe a choice should be allowed between the three-man and four-man crews. But the skipper must nominate before a championship whether a three-man or four-man crew will be used. That number must be kept throughout.

"I'm afraid that unless something like this happens, high performance two-man classes, the Cherub and maybe the 12-foot skiffs, are going to take over. And after all, what other three-man dinghies are there? Only the Sharpies." Ken believes that in drawing on the experience gained in use of the skiffs, a good three-man, one-design centreboarder of about seventeen feet could be developed for international competition.

He's sailed with and against some great skiff sailors and he divides them into two groups:

"There's the 'student' who is either the boatbuilder, the sailmaker, or the fanatic who is obsessed with finding out what really makes a boat go. I'd class Billy Barnett, Ken Minter, Jack Cassidy, Ron Gray, and Bobby Holmes among these; there are a lot more.

"Against them are the naturals, guys who don't necessarily know how to set up a boat, but what they've got at the starting line they get the best out of right through the race. These are the fellows like Billo Hayward, Vic Lucas, Jack Mitchell, Jack Lyons and Jim O'Rourke, and perhaps the greatest of them all, Ron Hendry, who came from

Queensland and won before the war four national titles in skiffs when he was only a kid.

"Hendry got the last inch out of a crew. I was sailing in his crew one day, on the trapeze, and he yelled for more power. I jumped and I was on my big toe on the gunwale, wondering what I was doing there. He had the knack of getting the most and the best out of men in the boat.

"There's a will to win and a pushing of opposition to the limit in this skiff movement. It works for the sailor when it is used in other classes."

Ken has moved into these other classes, sailing in the crew of the Twelve Metre *Gretel* during her unsuccessful campaign against *Dame Pattie* in the 1967 America's Cup trials, aboard ocean racers, in the 5.5 metres, and now, very seriously, in the Soling Class. In 1971, he and Lindsay Allsop, with an old Beashel crewman, Jim Gannon, who is working now in America, flew to New York to sail in the world Soling championship on Long Island Sound.

Before he left, Beashel said: "I used to think the greatest thing was to win an 18-foot or 16-foot skiff Australian championship and that a helmsman wasn't recognised as a good one until he did.

"But my attitudes have changed. The jet set has brought the international scene to our doorstep, so much so in recent years, that local recognition is no longer enough. My ambition now is to win a fair dinkum world championship."

Ken's first real encounter with the jet-setters was in 1970 when the world 5.5 metre championship was held on his home waters, off Broken Bay near Sydney. He was given the job of preparing the Bahaman entry, *John B.*, that was owned by Bobby Symonette. A series for the Australian Gold Cup was held on Sydney Harbour beforehand but Symonette was unable to reach Australia in time to compete. So Beashel skippered the boat with Symonette's crew. He sailed in his usual daredevil fashion; across the bows of ferries, under the stern of passing ships, shaving the rocks, and not hesitating to leave the tiller and run forward when something went amiss with the crew-work. Beashel finished a very close second to experienced Sydney 5.5 metre sailor Norman Booth.

And in the company of millionaires from America, Crown Prince Harald of Norway, and other very important people, Beasho didn't put a foot wrong socially; although some of his mates with long memories conjured up a nightmare vision of him arriving in shorts and white singlet, meat pie in hand, to receive his trophy at the Royal Sydney Yacht Squadron presentation dinner.

Stonehaven Cup twelve-foot Cadet Dinghies, originated in the early 1920s as a trainer class for Royal Clubs, are still going strong in Victoria, Tasmania, and South Australia. Jock Sturrock, Tony Manford, Norman Booth, and Jim Hardy all sailed in these

The champ on a day off. *Ragamuffin* reaches home for Sydney after a weekend cruise to Pittwater

THE OCEAN RACERS

HOW I LOST THE Hobart race. Did you ever hear about the time I lost the Sydney-Hobart race? Well, it's not the type of story I like to tell against anyone, much less against myself, but it's true and bears re-telling. It sums up what ocean racing is really all about in Australia these days. The lesson is that one mistake, one lapse in concentration for a few minutes in a 630-mile race is just as fatal as if you were racing around a 12-mile Olympic course.

I was recruited at the last minute, a pier-head jump, for this yacht; a fast one in conditions that suited her, although she had slipped back in the design race to the point where the owner was at the time having a new, bigger yacht built. So he wasn't taking this race all that seriously; that is, until we looked like winning the thing.

At first, it was an offshore yachtsman's dream. We ran hard for 500 miles under spinnaker before kind breezes, hitting a high average of better than eight knots for seventy-five per cent of the time. I experienced some of the most exciting sailing of my life at the wheel at night; with the needle going off the clock on the speedo, as the yacht lifted and skated in a mighty plume of spray down the face of an ocean swell.

Our tactics, a last-race fling of standing well out to sea, paid off as we realised we were enjoying much more consistently fresh breeze than the yachts inshore. Our navigator became more exasperated as it was obvious that officials back at the race headquarters in Sydney could not credit our progress. Or so we took it from the qualifications they handed out to the radio stations for news reports.

But we didn't care. The sun was shining; the nights were warm. We had faith in our navigator, the food was good, sleep came easily, and the company was fine.

A rotten thirty-five knot southerly ended this idyll on the fourth day, just as we were beginning to tot up how much booze we had won in bets from the other boats. For, at the time, we were the southernmost boat in the fleet with even a chance of being first into Hobart. Another few hours running and we might have made it for that would have allowed us to lay around the last great obstacle, the forbidding cliffs of Tasman Island, without having to tack.

But the southerly stopped us short. The headwind, and particularly the big sea, didn't suit the shape of our boat. Under reefed main and small jib, each sea would push her head away; she'd heel and slide away sideways, losing boat lengths at a time to leeward. It was bad enough being on deck; spray and rain stinging the face with shotgun pellet force and water finding its way through the "waterproof" gear and jumpers, that had remained dry for so long, to soak the skin. But worst of all was the realisation that this chance of a lifetime, winning the Hobart race, was slipping from our grasp.

At last, coming on dark, we made landfall and found smoother water under Schouten Island on the Tasmanian coast. A sail loomed from the rainsqualls closer to shore and elation rose again as we realised this was the fast English boat, *Prospect of Whitby,* which carried a much bigger handicap penalty than ourselves. We were still in the running. They changed to a bigger headsail when they saw us. *Prospect* was a beautiful machine to windward and it was soon apparent that she was chopping us to pieces as we beat along that rocky shoreline. Finally a decision was made to stand offshore again. This was probably as costly as my sin later. The skipper had been badly caught in a calm under the high land along this coast in the previous year, and reckoned the wind would die with darkness. It didn't and the further we went to sea, the worse the waves became and the slower we went. To top it all, the wind began to veer from south to southwest which meant that we lifted on the offshore tack, and would be knocked back on the inshore tack towards where we had started. But finally, we reached a point where we had a fighting chance of laying around Tasman Island and maybe saving ourselves.

At dawn, I had the wheel. The skipper and navigator, exhausted after a day and a night of sleepless bashing to windward against the icy blast from the Roaring Forties, went below to their bunks. I was cold and tired, but the boat was handling these smaller seas well. Gradually, to my horror, I realised that the bulk of Tasman Island, which had been looming on our starboard bow, was now falling directly ahead. A glance at the compass revealed the wind had headed us by five degrees. Then a rainsquall hit us and, there was no question about it, the compass swung ten degrees, and more. We knew we should tack, to gain the benefit of the shift on starboard. But this would have taken us offshore into rougher water again and, ahead of us, a couple of bigger yachts were absolutely rocketing along in smooth water.

I told the watch captain: "We've been knocked nearly twenty degrees, should we tack?"

He said: "Hang on, it might just be the squall, wait until it clears."

It passed, but the wind still headed us by twenty degrees. For reasons that I can only ascribe to fatigue, I didn't raise the question of tacking again. The watch captain took over the helm and continued on the inshore leg. I went below and the owner asked me if we were still laying Tasman. I said that we weren't and told him why. He asked, in a few terse words, what was wrong with me and demanded to know why we hadn't called him or the navigator to discuss the question of tacking? He indicated that this was the least he expected. I had no answer. By now, the proximity of other boats told us we had blown our chances in the race, although we did finish third.

My lapse was forgiven and in fairness to myself, it must be reckoned that this was only one of a series of mistakes that cost us the race. But I'll always be haunted by the thought that possibly it was THE one.

Ocean racing is a wonderful sport if you have a strong stomach, don't mind going without a lot of sleep, and living in wet clothes and wet blankets when the going gets rough. But if you love the sea, and to be a devotee you must, the rewards are great: creaming along through the whitecaps under the firm pull of the spinnaker before a kind following breeze; the sensation of power in the hull as it smashes its way to windward; the satisfaction of a change of sheeting lead which enables you to inch up on and then go past a competitor; yarning quietly through the long night watches with a mate, sailing old races, retelling ancient jokes, and settling the world's problems. And the miles slip by. At the end of each race, the payoff is a great sense of achievement, and of at least having bested the sea, if not the opposition.

The greatest reward of all for the masochistic effort of ocean racing is the companionship—being part of a crew, each man with a task, each dependent on all the others doing their job—which is just as strong ashore as afloat. The offshore crowd race hard, and play hard afterwards. A marathon of partying, on and in the yachts and pubs around Con-

Ted Heath, winner of the 1969 Sydney-Hobart race and Prime Minister of Great Britain

Dockside arrival party, with audience, at the end of a Sydney-Hobart race in Constitution Dock

300

stitution Dock, where they moor after the finish, is part of the Sydney-Hobart tradition. Having New Year's Eve falling at this time has something, but not all, to do with it. The yachtsmen treat it as an annual reunion, a time to swap experiences, talk about boats, renew old friendships and make new ones.

"It's a lot quieter than it used to be," someone told me last time I was in Hobart at the end of the race. He recalled some of the famous post-race happenings: the agile for'ard hand who ran up the mast of a big ketch and stood on the top for several seconds while the onlookers suddenly became very sober; the time the guy was blowing the bugle in Bert Dolan's when the fellows kept pouring beer into it and, every time he blew, a great spray of suds descended on the troops; and the time the Kiwis challenged the Aussies to a tug o' war in Dolan's back bar—and the Kiwi anchor man managed to get the rope out the door and throw a round turn and two half-hitches around a parking meter so that the issue was determined beyond all doubt.

"Yes, it's a lot quieter these days," said my friend. "Oh by the way, I did witness one social event of note this morning when big Siddie Brown felt like a little drink, with breakfast, at Dolan's. Someone filled up a sea boot for him. He's afraid it might have given him a bad dose of athlete's mouth."

Well, that friend, Tony Cable, truly a magnificent cook at sea if handed a can opener, decided that year to do something about reuniting the crews in Hobart. He was concerned that, with the bigger fleets, there wasn't enough room anywhere around the dock for all the crews to get together. He organised a crew get-together in an out-of-the-way pub, the Shipwright's Arms on Battery Point. It began with a yachtsman startling an elderly regular with the order, "Two hundred beers please, and keep them coming." The tally at the end of the day was 1,467 beers. That total was passed the following year when it reached 2,000, and subsequent totals were 5,000 in 1971 and 6,200 in 1972. Sing-songs, jokes, and lie-telling occupied the day. The crew from a visiting English yacht were so impressed that they invited Cable to liven up Cowes Week with a similar get-together happening. The august headquarters of British yachting will never be the same.

That side of it is fun, but ocean racing is a serious business in Australia today. Despite price tabs of up to $150,000, a steady stream of big, new offshore yachts has been emerging from boatbuilders' yards. Australian crews have reached a level of excellence in offshore racing that is unsurpassed anywhere. This excellence is based on non-stop effort and hard-driving tactics when winds blow. The crews work at improving their performance by regular gymnasium sessions, sail-handling practice, and a racing programme that runs year-round.

Ocean racing in Australia began with tentative outings from Sydney Harbour, the first recorded offshore event being from Sydney Cove and part of the Anniversary Day regatta of 1861. The winner of the prize of £300 was the fifteen-ton *Annie Ogle* from Australia, a remarkable

FACING PAGE: *Crusade*, 1969 Sydney-Hobart race

thirty-footer owned by Richard Harnett. Harnett designed her with identical symmetrical lines forward and aft of the midship section, taking her lines from a mackerel he caught especially for the purpose in Woolloomooloo Bay. Although unsuccessful in the Botany Bay race, probably because the bigger *Annie Ogle* had some advantage in the light winds and ocean swell of that day, Harnett's mackerel-design yacht was still winning races twenty-seven years later.

Xarifa, a thirty-tonner built on similar lines to the *Australian,* won in 1864 the first long-distance offshore race of 140 miles from Sydney to Newcastle and back; she beat *Chance*, a seventy-one-ton iron-hulled barque built in England and owned by the Commodore of the newly-formed Royal Sydney Yacht Squadron, William Walker. The owner of *Xarifa,* Charles Parbury, staked £100 to Commodore Walker's £150. The race was sailed in a southerly gale and *Xarifa* probably won because the wind shortened sail for her, snapping off her topmast while running off Narrabeen and breaking the gaff jaws, making it necessary for the crew to heavily reef. But this rig was ideal for the thrash back that night to Sydney Harbour. Meantime, *Chance,* which had run ahead out of sight, did not reef before turning off Nobby's, then broached while recklessly gybing all standing, and lost a lot of time reefing.

Little more is recorded of ocean racing, still in its infancy world wide, until the first Bass Strait race held in 1907. This stretched the 196 miles from Port Phillip Heads to Low Head at the mouth of the Tamar River in Northern Tasmania.

A trophy was put up for the event by the editor of the American magazine, *Rudder,* through a friend, Commodore T. A. Dickson of the Royal Geelong Yacht Club. *Thistle,* a forty-eight-foot yawl owned by Mr E. Newland, won. It finished in thirty-five and a half hours after being bedevilled by winds from all points of the compass and at all strengths. At times the yachts were becalmed, but later they were forced to reef to storm canvas. The event then lapsed for twenty-two years, probably because the wife of the owner of *Thistle*, who was aboard for the drama, was so shaken by the experience that she would never relinquish the trophy; perhaps she hoped to spare others the miseries of ocean racing.

The race was revived in 1929 by E. J. ("Doc") Bennell who won from six entries with his forty-two-foot ketch *Oimara.* Late in 1930 Bennell, of the Royal St Kilda Yacht Club, took *Oimara* to New Zealand where he challenged all-comers to race to Australia. His challenge was taken up by an ex-Norwegian pilot cutter, *Teddy,* a forty-footer more than forty years old that was on a world cruise with Erling Tambs, his wife and children. With a crew of four Auckland yachtsmen, Tambs won the race on corrected time from *Oimara*, with the New Zealand yacht *Rangi,* third. *Teddy* had a massive time allowance of ninety-six hours and the handicappers had obviously been misled by her great, beamy shape as she was extremely fine underwater. After her return from Sydney, she was wrecked on the New Zealand coast.

Oimara, under Bennell's son Frank, won the Bass Strait race held in

Highlander on Botany Bay. A keelboat with three men on the wire as well

1934 to coincide with the Melbourne Centenary celebrations. The race was revived by the Royal Yacht Club of Victoria in 1946 and has continued each year. From 1950 onwards it has been conducted by the Cruising Yacht Club of Victoria. The venerable *Oimara* gained a third placing in 1947 and still was sailing actively on Port Phillip Bay in the late 1960s.

But the real pattern for ocean racing in Australia was set out in 1945. Captain John Illingworth of the Royal Navy persuaded a group of Sydney yachtsmen, from the newly-formed Cruising Yacht Club, to make a race of their proposed Christmas cruise to Hobart. Illingworth, a committee member of the Royal Ocean Racing Club and an expert on offshore racing techniques and design, was at the time stationed in Sydney as Engineer Commander of the Garden Island Dockyard. He bought himself a yacht for the race, a thirty-four-foot-nine-inch cutter called *Rani*. It was designed by A. C. Barber, of Sydney, and was the light-displacement type that he favoured.

Besides talking them into racing, Illingworth showed the cruising men how to race as well. When the fleet ran into a sou'westerly gale off the New South Wales coast early in the race, the cruising men, as prudent seamen did in those days, hove to or ran for shelter. One crew even went ashore and shot rabbits while waiting for the gale to ease.

But Illingworth pressed on with his little yacht. When the crew suggested on one occasion that he reduce sail, he replied: "No, we'll only have to put it all up again." *Rani* beat the best of her bigger rivals into Hobart by seventeen hours. Besides founding a race that is today ranked as among the world's most important, Illingworth instilled in Australian offshore yachtsmen the hard-driving tradition that has made the Australian crews the toughest in the world; prepared to push past the limits of normal physical endurance in heavy weather.

The seaworthy but heavy cruising boats of those days, mixed with harbour-racing metre yachts converted to ocean racers, gradually gave way to yachts designed for the job. Some were from overseas, but Australian designs for a time became ascendant. This was due mainly to the work of young Sydney designer, Alan Payne, who was later to win fame as designer of America's Cup challengers, *Gretel* and *Gretel II*. Payne drew a thirty-six footer; fast, seaworthy, and designed to handicap well under the Royal Ocean Racing Club rule of measurement, called the Tasman Seabird class. One of the boats designed by Payne, Russ Williams' *Cherana,* won the 1959 race. Another Payne design, the mighty fifty-seven foot steel cutter *Solo*, skippered by rip-roaring Vic Meyer, won the race in 1956 and 1962 on corrected time. It took fastest time prizes in 1958 and 1959.

Vic was one of the first skippers to propound the philosophy of: "Leave it on until it blows out, and then put up another one," meaning he was a tough skipper to sail for, and went through crews very quickly, but anyone who raced on *Solo* came away better for the experience. Sid Brown, the big tough New Zealand fisherman who always seems to turn up on a fast boat in the Sydney-Hobart race, recalls one Hobart start where Vic gave him the helm and said: "Steer straight for the Heads and don't alter course for anything." Sid remembers: "It was a strong southerly and I couldn't see a thing for the spinnaker. We ran clean over a dinghy full of Greek fishermen off Shark Island. One of them was cursing Vic from the water, yelling 'You basta, I can't swim.' Vic waved his arms over his head, freestyle fashion, and yelled back: 'Quick, go like this!'"

Vic Meyer, an engineer who came to Australia from Switzerland at the age of nineteen, was a motor boat man who turned to sailing in his forties. He carefully built *Solo* himself, and quickly learned all the skills of yacht racing until there was nothing he couldn't do on that boat better than almost anyone else, although he would never take the helm during a race. He was forever working on *Solo,* re-siting fittings with his oxy-welder, striving to improve the boat. Her record grew quickly. Beside the Sydney-Hobart race victories, *Solo* won the 350-mile Montague Island race four times in five starts, taking line honours as well each

Rolly Tasker's *Siska*, a pencil-slim ocean racer converted from an inshore metre yacht

time. And she set a new record in winning the 1961 Trans-Tasman race, from Auckland to Sydney, in seven days, twenty-one hours, and twelve minutes.

Solo's greatest victory, over the fifty-seven foot American yacht *Ondine*, owned by Huey Long, in the 1962 Sydney-Hobart tends to be overshadowed, by the drama of the final race for the line between *Ondine* and Peter Warner's seventy-three foot schooner, *Astor*, and *Ondine's* establishment of the long-standing race record of three days, three hours, forty-six minutes and sixteen seconds.

But while *Ondine* pipped *Astor* by a minute, the home-made shark-like bow of *Solo* chased *Ondine* across the line within forty-three minutes. It was close enough to give *Solo* the race on corrected time. The local product didn't have the beauty of *Ondine*, nor her advanced sail-handling equipment. But through Payne's design skill and Meyer's ingenuity and effort in preparing her gear, she was just as efficient.

Astor, a truly beautiful schooner, was built in 1924 in Scotland from Burma teak to the design of William Fife for Sydney surgeon Sir Alexander MacCormick. The next year she sailed across the Pacific to finish fourth in division A of the Los Angeles to Honolulu TRANSPAC race. She was first to finish three times in the Hobart race and, while Peter Warner retired from active racing after selling *Astor* to an American, the crewmen spread their influence through other top boats in the offshore fleet. They had developed great skill in handling the big gear of *Astor*.

Vic Meyer was another who tired of racing, but he took on long-distance cruising with enthusiasm. He began, in 1962, by circumnavigating Australia. He covered 12,500 miles in thirteen weeks. His boat roared home across the Great Australian Bight. There was a gale behind her and a terrified pickup crew—Vic had only one permanent crew-man on that voyage—hung on grimly. Finally the cruising mainsail blew clean out of the bolt ropes. "Thank God," breathed the crew who hoped for some respite. But Vic rummaged below for another sail. It was not the storm main he wanted but the racing main. "Get the bloody thing up," he thundered and they were on their way again.

He's since been around the world a couple of times, almost losing *Solo* at Punta Arenas at the southern tip of South America; she broke free from her moorings and battered against a seawall in a gale in 1970. But Vic put her aboard a freighter, shipped her to Germany where she was repaired, and continued his cruise.

Through the early sixties, the Sydney-Hobart race dominated the style of Australian offshore yachtsmen. Graham Newland, a young engineer, won the race twice, in 1958 and 1960, in a new English designed Robb Lion Class thirty-five footer. Sailing with Graham on *Siandra* was Ron Swanson who later turned designer, with great success. One of his designs, *Cadence,* won the 1966 race. With his own *Camille,* he won a place in the first Admiral's Cup team to visit England in 1965. His Swanson 36 design, a thirty-six footer, was one of the first successful stock fibreglass yachts produced in Australia. Smaller stock yachts, the Swanson 27, 32, and Dart 22 day sailer followed.

But Ron's ambition of winning a Hobart race was thwarted by the successes of the brothers, Trygve and Magnus Halvorsen, who did much to direct Australian racing into its present phase of non-stop concentration and physical effort. The brothers won the Sydney-Hobart four times; first in 1957 with *Anitra V* and then three in a row with their remarkable double-ender, *Freya,* in 1963, 1964, and 1965. They built and designed their own yachts. Another of their boats, *Solveig,* won the 1954 race, but neither brother was aboard. They were ill and the skipper was her incomparable navigator, Stan Darling.

The Halvorsens built their victories on an inherent ability to handle any situation at sea. They had a vast store of experience to draw on, that went back to childhood. Trygve and Magnus are two of the five sons of the late Lars Halvorsen, a Norwegian boatbuilder who immigrated to Australia in 1924. He founded one of the country's biggest and most successful boatbuilding businesses.

While others complained of hard-luck "holes" in the wind, shifts, and calms, the Halvorsens, with the help of Stan Darling, framed their race tactics perfectly against prevailing and anticipated weather patterns.

TOP LEFT: Bob Crichton-Brown: owner-skipper who led a winning team in the Admiral's Cup. TOP RIGHT: Gordon Ingate: ocean racer, one-design helmsman, and rules expert. BOTTOM LEFT: Ron Swanson: designer and ocean-racing skipper. BOTTOM RIGHT: Bill Lucas: champion Western Australian inshore skipper

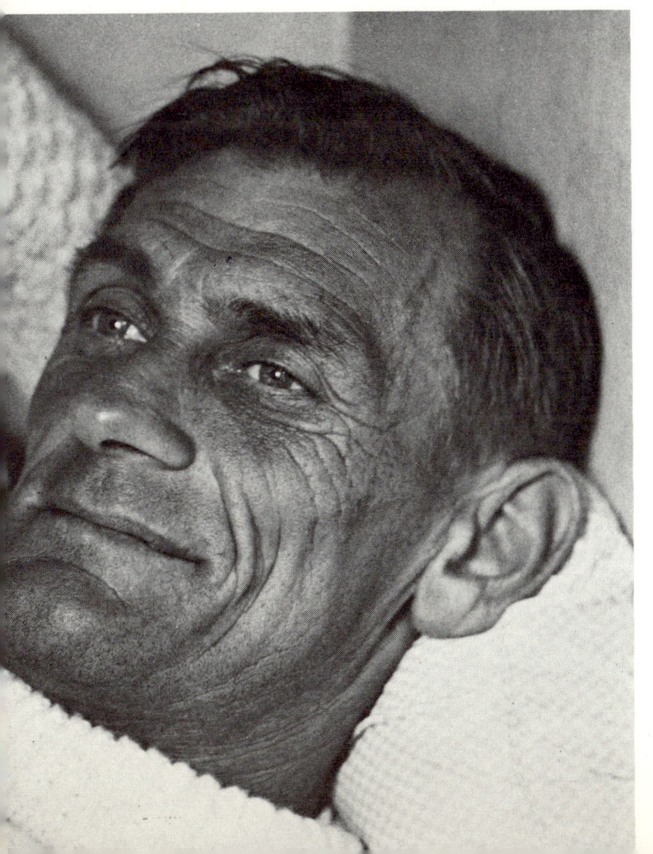

The Halvorsens always seemed to go the right way and always gained on the fleet at night. Others gradually saw that the brothers made the extra effort to tend sheets and were alert to the need to change sail in the hours of darkness. Then temptation is strongest to let things be and to huddle in the shelter of the cockpit.

In the year they completed the hat-trick of Hobart wins, the Halvorsens joined the first Admiral's Cup challenge. Ironically, and no one realised it at the time, participation in this international offshore teams championship was to lead to a great period of change in Australian ocean racing. It led to a swing away from local designers, like the Halvorsens, to overseas designers. This has virtually put many of the locals out of business and it led to a jump-up in the cost of new boats so that Admiral's Cup participation was put out of reach of any owner not a millionaire.

For, until 1965, the Sydney-Hobart race governed offshore development and design. To win a Hobart race, a yacht had first of all to be able to run hard, carrying spinnaker and full mainsail, in big seas to make the most of the nor'easter wind pattern down the New South Wales coast. It then had to drive hard to windward through the sou'westers of Bass Strait and the Tasmanian coast. So the rigs tended to be squat and hull design was slanted heavily to downwind and strong wind performance.

The Admiral's Cup is held in England every second year to coincide with the "Fastnet race." It is competed for by teams of three yachts from each nation.

First two selections for the 1965 Admiral's Cup team, after trials in strong to gale force winds, were *Freya* and Ron Swanson's *Camille*. Just scraping in by one point, from Arthur Byrne's more modern *Salacia*, for third place in the team was Gordon Ingate's *Caprice of Huon*, then thirteen years old and built to a design which Robert Clark of England first had on his board before the second World War.

But, although there were mutterings about her selection, *Caprice* and the dashing Ingate were the stars of the show at Cowes. *Caprice* won the first three of the four Admiral's Cup races in winds tending light to moderate on smooth water which suited her fine, metre-yacht lines. And Ingate, a graduate from the dog-eat-dog world of one-design racing, a bundle of nervous energy with an engineer's talent for getting the best from a yacht, was in his element. The rough-and-tumble of racing on the Solent, dodging non Admiral's Cup racing yachts, ferries, day-tripper launches, and shoals, amid a swirling three-knot tide, didn't worry him, or *Caprice*. But *Camille* and *Freya* weren't at home. They sailed well enough for Australia to have had a chance of taking the cup when it came to the decisive Fastnet race which scores triple the value of the shorter races. Rounding Fastnet Rock, the Australians were reckoned to be ahead on points. But they stood into the Irish Sea, anticipating a wind shift that never came. Instead, the wind veered back into the south-east, to the advantage of the British yachts which had sailed out into the Atlantic. Two of their yachts, *Quiver IV* and *Noryema IV* were first and third among the Admiral's Cup boats;

Camille was fifth, *Caprice* seventh, with the remaining British boat, *Firebrand*, eleventh, beating *Freya* into twelfth place.

Australia finished in second place, forty-four points behind Britain and ahead of Holland and the United States. The English yachtsmen who had welcomed the Australians warmly but with some condescension —"Sporting of you fellows to bring your old yachts over here," and that sort of thing—gained new respect for them. "Australia must challenge again for the Admiral's Cup" read a footnote to the account of the racing in that year's Sydney-Hobart race programme and the build up began almost immediately for the victorious 1967 challenge.

Two new boats, really different to Australian eyes, won through the selection trials for the 1967 team with the veteran *Caprice of Huon*.

Bob Crichton-Brown had built a forty-six footer, *Balandra*, to the same design as *Quiver IV*, England's top performer in 1965. She was a handful downwind, but the fastest boat of her size to windward seen until then in Australia. The other new boat was a minimum-rating forty-footer, *Mercedes III*. This was designed by her owner, Ted Kaufman, with the help of Bob Miller. Builder Cec Quilkey, by following the cold-moulding technique, laminating thin skins of oregon planking, probably made an important contribution. The result was a strong, lightweight yacht, shallow in form with the tight turn at the garboards to her keel making her almost a fin keeler. She was ahead of her time, in Australia at least, anticipating theories of the top American designers, Olin Stephens and Dick Carter. She was a brilliant boat right from launching. In her first fourteen starts, she scored nine wins, a second, two thirds, and a fourth.

Caprice was under charter to Gordon Reynolds who had sailed in her crew in 1965. Ingate was tied up at this time as helmsman for *Gretel*, in her unsuccessful campaign against *Dame Pattie* to be America's Cup challenger.

So with better boats for the lighter winds and smoother seas of the English coast, and a new attitude to ocean races with more emphasis on windward work and round-the-buoys tactical performance, the Australians went back to Cowes in 1967. They won by a record margin of 104 points from Britain. They won through completely consistent performance against yachts which may have, individually, been faster. And the reason for this consistency was their approach as a team. Drawing on the experience of *Caprice*'s navigator, Bill Fesq, the Australians came to terms with the conditions. Fesq had studied the English coastal waters as a navigator during the war and later as a commander of torpedo boats. The sailing experience of other 1965 veterans such as Reynolds and Graham Newland gave more advantage to the Australians. Then practice together brought boats and crews to a keen pitch before the series began, while the other nations tended to turn up just to race as individual boats. The series showed as well that Australian sails, with the work of Joe Pearce predominant, were excellent and our masts, winches, fittings were, if anything, better than those on the boats of other

Sir Max Aitken's *Crusade* at the start of the Southern Cross Cup ocean race

nations. These days, the leading Australian winch-maker sells most of his output overseas, and aluminium yacht masts and fittings from Australian manufacturers also find ready export markets.

In 1967 the Cruising Yacht Club of Australia instituted an Admiral's Cup contest of its own in an endeavour to attract more entries from other countries to the Hobart race, three shorter races beforehand were provided as an incentive. Called the Southern Cross Cup, the contest is held every second year between teams from the Australian States and visiting nations. In its first year, it attracted the strongest New Zealand contingent to ever cross the Tasman. And while New South Wales beat the New Zealanders by forty-four points for the cup, one of the New Zealand entries, Chris Bouzaid's *Rainbow II*, won the Sydney-Hobart race. She was the first overseas entry to win the Sydney-Hobart since Illingworth's *Rani*.

The next Southern Cross Cup, in 1969, brought out a full English team: *Prospect of Whitby,* owned by Arthur Slater, a forty-one footer from the Admiral's Cup team of that year, Sir Max Aitken's sixty-two-foot cutter, *Crusade,* and Rodney Hill's thirty-four footer, *Morning After.* Again, New South Wales won from Britain, with New Zealand third, and again an overseas visitor won the Hobart race. This was Edward Heath's *Morning Cloud*, a Sparkman and Stephens thirty-four footer. Later that year, Heath's Conservatives won the election and yachtsman Ted Heath became Prime Minister of Great Britain. His "double" victory of that year will probably stand in the record books forever.

Rainbow II's 1967 win was also the first by an overseas designer—Olin Stephens, USA—in six years, and in that same year a decision was made that was to accelerate in Australia the trend from local designers to overseas designers. The trend swung especially to Olin Stephens. Syd Fischer, a yachtsman with some seven years' experience in ocean racing, having made a fortune as one of Sydney's biggest building developers, wanted to buy a new, big yacht. Syd, a completely practical man, was undecided between Stephens and Warwick Hood. The latter was a young naval architect who had understudied Alan Payne and recently taken over Payne's practice. Payne was temporarily out of yacht design. Hood had designed the 1967 America's cup challenger, *Dame Pattie,* to meet the Stephens defender, *Intrepid. Intrepid* won comfortably and so Stephens got the nod to design Fischer's new forty-eight footer, *Ragamuffin.* This was the yacht that was to call the tune in Australia for the next four years. Cec Quilkey set to work, building in the same cold-moulding process that had proven so successful with *Mercedes III*, while Fischer began assembling a crew. He used the same canny talent for assessing a man that had helped him build up the multi-million-dollar Australian Development Corporation of twenty or more companies from a one-man house-building business.

First he chose Graham Newland, for his great practical knowledge of big-yacht engineering as well as his sailing skills. Graham Newland, with the approval of Olin Stephens, designed into *Ragamuffin* improvements in fittings and engineering. One innovation was a method of running the propeller shaft uphill, through a series of three shafts, from the motor set low in the boat and directly over the keel, to aperture between the rudder and skeg aft. This gave an improved rating and minimum drag. The original plan had the shaft spearing straight out of the underbody of the boat with the propeller in front of the skeg. Such refinements, with some thoughtful construction, enabled a significant improvement on the designed ballast ratio.

With Graham Newland came Doug Patterson; they had been inseparable sailing mates since 1958 when Doug shipped aboard *Siandra.* Doug Patterson is a real student of every aspect of yacht racing; excellent sheet trimmer, good tactician, you name it, he can do it. From the foredeck of *Dame Pattie* came Tony Ellis; from the waist of *Gretel,* Frank McNulty; Peter Hemery from *Balandra*'s Admiral's Cup team crew; Jack Christoffersen who had sailed with Syd Fischer on his previous boat, the Lion Classer, *Malohi;* Jim Mason, Sydney-Hobart winning skipper of 1966 as navigator, and John Noakes from *Bacchus D.*

One by one, Syd Fischer assembled the nucleus of his crew: "I always ask myself before selecting a crewman, what the man can contribute to the boat and if he will fit in," Syd explained. "And the last part of the question is just as important as the first. You must have blokes who can get on together, under all kinds of difficult circumstances, and who will be a little bit forgiving of the others' weaknesses.

"But they must also have the will to win. I like to have in my crew a man's man; a fellow with some courage who will work hard and who doesn't get upset if things are not going his way, and a man who will fight his way out of a corner if necessary."

That comment pretty well sums up Syd himself. It was made just after he returned from Auckland where he shocked the New Zealanders by winning the One Ton Cup. More of that later, but by that time, March 1971, Syd Fischer rated as Australia's most successful ocean-racing skipper. His *Ragamuffin* had top-scored for Australia in the 1969 Admiral's Cup, won the major points score trophies at home, and was number one selection for the 1971 Admiral's Cup team.

Syd didn't buy himself into ocean racing, as he could have, but learned the hard way. He enjoyed tough sports. He had been a first-grade Rugby League forward in Sydney with Manly and a surfboat sweep at North Steyne and Bilgola surf clubs. "I was getting a bit old for the surf boats and looked around for another sport," he said. "I tried water-skiing but didn't like that. And then I found in ocean racing the kind of blokes I was used to in football and surf clubs—the types who had a go and liked a bit of fun."

Syd's interest in ocean racing began with a sail he had aboard *Caprice of Huon* in the late fifties when Bill Northam owned her. He had taken a few sailing lessons from Jim Bruton's sailing school and Jim, who was crewing on *Caprice,* invited him out on a training sail. "I was hooked," Syd said. He bought from a deceased estate, *Carefree,* a forty-one footer that had been lying at the Cruising Yacht Club for three years. He renovated the hull, put on a new deck, made a mast, "and learned a lot about the construction of boats." He went straight into ocean racing and then, in 1962, bought from Nev McEnally *Malohi.* This is a sister-ship to Graham Newland's *Siandra.* He enjoyed moderate success with her and scored fifth placings in the 1962 and 1966 Hobart races.

Then he had *Ragamuffin* built. On her first race, the 350-miler to Montague Island and back from Sydney in 1968, she was fresh from the builder's yard, full of shavings, odd carpenter's tools, had a stove that didn't work, and she leaked through the deck seams. The crew had a cold, miserable, and hungry thrash home through a northerly gale that forced ten retirements in the fleet of thirty-four. *Ragamuffin* was second in division one for Admiral's Cup boats to the veteran *Caprice of Huon.* But boat and crew quickly found form.

The 1969 Admiral's Cup team comprised *Ragamuffin*, *Mercedes III*, and another new boat, *Koomooloo*. The latter was a slightly bigger version of *Mercedes III* that was designed by Ted Kaufman and built by the Quilkey brothers for Dennis O'Neil.

They were well prepared, practised hard as a team under the astute leadership of team-captain Gordon Reynolds, but were beaten in the end by the Americans. *Ragamuffin* won the first event, the 225-mile Channel Race, from Dick Carter's lifting-keel forty-one footer, *Red Rooster,* star performer of the American team. *Mercedes III* was fourth and *Koomooloo* seventh, giving the Australians an early points lead. They lost ground in the two shorter races, with *Ragamuffin* scoring a seventh and a third, *Koomooloo* sixth and fourth, *Mercedes III* thirteenth and tenth, and went into the last race of the series, the Fastnet, with a small points lead from Britain and America. At Fastnet Rock, the Australians were well in it, coming through the fleet as the breeze freshened following two days of light winds and calms. But towards the end of the race, a vast and complete calm settled over the whole fleet. *Red Rooster*, her keel retracted, had shot back across the Irish Sea like a dinghy to finish before the wind finally dropped completely and she won on corrected time, with *Ragamuffin* second. But the smaller Australian yachts were hopelessly becalmed near the Scilly Isles and drifted home in nineteenth and twentieth place. The British went down the drain in the same calm; thus leaving the Americans whose bigger yachts, *Carina* and *Palawan,* had come home in third and eighth place on corrected time, as winners from Australia by fourteen points, with Britain another eleven points behind.

The final result was hard luck for the Australians. But the Admiral's Cup that year did show us that *Ragamuffin* was truly a great boat; she had gone away virtually untested because there were no boats of similar size and type for her to race against in Australia. The locals took a closer look at *Ragamuffin* because here was the most efficient big ocean-racing yacht we had ever seen. Much of this was due to the crew. They worked hard, then and since, with a constant search for improvements in sail-handling, sail combinations, and racing techniques to keep *Ragamuffin* on top. Once a week they turned out to train at a Sydney gymnasium for an hour and a half with owner Fischer himself setting the pace.

Syd Fischer gained a pace-setter when Arthur Byrne, the man who just missed selection with *Salacia* against *Caprice of Huon* in 1965, decided to build a new boat. Arthur, who like Syd made a fortune from nothing but the skill of his hands and business sense, bravely chose a boat just like *Ragamuffin*. It was virtually the same design but uprated by Olin Stephens to take advantage of the new International Offshore Rule, which came into effect world-wide in 1970. Previously, American yachts raced to two main handicap systems based on measurement: American yachts to the Cruising Club of America Rule; and Britain, Australia, and most of Europe raced to the Royal Ocean Racing Club Rule.

The duels between *Ragamuffin* and *Salacia II* made the 1970-71 season an absorbing one with *Ragamuffin* still on top but *Salacia II* was closing the gap. These boats finished first and second in the selection trials for the 1971 Admiral's Cup team. Third team-member, *Koomooloo*, under new owner Norman Rydge Junior, with Jock Sturrock and Mick Morris aboard as specialist helmsmen, was extremely well sailed during the trials to beat a number of newer designs. She had won the Sydney-Hobart in 1968 under her previous owner, Dennis O'Neil.

The 1971 challenge was another hard-luck story. *Koomooloo*'s rudder sheared from its stock when she was running home from Fastnet Rock, with the Australian team in a winning position. Britain took the Cup with 825 points from the USA (782), Australia (719), Argentina (680), Holland (653), South Africa (574), Italy (566), and Bermuda (547). Teams from Brazil, Germany, Ireland, Belgium, New Zealand and France also competed. The Admiral's Cup that year truly became an international championship. Britain had a team of fast yachts, all brand new designs by the American firm, Sparkman and Stephens, that had a distinct edge on the Australians and Americans in light to moderate weather. The British team was captained by the Prime Minister, Ted Heath, at the helm of a new forty-foot *Morning Cloud*. Arthur Slater was in it with a new forty-five-foot *Prospect of Whitby*. The third yacht was *Cervantes IV*, owned by Bob Watson, an unobtrusive boat with her white topsides against *Morning Cloud*'s gleaming clear-finished topsides and *Prospect*'s royal blue enamel, but a brilliant performer.

Britain jumped to a good points lead from the first race of the series, the Channel Race, when *Prospect of Whitby* won from the outstanding new American fifty-five footer, *Yankee Girl*. Australia's placings were *Salacia II* fourth, *Ragamuffin* thirteenth, and *Koomooloo* nineteenth. *Ragamuffin* was caught pinned on the wrong side of a wind shift on the English coast; *Koomooloo* suffered from an error in her compass. Australia's performance in the second race did not help improve her position. *Ragamuffin* was seventh, *Koomooloo* ninth, and *Salacia II* twenty-first after a very bad start. But a hard wind blew the Australians back into the running in the third race, another inshore event, a tight, thirty-mile course. They handled the wind and nasty seas of the tide-ripped Solent perfectly while other yachts broached helplessly out of control. *Salacia II* finished second to the Dutch yacht *Belita VII*, *Ragamuffin* was third, and *Koomooloo* fourth.

Some ground had also been won back for the Australians by *Cervantes IV* being disqualified from the first race on the protest of *Koomooloo*. *Koomooloo* claimed that on the starting line, while on the right of way starboard tack, she had to pull away to avoid colliding with *Cervantes IV* on port tack.

Britain went into the Fastnet race with a twenty-two point lead over Australia. *Ragamuffin* won the Fastnet, the first Australian yacht ever to do so, with some astute sailing through variable winds on the first night out and a do-or-die spinnaker run home in the best Illingworth-Meyer-Halvorsen tradition. She blew out two spinnakers, one in a dangerous

Cedallion, a South Australian ocean racer

all-standing gybe at night in a forty-knot wind in the middle of the Irish Sea, and ran down waves like a surfboat at times "doubling" the wave in front, jumping its top and running down the face.

Salacia II was eighth, after losing ground with steering gear failure under the pressure of the hard run home across the Irish Sea. At the Fastnet Rock, as usual, Australia looked to have the Cup won. *Koomooloo* had only to finish better than thirteenth. Then, under the strain of constant hard wheel winding against a quartering sea, *Koomooloo*'s rudder failed. Stainless steel bolts pinning the blade to the stock, possibly weakened by a grounding during training off Cowes, snapped like carrots.

Britain sent its Admiral's Cup team to Australia later that year for the Southern Cross Cup, complete, except for its captain, Ted Heath—Sammy Sampson skippered the boat in his stead. They were favourites, but the New Zealanders made a clean sweep of both the Southern Cross Cup and the Sydney-Hobart race. The New Zealand team yachts, all of the One Ton Cup Class, were sailed with extraordinary consistency.

The three of them crossed the finishing line in Hobart within an hour and fourteen minutes of each other. The winner was *Pathfinder,* a new Sparkman and Stephens designed thirty-eight footer, skippered by Auckland boat-builder, Brin Wilson. Runner-up was *Runaway*, designed, built, and skippered by Wilson's brother-in-law, John Lidgard. Ray Walker's *Wai-Aniwa,* skippered by Chris Bouzaid was third in the Hobart and top points scorer for the Southern Cross Cup. New Zealand won the series with 376 points from Britain (353) and New South Wales (314).

Early in 1971 Fischer won the One Ton Cup, a prized international trophy. This feat won Syd recognition as Australian Yachtsman of the Year. The circumstances were unusual. The One Ton Cup is an ancient European trophy whose name bears no relation to the size of boats which presently race for it. An ornate creation fashioned from a twenty-two pound block of silver, it was presented to the Cercle de la Voile de Paris in 1898 for small yachts conforming to the restricted One Ton Class Rules. Later it became an important trophy for the International 6-metre Class. In 1965 a French yachting visionary, Jean Peytel, organised the presentation of the One Ton Cup for a new concept in ocean racing, the competition between yachts of similar size racing without handicaps. This was done by selecting a handicap rating, originally 22 foot waterline rating under the RORC rule, now 27·5 foot under the International Offshore Rule, to which all yachts had to conform. This gave room, within the rating formula, to experiment with hull shape and sail area, providing the answer came out the same. The yachts it produced, called One Tonners after the trophy they race for, are around thirty-nine feet overall, swift, and because of the close boat-for-boat racing, efficient, and very well crewed.

Until 1971 Australia hadn't made any significant showing in the One Ton Cup. Ron Swanson tried in 1966. He took *Salome,* a yacht he designed and built especially for the Cup, to Copenhagen. But she was outclassed and finished fifteenth. A Swanson 36, *Wathara II,* owned by Bruce Cameron, and a Sydney Sparkman and Stephens boat, *Maria Van Diemen*, owned by Peter Hill, went to Le Havre in 1967, to be soundly beaten into sixteenth and twentieth places. But the New Zealander, *Rainbow II*, encouraged by her 1967 Sydney-Hobart race win, went to Heligoland, an island off the German coast, to finish an encouraging second in 1968. Then, in 1969, Chris Bouzaid and his snappy young crew, carried off the Cup to a hero's welcome in Auckland. Chris and his crew were the slickest yacht-handling combination I have ever seen. From Heligoland in 1969, they took *Rainbow II* to England for Cowes Week and the Fastnet race which maybe they would have won had it not been for the calm. I watched them sail rings around the Australian Admiral's Cup team in a training session at Cowes one day. Through a tack, their sheets snapped home so quickly that the yacht hardly dropped a fraction of a knot.

To defend the One Ton Cup in March, 1971, the New Zealanders began frantically building new boats and training crews to the high standard set by the *Rainbow II* bunch. The Royal New Zealand Yacht Squadron, celebrating its Centennial Year, made a supreme organisational effort, offering accommodation and transport incentives which attracted the best overseas One Tonners; a fleet of seventeen representing nine countries, with entry limited to three yachts from each country, finally faced the starter.

Against this, Australian enthusiasm for One Tonners had run down. From a promising fleet of a dozen or so, boosted by the popular Swanson 36s, interest sharply dropped after the IOR rule was introduced in 1970. The new formula had made the older One Tonners obsolete. From a possible twelve to fourteen entry list, only five contested the Australian trials. But one of these was an up-to-the-minute IOR design by Olin Stephens, *Stormy Petrel,* owned by Charles Curran and built by Swanson Brothers. Graham Newland, now a full-time design and tuning consultant, had added some extra magic in the form of 1,800 pounds more lead ballast, and a heavy 625-pound engine to sink the waterline and enable the sail area to be pushed up two feet within the rating formula. The extra weight gave her an ability to carry her way in sloppy seas, and the tall rig helped her light weather performance.

Stormy Petrel easily won the Australian trials. But in the Hobart race which followed, the boat took a thrashing in gales which knocked out fourteen of the sixty-one starters. Her main bulkhead under the mast fractured, and the cockpit-coachhouse moulding tended to twist away from the fibreglass hull, causing bad deck leaks. She needed a good deal of work to be put right and Curran, with heavy business commitments and the demands of a young family on his time felt himself unable to do the boat justice in the One Ton Cup. He was devoted to the boat, prepared to do anything to see her do the best she could, even if it meant selling her. So he offered her to boat owners he thought could do well with her in Auckland; Syd Fischer was the one to snap her up.

Fischer stacked a strong crew aboard: Graham Newland, Pod O'Donnell, Hugh and Ian Treharne, and Butch Dalrymple-Smith. The Treharnes were brothers who had won a world 18-footer championship and they had sailed aboard *Stormy Petrel* in the trials. Butch Dalrymple-Smith was a technically-minded and very experienced young English hand who had remained in Australia after arriving as a crew-hand on *Prospect of Whitby* for the 1969 Southern Cross Cup.

While these men had great confidence in the ability of the boat, there was no opportunity to train on her seriously beforehand. She was sailed straight to Auckland from Hobart after repairs. Strong winds, right up to the beginning of the series, prevented any worthwhile crew training.

Meantime, the Aucklanders were expecting another Kiwi victory. They were buoyed up by an exciting trials series in which the hero of 1969, Chris Bouzaid, had to struggle to make the team with a late run aboard *Wai-Aniwa*, a brand-new Dick Carter design boat built in aluminium. And the other two New Zealand representatives were

The Duncanson 34 fibreglass yacht is a fine example of the Australian trend to stock production

Young Nick, skippered by Alan Warwick, who had been Bouzaid's right-hand man aboard *Rainbow II* in 1969, and *Escapade*, by Gil Hedges. Both were brand new Sparkman and Stephens boats of the same Swan 37 design as *Stormy Petrel*. The crews of these boats had trained hard for months and the Kiwis were clear favourites to win the series.

So the whole country, with newspapers clearing their front pages to relay the news of the racing, tack by tack, was stunned when *Stormy Petrel* stole the bacon, winning the first race over a 27.5-mile Olympic course; then winning the second, a 150-miler around the beautiful Hauraki Gulf, dropping to sixth in the second Olympic course race but clinching the series with a win in the 270-mile marathon which scored double points. She finished sixth in the fifth race on the Olympic course, which completed the series, but by then she had accumulated enough points to win the Cup without starting in that race.

Stormy's extra weight and taller rig kept her moving in the light winds and lumpy seas which prevailed for most of the racing. Some in-fighting between the New Zealand crews probably helped, too. Convinced that one of them would win the series, the New Zealanders spent a good deal of time watching each other instead of adopting their tactics to cover the fleet as a whole. Warwick protested and secured the disqualification of Bouzaid from the 150-mile race. Warwick alleged he had to alter course while beating up to a mark on starboard tack to miss Bouzaid who was running away from it on port. There was no collision, no other boat noted the incident, and while they were within the letter of the rules, Warwick's actions seemed to many to be playing the game too hard. It seemed especially so when he went against a countryman. Hanging on Syd Fischer's wall is a photograph of a caricature tableau of papier-mache figures. There's Syd, with a big grin on his face, looming over the figures of Warwick jabbing a finger in Bouzaid's eye. The photograph was published in a New Zealand yachting magazine. It didn't have a caption because it didn't need one. That was the way the Kiwis felt at the time.

Syd, besides being new to the boat, had difficulty adapting to *Stormy Petrel*'s tiller steering, and she's inclined to be hard to steer anyway. This led to his famous quote after the series ended: "She's a bitch, but she sails well!"

Four helmsmen shared the steering: Newland, Hugh Treharne, O'Donnell, and Fischer. Each spent only an hour at a time on the helm during the long races, but they kept the boat moving all the time. "We had a bloody good crew," Syd said. "Some of the jet setters from Europe couldn't understand us when we spent four days before the races, in our oilskins most of the time in pouring rain, rubbing *Stormy* down on the slips."

Fischer believes that the sails, made by Hugh Treharne, were a little fuller than on some of the other boats and this helped the boat punch through the chop. "The sails were good and we trimmed them constantly," Fischer said. "I can't speak too highly of Hughie's ability on the boat and as a sailmaker. He worked long hours, at night sometimes, on improving our sails."

Syd Fischer, who celebrated his forty-fourth birthday on the day *Stormy Petrel* hit the front in the long race—he kept quiet about it until after the finish so as not to break the spell of concentration—had again selected a winning crew. He leads in an unobtrusive way, without shouting and yelling as some skippers do. He and Graham Newland computed information and opinion on situations from the trained eyes and brains of their crew and reach decisions in the cockpit.

"No one plays the big boss," says Syd. "It's a kind of mutual co-operation. I don't think I've ever had to stand anyone up in front of the others. Once or twice, I've had to pull someone into line, and then it's just been a matter of having a quiet word with the bloke. They know what to do on the boat better than I do. And if we make a mess of something, they are as embarrassed as I am."

Stormy Petrel's win brought the One Ton Cup to Sydney in December 1972. Fifteen yachts representing nine countries fought out the closest

An afternoon cruising party, off Manly, Queensland

series in the modern history of the Cup. By the fifth and final race there were four winners. And in that twenty-seven-mile race, the winner of the Cup was decided only two miles from the finish. Then, *Pilgrim* (Graham Evans, Australia), which held a narrow points lead going into the race, made the tactical mistake that cost it the Cup and presented it to the doggedly-sailed New Zealander *Wai-Aniwa*, again skippered by Chris Bouzaid for Ray Walker.

Pilgrim had only to finish better than seventh in this race to win the Cup. After struggling all day in mid-fleet in the eight to ten knot nor'-easter, it rounded the last mark in sixth place. *Pilgrim* looked secure, carefully but easily covering the seventh boat *Bushwhacker* (Harry Smith and Bob Hartwell, USA). The eighth boat, *Escapade* (Rodney Hill, Britain) posed a distant threat on the opposite side of the course. *Pilgrim* broke off its cover of *Bushwhacker* and tacked into mid-course to try and cover both *Escapade* and *Bushwhacker*. *Bushwhacker*, moving faster as the wind died slightly, easily crossed in front of *Pilgrim* when next they met. *Wai-Aniwa*, whose tactics earlier had been to hold *Pilgrim* back behind the fateful seventh-place line, crossed the finishing line in fourth place and sat waiting for *Bushwhacker* to decide the outcome of the One Ton Cup. As *Bushwhacker* finished sixth, ahead of *Pilgrim*, the horns and cheers at last rang out for the New Zealanders.

Wai-Aniwa ended the series with 74.5 points to *Pilgrim*'s 73.875. Third was *Pathfinder* (Roy Dickson, New Zealand) with 66.75, and fourth *Ydra* (Hans Beilken, Germany) with 62.5. A broken forestay rigging screw eight hours after the start of the longest race of the series, the 270-miler, cost *Ydra* her chances. This new Dick Carter design was the outstanding boat of the series and had she finished better than tenth in the long race, she would have won the Cup. *Wai-Aniwa* ground her way to the top of the points score with determined, thoughtful handling by

Bouzaid and his crew rather than boat speed. Bouzaid always had doubts about the full-bodied *Wai-Aniwa*'s ability to handle the peculiar sloppy seas off the New South Wales coast. But he never gave up. *Pilgrim*, a big-bodied Sparkman and Stephens design, was sailed well by a young crew and steered with great accuracy by sailing master Jim Burke. She had the speed and the crew had the will to win. Lack of experience in big-time racing over the shorter Olympic-style course let them down.

The close finish and close racing of the One Ton Cup made Australian yachtsmen aware of the excitement of level racing. But with a new One Tonner costing up to $60,000 building activity in this class slowed to a stop in 1973. More interest was being taken in the smaller level-racing classes, Half Ton (21.6-foot rating) and Quarter Ton (18-foot rating). A top Half Tonner could be launched for $20,000, and a Quarter Tonner for $6,000 to $10,000.

These boats fall into the offshore substructure known as the Junior Offshore Group (JOG). The JOGs, of less than twenty-four foot waterline, with improvements to hull design, rig, and equipment, are becoming faster and more suited than they used to be for offshore racing. Captain John Illingworth was a founding father of the JOG in England in 1950 to promote racing for yachts of between sixteen and twenty-four feet on the waterline. In Australia the JOG movement is booming.

They, too, have international aspirations. The Captain James Cook Trophy was presented by the Australians in 1968 for international JOG competition along Admiral's Cup lines. Australia sent a team to the first challenge, in England in 1968, which the French team won. But the Australian JOGers, after this initial burst, were unable to organise themselves sufficiently to mount another challenge. Now, with full-scale support from the clubs, the JOG association has realised its basic aim to have the little fellows taken seriously in Australia and no doubt more international involvement will flow from this.

With crews of three or four, an overnight race in these bounding small boats is just as demanding as in a big ocean racer and, usually, more fun with everyone on board having to take a crack at every task.

Going into the seventies, the JOGs were the growing force in an ocean racing scene that had changed dramatically in five years. For by then, the "battlers" of the early days, the yachtsmen who had designed and built their own boats, like Ron Swanson and the Halvorsens, had all but disappeared from the scene. In their place in the winning lists stood the millionaire yacht owner with the latest overseas design, the best equipment and sails that money could buy, the paid hand aboard to constantly scrape, varnish and paint, and keep the advanced equipment in working order. Granted this same millionaire was usually a great bloke who mixed well with his crews. And there's nothing like ocean racing to level out pretentions; ever tried to be pretentious in the middle of a Bass Strait gale, with only wet blankets to lie in and every stitch of clothing wringing wet? The monied man gave cheap sailing to a number of yachtsmen who couldn't afford to own boats.

But it was sad to reflect that in the race for the services of Stephens, Carter, and others from overseas, the good local designers like Payne, Hood, Swanson, Halvorsen, and Miller were given the go-by.

I had a sad beer or two with Ron Swanson in the Middle Harbour Yacht Club one day in 1970. We had been for a sail in one of the little twenty-two-foot fibreglass day-sailers that are bread and butter to the Swanson Brothers' yard.

"You know," said Ron, "we could never afford to build another Admiral's Cup boat for ourselves, let alone take her to England if we were selected. The game's beyond us now."

A few weeks later, Ron left to ferry *Sundowner*, his hope for the 1969 Admiral's Cup trials, to America and sell her there. He had been unable to find a buyer in Australia. The previous year, the famous *Freya* had been sailed to the same Valhalla by Magnus Halvorsen.

While Ron was away his brothers, Ken and Jim, kept the home fires burning. Their main job was building a new one-off forty-five footer to an Olin Stephens design.

An era had ended.

In 1973, the success of the Bob Miller designs, *Ginkgo* and *Apollo II*, the popularity of the designs of Peter Joubert of Melbourne, and the return of Alan Payne with a commission to draw a new Half Tonner, give promise of greater recognition for Australian designers.

Graham Newland: builder, rigger, and tuner of big yachts

Graham Newland

"I've been spoilt."

GRAHAM NEWLAND'S CAREER in ocean racing spans the transition period from the 1950s, when fleets were filled with cruising yachts and inshore yachts made over as ocean racers, to the 1970s where specialised ocean-racing "machines" dominate the racing. And as a professional consultant on building, rigging, and tuning big yachts he's become very much the man that makes all the beautiful machinery tick.

Newland, an engineer, became so involved in the mechanics of setting up big yachts for other people that, in 1970, he was able to sell up his marine dealership and devote himself to the task full-time.

He's a tall, thoughtful, efficient fellow; one of the unspectacular workers of the sport. But his influence, through the new big breed of Admiral's Cup boats, and the One Tonners, has been important to the success of Australian yachtsmen in these classes. As the man in Australia for Sparkman and Stephens, the American design factory presided over by the "dean" himself, Olin Stephens, he's right at the heart of offshore progress.

Think of him as an obstetrician to the birth of big yachts. He fills in the communications gap between the designer on Madison Avenue, New York, and the Sydney boat-builder; translating the Stephens vision to the owner and the builder, rounding up all the bits and pieces the builder must have, and where he can, devising improvements in the complex engineering of these modern yachts.

He was able to institute changes to *Ragamuffin* which gained her small but valuable advantages to rating and speed. He advocated the extra ballast of around 1,800 pounds, which helped give *Stormy Petrel* the edge over two identical Sparkman and Stephens designs in the New Zealand One Ton Cup team. Arthur Byrne engaged him to preside over the birth of his new Sparkman and Stephens forty-eight footer, *Salacia II*, and Newland has since been busy with a whole new group of Admiral's Cup boats and One Tonners building in Sydney.

In love with his job, with sailing, and short of being able to field a boat of his own in these new "gold plater" fleets, he is content.

Besides tuning yachts, Graham Newland knows how to sail them. He's twice won the Sydney-Hobart race, with his own thirty-five foot Lion Classer, *Siandra*, in 1958 and 1960. He has sailed in every Admiral's Cup challenge and was aboard *Stormy Petrel* in her One Ton Cup win as right-hand man to Syd Fischer, as he had been aboard *Ragamuffin* from launching.

Aboard a boat and ashore, Graham Newland gives out an impression of steadiness, a man who knows where he's going and who will be cool in a crisis. There is a story told of his early days, of how in racing up to Lake Macquarie, Newland handed the tiller to a new crew-member with instructions to sail for Norah Head lighthouse. The crew was roused from a pleasant doze by the tyro asking whether he should pass the lighthouse to the left or the right! On deck, they found the yacht in the first line of breakers. She was gybed, all standing under spinnaker. After the mess was cleaned up, Graham Newland spoke his first and only words on the incident: ". . . that was close."

I first met Graham Newland at the finish of the 1960 Sydney-Hobart race. He was wandering nervously about Constitution Dock, knowing he had a good chance of winning the race but waiting for the time to run out for other yachts who had a chance of beating him on handicap. Ron Swanson, something of a wild young fellow in those days, who had sailed with Graham aboard *Siandra* for the race, was steadying his nerves in the nearest pub. Graham related how in heavy fog *Siandra* had taken the inside passage between the dangerous Hippolyte Rocks off Tasman Peninsula and the shore.

"We saw the rocks and realised they were the Hippolytes. We turned up the Pilot Book and it said the passage inside them was on no account to be attempted. But by that time, we were halfway through anyway," Graham said. We chatted for a while. Graham impressed me then as a serious-minded student of yachting who stood out from the rip-or-bust school of the time. At the same time, when it became apparent around noon that *Siandra* had won, Graham joined Ron in the pub.

Graham Newland was a late starter to sailing, taking it on when he was about twenty-seven. Gordon Ingate introduced him to it. His family

and the Ingate family had been closely associated since the first World War when the fathers had served overseas together. Graham grew up with Gordon's elder brother Jack and one day Gordon asked Graham to go for a sail aboard *Jasnar*.

"I was bitten by the sailing bug and bought a twenty-eight footer, a straight-steamer called *Firefly* which I began racing with the Sydney Amateurs," he said.

"I started cleaning up with her right away, but she leaked like a sieve.

"I entered for a race to Long Reef and—I'll never forget this—Cliff Gale (an official of the club) rang me up and said:

"'I don't know how to say this. I would rather criticise a bloke's wife than his boat. But we can't accept your entry. *Firefly* leaks too much!'

"That was true, and that was it. I had to put her up on the slips and have her re-timbered, and new keel bolts fitted. And that was how I came to meet Ron Swanson.

"I went up on Ford's slips at Berry's Bay and Ron was there at the time building himself an 18-footer, one of his first boats."

This friendship between the two men grew when Graham Newland decided to go for a better boat, chose Arthur Robb's Lion Class design, and employed Ron Swanson on wages to help him build it. *Siandra* was launched in June, 1956.

"Ron and I had built up a good friendship over the building of the boat and he came into my crew with Frank Likely and Pod O'Donnell. For all of us, it was our first crack at ocean racing. Poddy was still at school. Peter Mounsey also did a lot of races with us and Doug Patterson joined us in 1958.

"*Siandra* began to percolate right away. She was pretty well rated and we won our share of races as our own progress in ocean racing caught up with the potential of the boat.

"We took our racing seriously and trained for it. We would go out on Friday nights for an all-night training sail, and we spent some pretty uncomfortable nights out there, bashing to windward and then running home in the morning. We had meetings at home to kick ideas around. I think we were probably one of the best-prepared crews of those days.

"After the first season, I converted *Siandra* to masthead rig, a pretty advanced step in those days, and we were one of the first boats to put a vang on our boom; simple things like that were all part of the boat's success."

Making fittings for *Siandra,* winches, and roller-reefing gear, gradually led the Newland engineering business into making yacht fittings and finally into retailing.

Graham sold *Siandra* suddenly, at the height of her success in the 1960-61 season, to Mike Boyden, the brother of Tony Boyden, who owned the 1964 British America's Cup challenger *Sovereign*.

Graham explained: "He asked me for a look over the boat, then said, 'Do you want to sell her?' I told him I had no idea of selling at that time but he produced a cheque already made out for a lot more than I con-

FACING PAGE: The bosun's chair provides a good view of the activities on the wharf

sidered she was worth. Next morning, I agreed to sell provided we could complete the season. We won the points score, and Mike Boyden took it over from there.

"Jim Samson asked me to sail *Anitra* for him—he had bought it from the Halvorsen Brothers—and that started me on the trail of sailing other people's boats."

Graham sailed with Gordon Ingate again, aboard *Caprice of Huon* in the 1965 Admiral's Cup, then with Gordon Reynolds aboard the same boat in 1967, after sailing aboard *Gretel* in the America's Cup trials against *Dame Pattie*. Syd Fischer asked him straight after that to join his new boat.

Meantime, his business, now that he was heavily committed to selling fibreglass powerboats and outboard motors as well as yacht fittings, had grown. But it was more demanding on the ocean-racing spare time of Graham Newland, so finally, in 1970, when he was offered a good price for the valuable Johnson outboard motor franchise, he decided to sell up and get out.

"I'm not a selling type, particularly the hard-selling needed for outboard motors and boats and each year the business was getting harder for me. I found it was very time-consuming, calling for a seven-day-week effort, and I am too lazy to become that involved. So when someone made me an offer for the Johnson franchise, I more or less jumped at the opportunity.

"I had by then made up my mind to devote myself to setting up new boats. Frequently people would ask me to help with the construction of new boats—this happened with *Ragamuffin* on a love basis, something I could not repeat as it cost me too much time. Next, Arthur Byrne came up with the offer of helping with *Salacia II* on a business basis.

"And I thought: 'Well, that does it; I'll hop right out of the marine retail trade and I will try to make this a business. It is something I enjoy doing and I can make some sort of an income from it.'"

After *Salacia II*, he worked on Lou Abrahams' new Admiral's Cup triallist, *Vittoria,* the One Ton Cuppers, *Stormy Petrel* and *Kerkyra IV,* the 1971 Italian One Ton Cup entry, the new Sparkman and Stephens forty-five footers, *Meltemi* for Bill Psaltis and *Queequeg* for Rick Dowling, and the 1972 vintage One Tonners, *Pilgrim* and *Mark Twain.*

Newland doesn't share the fears of some other yachtsmen that Australia, after a burst of success that won it the Admiral's Cup and One Ton Cup, is slipping behind America and Europe in ocean racing.

"We are right up to world standard in many departments because most of our people are much more dedicated than the average boat-owning type of person overseas. I think here, where the bulk of our fleet actively race, the position is completely the reverse to England and the States. The bulk of their fleets are basically cruising boats and in the Bermuda race, the committee have even had to issue a circular to all competitors about the number of dropouts. If anyone drops out, they have to give a good reason why, otherwise they might not be allowed to compete again in future years.

"This is just a sign that a lot of people in the Bermuda race consider it a bit of a jolly, and go along with their wives and girl friends just for a cruise.

"I believe the only area in which we have yet to match them is in the design of the hulls. Our naval architects unfortunately don't get the through-put of work that will keep them right up to world standards. They can't afford the research, and so forth. But in other areas I think we are right up with it, particularly in crewing."

I asked Graham for some impressions of the bigger events he had been involved in with his more recent sailing.

It's 3 a.m. and *Crusade* and *Apollo* raft up for an inquest after finishing in the Sydney-Hobart race

"In the first Admiral's Cup, we just didn't have the boats. Our yachts were too tailor-made for Australian conditions and while *Caprice* was an English design, and did do well in England, the other two were boats that were slanted heavily towards Hobart race conditions. The English conditions just didn't suit them," he said.

"We won the second challenge through our crews and our boats. I don't think there was a better team in all three series than the Australian team that time. We were right up there all the time. Everything was going for us. We had a good, well-balanced team of boats, the best team of crews, and our preparation was just right. Also, we didn't have any unlucky breaks as we did in 1969.

"We were robbed in 1969. Again, we were of world standard, without a doubt, as a three-boat team. It was just sheer bad luck that the weather went the way it did. This robbed us of any chance. It also robbed the second best team of any chance and the third or fourth best team won the series.

"In 1971, we had the potential to win and were unlucky in the end. But we wasted a lot of time on crew training in Australia that would have been better spent in getting to know our boats and tuning them for top speed. The crew training is important, but it could have been left to the quite substantial spare time we have before the races in England. In the end, a lot of this time was used in trying to make the boats go faster, instead of crew training."

Graham recalls his 1967 experiences on *Gretel* as "Eighteen months of heartbreak with the Twelves."

But he adds: "It was an experience I don't regret. I learned a lot in that eighteen months about big boats and worked with Alan Payne in the tank up at the University for a while. I learned something about the facets of design and tank-test work. It added to my general knowledge a helluva lot. But looking at the other side, there were too many frustrations and political problems, plus things associated with the deal, that would make me think twice before being involved in such a race again.

"But I really think Australia could win the America's Cup. I don't really go for the attitude that America has this so-called technology that is supposed to be very superior. I'll try not to pat myself on the back, but the technical side of some of the Stephens designs I have been associated with were almost thrown overboard, along with their hardware. And I am quite convinced that what's gone on in its place, from Australia, has been quite superior. And Olin is the guy who designs the American Twelves.

"I don't agree with a lot of the American hardware. It's unnecessarily heavy, cumbersome, not very efficient. I think Olin Stephens puts an extra effort into the Twelve Metres, but I can't see any of the equipment being so radically better, or far enough advanced to be the winning factor.

"I think the one big thing that the Americans have got that we have yet to equal is sail-cloth. But in every other department, I don't see why we couldn't be at least as good.

"I reckon our yachtsmen are just as good. We might lack the helmsmen who have had as much keen competition as some of theirs, but I think that is fairly easily remedied."

Was big-yacht ocean racing going to be priced out of existence?

His answer: "Yes and no. I think we are going to see a lot more smaller boats, but this is going to be mainly because of the affluent society. More people with a reasonable amount of money who can afford Quarter Tonners, or Half Tonners, and maybe One Tonners. And I think the level of big-boat numbers probably won't drop, but it won't increase dramatically as it will in the small classes. I think the Half Ton class is one worth watching because it is going to be a tremendous design class. You can afford to do a lot of things in a Half Tonner that you couldn't experiment with in a *Ragamuffin* sized boat."

How important is the crew to the success of a boat like *Ragamuffin*? "A lot of us on the boat had a fairly long relationship. Doug Patterson started sailing with me right from school. He was one of the strong hands I had on *Siandra*. He sailed with me on *Anitra* and *Tahuna*, and all the boats I have sailed. But the whole crew was a crew of thinkers as well as doers, always trying to work out better ways of doing something, whether it was how to sheet a sail or hoist a spinnaker. But more than that they worked on assembling information about the boat; what direction it liked being pointed in what breeze. We were collating it all the time and talking about it all the time. The crew was contributing all the time and consequently we got more and more out of the equipment."

How much time was involved in campaigning a boat like *Ragamuffin*?

The moment every Sydney-Hobart racer lives for: entering the dock for Hobart's warm welcome

"Our typical pattern was to sail every weekend, at least one day in a race, and most of us would also cruise on the boat on a Sunday with our wives and girl-friends, in which time we tried out a few ideas. And we saw each other at least once a week. We went to a gym and were fairly constantly in touch with each other by phone. If anyone had an idea, we rang each other up and tossed it around a bit. Perhaps we would try it out the next weekend. So we were a pretty close sort of a team in a lot of ways."

How did he come to terms with the millionaire owners he had sailed for or advised? Were there personality problems?

"The problem with big-yacht racing is that you need a man who has been a tremendous success in business so that he has made enough money to buy the boat. If he has been as dedicated as that, he won't have time to be involved very deeply in yachting.

"On the other hand, you have the fellow who has not been prepared to sacrifice himself to business and who consequently hasn't got the money to own the boat he wants, but has dedicated himself to yachting and has acquired all the knowledge that's needed to run a big yacht.

"So you have to marry these two sorts of people. A successful businessman who buys a boat finds it hard to understand that there are a lot of things he doesn't know about yachting initially. And so there is a period where there can be personal difficulties.

"But he has only to be beaten a few times, or to have things pointed out to him, and he soon realises that he is equally dependent on a crew that has been able to acquire the knowledge he hasn't got.

"And if he is typical of the business person with a yacht, he quickly learns. He is trained through his business experience to assess a situation. It doesn't take long for the man to be at least a top-average yachtsman. He may never become a Paul Elvstrom but he learns."

I could not resist asking Graham Newland if he ever feels the desire to own his own boat again?

"Oh sure. I'm afraid I've been a bit spoilt. I have considered building a new boat a number of times since I sold *Siandra* but each time I have, my ideas have grown quicker than my pocket. So it's always a case of wait another year. And also, I love big boats, so the sort of boat I'd like would be forty-five to fifty feet, and I'm afraid I haven't got that sort of money as yet. I've had to be content with letting other people pay the bills."

One of those days—being towed ashore with a bad wineglass in the spinnaker

FD
KA166

THE OLYMPIANS

SAILING A YACHT is no easy way to making an Olympic Games team. Unlike other sports, only one crew can be selected from each of the Olympic classes, and the competition is fierce. To stay in the running in an Olympic class, you must be able to keep tabs on what the top-liners overseas are doing; firstly, it is necessary to be in amongst the overseas boats if you are aiming to be selected for the Games and, secondly, this is important, so that an Australian competitor doesn't cotton on to some important overseas advance in equipment or technique before you do.

So to ensure they remain competitive with fleets in other parts of the world, the Australian Olympic classes send their best crews away to world championships and other important events in off-Olympic years. This costs money and, besides having his hand in the pocket all the time to keep his boat up to scratch, the Australian Olympic class yachtsman finds himself having to kick in fairly regularly towards these overseas trips. This is done either through straight donations or by devoting a good deal of time and effort into fund-raising activities such as raffles, dances, barbecues, wine-bottling sessions, and so on.

While some of the classes are not common to all States, the Olympic movement is strong in every State. It has been one of the main unifying influences of the sport, bringing together as it does, officials from all centres, to determine questions of team selection and finance.

The Olympic movement led directly to the formation of the Australian Yachting Federation with the allocating of delegates from yachting associations of all six States in 1950. And while the Australian Yachting Federation has since become concerned with administering the sport, the influence of the Olympic classes had much to do with Australia gaining direct affiliation with the world governing body for yacht racing, the International Yacht Racing Union, in 1967. Until then, our voice was

FACING PAGE: A Flying Dutchman in perfect trim for windward work. Extra ounces of power are being gained by the hands clasped behind the head

heard on this international policy-making body only through an English representative. When the growth of the sport threatened to outstrip the administration in Sydney, a full-time professional secretary, Tony Mooney, was appointed in 1969 by the Yachting Association of New South Wales.

Olympic-class sailing means working steadily through the four-year cycle between Games, maintaining or building up to a peak of performance through Australian championships and other intermediate goals. Hours must be spent working on the boats at night, sailing through the chill of a winter, out with a mate tuning and training into darkness after hurrying home from work midweek, racing both Saturday and Sunday most weekends during the season. But knowing that you are part of an international sailing movement; that others in the same boats are doing the same sort of things in dozens of overseas countries, helps make it worthwhile, even if you never win that Olympic medal.

Olympic yachting in Australia began with Alexander Stuart ("Jock") Sturrock who, besides winning a bronze medal in the 5.5 metre class at the 1956 Olympics, later gained wider international fame as skipper of the America's Cup challengers, *Gretel* and *Dame Pattie*.

His father, also Alexander Stuart (the "Jock" came to prevent confusion), was a leading skipper in the twenty-one-foot restricted class. This was a ballasted centreboarder carrying big sail area on overhanging booms and long bowsprits which, until Australia became international-class conscious after the second World War, provided keen interstate competition for the Forster Cup. As an eight-year-old Jock began his sailing in the dinghy of his father's twenty-one footer, *Idler*, from the shore near his home at Brighton, a Melbourne bayside suburb. He rigged it with a spritsail and jib, shoved an oar out the back, and as the dinghy had no centreboard, filled it half full of water to stop it from blowing sideways.

By the time he was twelve, Jock was sailing a proper boat, a twelve-foot Cadet Dinghy, and soon he was winning State competitions until finally the Australian championship in 1933. One of his opponents was a youngster called Norman Booth, from Sydney, later to become one of his greatest foes in the Dragon and 5.5 metre classes, and yet one of his greatest friends. They sailed together in the afterguard of *Dame Pattie*.

After a brief spell with the fourteen-foot skiff-type dinghies Jock, at the age of eighteen, helped start the International Star Class in Australia. He had one of the first three of these boats built in Australia. Interest grew in the Stars, a fast, two-man, twenty-two-foot-eight-inch sloop and in 1938, twelve were racing on Port Phillip Bay.

In 1948, after a run of championship wins broken by the war (when Jock served in New Guinea with the infantry, rising from private to captain), Jock and his crewman, Len Fenton, won nomination for the Olympics. Yachting was not recognised in Australia as an Olympic sport at the time and they had to raise their own expenses to send their Star, *Moorina*, to the Olympic regatta at Torquay. They raised £1,000 in one great night in the Brighton Town Hall when Walter Lindrum, the world's champion billiards player, gave an exhibition, and yachtsmen from all over Victoria bet on the shots and the money flowed.

Sturrock and Fenton finished a respectable seventh out of eighteen boats at the Games. They were leading in the first heat but fouled out when *Moorina* laid over in a puff and touched the American entry rounding the last buoy.

"We were only good for the hard weather," Jock recalls. "We didn't have the sails for the light stuff." They won the last heat when the wind blew up to thirty knots. Later, they sailed in the world championship at Portugal, finishing eighth after a dismasting.

Sturrock moved on to the Dragon Class in 1951, then in its infancy in Australia with about eight boats racing, and won selection for the 1952 Olympics in Finland with Kev Worcester and Doug Buxton as crew. They couldn't afford to take their own boat and the Dragon they chartered in Helsinki was old, heavy, and hopelessly outclassed. They finished twelfth. On return to Australia, they won the first Prince Philip Cup, presented by the Duke of Edinburgh, for the Australian Dragon Class championship, in 1954. In 1955, Dave Bingham, owner of the 5.5 metre *Buraddoo*, asked Jock to sail her in the trials for the 1956 Olympics. He won the trials, narrowly defeating the Royal Sydney Yacht Squadron's *Kirribilli*, skippered by Pat Taylor.

Rolly Tasker, dedicated to making boats sail faster

The 1956 Olympics, held in Melbourne, were the first in which Australia was represented in all classes. And, by bringing the world's best Olympic class sailors, they sparked off great interest in the Olympic classes. *Buraddoo* won a bronze medal, losing the silver by twenty-two points in a total 6,000 to Britain's *Vision*. The Swedish yacht *Rush V* was the winner.

Rolly Tasker from Perth went as close as anyone can to winning a gold medal. With Malcolm Scott a strapping crew, he tied with the New Zealander Peter Mander (with Jack Cropp as crew) on 6,086 points in the 12 Square Metre Sharpie Class. A countback of placings found in the New Zealanders' favour as they had three wins to Tasker's two. And Tasker had actually lost the gold medal by being caught port and starboard by France in the last heat. Tasker claimed he had been unable to tack because of the proximity of Canada on his port side although he had hailed Canada about. Had he then tacked and fouled Canada, he had a chance of winning a protest against Canada. But after the collision with France, he had little hope of surviving France's protest.

Tasker was the first of the totally-devoted Australian dinghy sailors. By involving himself and his crew completely in preparing the boat and perfecting team work he put together a record of thirty-three wins in Australian titles. Most of these were in the Sharpies; he had 180 wins with one of his boats, but later he dominated the Flying Dutchman class, the nineteen-foot-ten-inch speedster which, after the Melbourne Olympics, replaced the Sharpie.

Rolly (short for Rolland) began sailing at eleven in the tender for his father's launch. He raced VJs and a 16-foot skiff before going into the Sharpies.

He built his own boats, designed his own fittings, and made his own sails. This latter talent finally induced him to give up his career as an accountant and become a full-time sailmaker. He became one of the world's biggest sailmakers with lofts in France, Hong Kong, America, and Sydney, as well as the home loft at Claremont, Perth.

He won Australia's first world championship in the Flying Dutchman Class in Austria in 1958 with Ian Palmer as crew. He first heard of the Flying Dutchman at the 1956 Olympics when a competitor showed him the plans, and almost immediately began building one. As soon as the Flying Dutchman was named as the new Olympic class, Tasker took his boat to Europe, at his own expense, to gain experience. Both masts were crushed in shipment.

"We found an ancient boatbuilder, he must have been eighty or ninety years old, on the shores of Lake Attersee, who would build us a new pine mast in a hurry," Tasker said. "But our preparations for the championship were set back four days. So for the next eight or nine days we sailed from seven in the morning until five at night, to get our mast-sail combinations right.

"In the end, they called the world championship regatta off because we got so far ahead on points. We beat forty-eight boats from twenty-seven countries."

Tasker was untroubled to win the trials on Port Phillip Bay for the 1960 Rome Olympics, building up sufficient points in the early heats to gain selection without a seventh heat being held. There were some rumblings from the other competitors that Tasker had used big Andy White as crew in the trials but intended taking the lighter Ian Palmer to Naples for the Olympic regatta. However, this move was officially approved. At Naples, Tasker was a disappointing nineteenth. He just couldn't master the light Bay of Naples breezes.

He all but won the Flying Dutchman world championship for the second time at Florida in 1962, with Andy White on trapeze. They were, in the end, up against Hans Fogh of Denmark with the world's greatest sailor of modern times, Paul Elvstrom, crewing and calling the shots. Going into the final heat, the Danes held a lead of 200 points (under the old high-scoring Olympic system) and the Australians had to finish fifth or better to take the title. But Fogh and Elvstrom boxed them in from the starting line, holding the Australians back to twelfth place at the first windward mark. They recovered well, but not well enough, to finish sixth with the Danes way back in sixteenth place but winners of the championship by ninety-eight points.

From that time, pressures of his growing business, and from the greater frequency of competition, told on Tasker. He was beaten in the 1964 Olympic trials by John Dawe of Melbourne, an intense competitor who won through consistency rather than the Tasker-type bursts of individual brilliance. And after that, Tasker slipped out of the dinghy classes, apart from a foray into the catamarans to win the "world" B class championship in Melbourne in 1966 (world in parentheses because lack of overseas participation hardly enabled the event to justify the title). In more recent years, he has turned to big-yacht racing, first in a fifty-foot ketch, *Siska*, and the 1971-72 season in a lightweight sixty-foot ocean racer, *Siska II*. Both *Siska*, converted from an old Sydney metre yacht, and *Siska II* were evolved as pure speed machines. Getting there first is regarded as more important in Western Australia than winning handicap prizes.

At the ceremonial opening of the 1960 Olympics in Rome, Jock Sturrock was chosen to carry the flag for the Australian team. Besides recognising Jock's achievement in representing Australia at all three Olympic regattas since the war, this gesture showed that yachtsmen had earned a rating of excellence with the top Australian swimmers and athletes. Jock, again sailing *Buraddoo,* finished sixth in the 5.5 metre class. The boat was just out-designed in this three-man keel yacht development class where hull shapes may vary slightly but decisively within the design formula.

A strong young Queenslander, Ron Jenyns, whose jutting jaw-line spoke for his determination and self-discipline, was fourth in the Finn Class. The Dragon crew from Victoria, led by Mick Brooke, was tenth and the Star Class crew of Bob French and Jack Downey, twentieth.

Brooke, a benign veteran with a natural touch for steering a boat despite the handicap of having the use of only one arm with the other withered from childhood, found himself the centre of a storm at Naples where the Olympic regatta was held. The boat he took there, *Ghost III*, was barred from competing, twenty hours before the first race, on the grounds that she was too small in a stern measurement. Brooke was dismayed. He had gone to Naples with a valid measurement certificate which, he believed, reinforced by a ruling in the class rule book, would stand for all time unless major repairs were made. He claimed the Olympic measurers had originally passed the boat at Naples and that she had not been thrown out until she began to sail particularly well in tuning brushes against the other boats before the regatta.

Ghost III was altered on her return to Melbourne, a new measurement certificate issued, and Brooke, by taking off the Prince Philip Cup in 1961 at Hobart, slayed suggestions that a "sneaky stern" had helped him win the Olympic trials.

The Dragons by this time had become Australia's keenest keelboat class. This twenty-nine-foot-two-inch sloop of classic lines and with gleaming clear timber finish is beautiful to the eye. She was designed back in 1928 by the Norwegian naval architect, Johan Anker, for weekend racing and family cruising. In 1948 she was adopted as an Olympic class and once the racing men really got hold of her, her cabin top was reduced to a minimum and all the cruising appointments skinned out.

As a pure racing class, the Dragon won a staunch following all over Europe and in Australia where her sail plan, moderate by modern

Solings in a light weather spinnaker battle on Broken Bay

standards, suited the stiffish breezes. The close tactical racing, with one slip in crew work inevitably resulting in a lost place, also appealed to Australians.

Into the 1970s, the Dragons were declining in Australia because of the increasing costs of building and maintaining them, and the competition of the less expensive fibreglass Olympic newcomer, the Soling.

Through the 1960s, however, the Dragon attracted the best yachting talent in Australia and it was in this class that the realisation first firmly grew that to stay at the top in home fleets, it was necessary to keep in touch with what the rest of the world was doing. Jack Linacre led the search for knowledge overseas by taking *Gustel XI* to Trieste for the European championship in 1959. Jock Sturrock skippered her, Rolly Tasker sailed for'ard, and they finished fourth in a fleet that included three world champions.

Then Norman Booth, of Sydney, under the inspiration of the clubs abroad of his friend, Jock Sturrock, sailed *Adios* to second placing in the Dragon Gold Cup world championship in Scotland in 1961. Crewing with him were Billy Barnett, the boatbuilder and former 18-foot skiff champion, and Neil Bennell, a young Victorian, who was son of *Oimara*'s owner, Frank Bennell. Neil Bennell was working in England at the time. On his return, Booth showed how travel broadens the mind by winning the Prince Philip Cup with four victories in five heats on Sydney Harbour. Booth had in his crew, Carl Ryves, a youngster of great natural sailing talent. Ryves was later to represent Australia with distinction at the Olympics in the Flying Dutchman class. Booth took off for Europe again in 1962, with Ryves and John Lawson in his crew, and won the British championship. Jack Linacre was back there, too, and won the English Speaking Union Cup in Scotland.

Linacre's win brought this important trophy to Australia where the competition was held at Hobart in November 1963. Five times world champion, Ole Berntsen of Denmark, won the trophy but left Australian opponents inspired by his tactical skill, and by the teamwork of his crew. This was developed by sailing long weekday hours in the Scandinavian twilight.

The Olympic trials the following year held a sensational prelude for a sensational final result. They were split, with the Dragons and Flying Dutchman in Adelaide, 5.5s and Stars on Lake Macquarie in New South Wales, and Finns on Moreton Bay in Queensland.

The Victorians triumphed in Adelaide. Graham Drane, the 1956 representative, a skipper capable of complete self-analysis of why he wins and loses—so much so that it used to be embarrassing listening to him describing a bad day—won the Dragons. John Dawe and Ian Winter, sailing fast and consistently, won the FD trials.

Up in Brisbane, Colin Ryrie, the 1956 representative, wrested the Finn nomination from Ron Jenyns. Ryrie, a man of extraordinary determination on the water, had gathered some valuable tactical information from his friendship with Paul Elvstrom, built up first at the Melbourne

Olympics and later by a business association in which they opened a branch of the Elvstrom sail loft in Sydney. Ryrie's duels with Jenyns in the demanding single-handed Finn class—a fourteen-foot-nine-inch handful under a 107-square-foot sail—enlivened the class until Ryrie quit it for the Dragons in 1966. In the Brisbane trials, Jenyns crossed the line first five times in seven races but was disqualified from one for a breach of the overtaking rules and had to include a seventh and a tenth in his points tally while Ryrie, a model of consistency, had a win, four seconds and a third to count.

But the real drama of 1964 was the 5.5 metre trials series on Lake Macquarie. A talkative old fellow called Bill Northam, in his sixtieth year and with no previous experience in one-design racing, beat the mighty Sturrock, and Norm Booth, who were both sailing brand new boats. Jock's was *Pam*, especially built for the trials and owned by Otto Meik, Commodore of the Royal Melbourne Yacht Squadron and a strong patron of Olympic yachting in Victoria. Otto also owned *Cambria*, the Dragon Graham Drane was sailing to victory in Adelaide, and at the time owned or part-owned a dozen or so other craft. Otto, known as the "Patron Saint of Yachting" had imported a 5.5 designed and built by Ohlson Brothers of Sweden. This was for Jock who went into the trials as odds-on favourite.

But Northam had also gone to a top designer, Bill Luders of America, assembled the best sails he could lay hands on and secured a first-class crew in Dick Sargeant and Pod O'Donnell, two young yachtsmen fresh from campaigning aboard the America's Cup challenger, *Gretel*.

Northam's *Barranjoey* beat *Pam* in the Australian championship which preceded the trials with two wins, a second, a third, and a disqualification against Sturrock's two wins, two thirds, and a disqualification. The trials themselves were even closer. At the start of the last heat, Northam had to finish second or better to defeat Sturrock or Booth on points. And he came from third on the last beat, after shrewdly working lifts in the wind on the north-eastern shore of the lake, to gain the second place he needed.

The result left a good many people dissatisfied. *Pam* had scored more total points over the seven races, 5,403 against *Barranjoey*'s 5,336. But *Pam* had to discard a fourth as her worst performance while *Barranjoey* had a seventh to discard, leaving the final result *Barranjoey*, 5,126, *Pam* 4,950 and *Southern Cross* 4,598. There were moves for more racing before the Australian Yachting Federation made a final choice; it had reserved the right to select any boat for the Olympic team regardless of the points standings. But Northam declined to compete in a further series; he had *Barranjoey* up on the slips for alterations, mainly to make her cockpit larger.

And so Bill Northam left for Tokyo against the misgivings of some critics, including myself, who felt that Sturrock should have been sent because the result was so close, and his experience in top one-design racing so much greater. Well, we were all wrong and I was happy to eat my words as Bill Northam became the first Australian yachtsman to win an Olympic gold medal.

He sailed an excellent series, helped by his great crew and his own shrewd brand of gamesmanship, to win with 5,981 points from Sweden (5,254) and the USA (5,106). Bill, in recounting his win, likes to suggest he needled his crew to excellence. But Dick Sargeant says: "I don't want to spoil a good story, but Bill was very good with us, the quietest skipper you ever saw.

"We got on really well together. He'd let us do whatever we wanted with sail selection and trim. Pod would call most of the tactics and Bill would just steer the boat. But he steered well.

"He would concentrate more than anyone I have ever sailed with going to windward. He gave it the lot, pointing with the best of them and footing with the best of them, so intent on his steering all the time that when he got to the weather mark, you'd have to tell him whether to turn left or right."

The for'ard hand gets the water treatment while the skipper stays dry

Colin Ryrie finished sixth in the Finns, a little unlucky after being positioned to win a medal at the start of the final heat.

Next best was a tenth in the Star Class by *Maryke,* skippered by aggressive Martin Visser who was spurred by a sense of indignation that no one in Australia gave him and crew, Tim Owen, a prayer of a chance before they left.

John Crosbie, manager, recorded in his official report: "*Maryke* did very well to finish tenth in this class. She always performed well to windward but was at a disadvantage downwind against the more modern Stars. A great deal of work was done on *Maryke* before she left Australia and Martin Visser undoubtedly reaped the benefit of his visit to the world championship the previous year."

The Dragon, *Cambria,* was a disappointing twelfth and the Dutchman crew, after appalling luck which forced them to retire in three races, fourteenth.

In 1965 there was the customary post-Olympic let-down period but Norm Booth was off to Europe again, and again runner-up in a world championship, this time for the 5.5 metre class in Naples. With him were Carl Ryves, who now worked for his car retailing company and Peter (Pod) O'Donnell, who had become his son-in-law. They sailed in a number of European regattas, won the Coupe de France, and then took delivery of Booth's new Dragon from the Danish builder, Borresen, to win some races in a regatta at Sandhamn, Sweden.

While this was another important campaign for Booth, it was also feeding the Ryves talent with more valuable international experience.

Carl Ryves is one of the lucky sailors who can make any boat go with a minimum of tuning agony which the plodders of the sport must painstakingly endure. Before joining Booth's Dragon crew in 1962, Carl had won three New South Wales titles in the Flying Dutchman Class and finished third in the 1960 Olympic trials to Tasker and Noel Brooke when he was only eighteen. He began sailing Olympic yachts at fourteen when his father, Jim Ryves, built him a Star.

His sailing association with Booth began at the 1960 Olympic trials when Booth carried Ryves' Dutchman down to Melbourne on top of his Dragon. And when Booth heard Ryves and his crew Steve Auland had nowhere to stay, and were contemplating sleeping on the beach, he offered them beds at the place he was renting for his own crew. After four years with Booth, Ryves returned to the Dutchmen, in 1966, with a for'ard hand who had never even sailed in a dinghy before. But what a hand was Dick Sargeant, with a mile of experience behind him in ocean-racers, aboard *Gretel,* and with Bill Northam. Sargeant, who was also working for Booth, quickly fell into the skilled ways of crewing an FD. Ryves says of Sargeant: "He is a complete yachtsman, a great assistant ashore and all round the course with his knowledge of sail-trim, tactics and tuning." They built Ryves' new Dutchman, *Sidewinder,* together and the new *Sidewinder* which took her place in the 1970-71 season, and worked together on getting them going.

Through the 1966-67 season, the forces began assembling for the Olympic trials the following season. In Sydney, Ryves and Sargeant battled Craig Whitworth and Bob Miller for supremacy in the Flying Dutchman class. Miller and Whitworth, by winning the Australian championship in Perth that season, gained sponsorship from the Australian Flying Dutchman Association to the world championship at Montreal, Canada, the following year. They were going well and hopes were high for another Australian victory. But after being in third position after the second heat, behind John Oakeley and David Hunt of England and Geoff Smale and Ralph Roberts of New Zealand, they went down the drain to mid-fleet obscurity as the wind vanished and the waters of Lake St Louis settled in a glassy calm. Two of the seven heats were called off when the five-hour time limit expired. The fifth and sixth heats were sailed on the same day, both just finishing within the time limit. A first and a third in these two races clinched the title for Oakeley and Hunt. Craig Whitworth returned home acutely aware of the deficiencies of Australian yachtsmen in really light airs and suggested more visits overseas to sail with fleets in England and on the Continent.

That season, Tony Manford of Perth became the first Dragon helmsman to win the Prince Philip Cup four times, beating Jock Sturrock's record. Manford, together with his crew, Tam Thompson and Bob Day, were the outstanding Dragon combination of the period. Each had a share in ownership of the boat, *Leander,* and this helped forge their understanding in crew-work. That year, at home in the hard breezes of home waters of Cockburn Sound as they won the Prince Philip, it looked as though they had the form to win the Olympic selection.

But of equal portent was the performance of the Queenslander, John Cuneo, in steering the sixteen-year-old *Marjorie Anne* into second place to Manford. Cuneo, with seven titles in the Sharpies and an Australian 505 title behind him, had been in the Dragons only ten weeks. The class was at the time taking hold for the first time in Queensland. Later in 1967, realising the potential of Cuneo as an Olympian, a group of Royal Queensland Yacht Squadron members formed a syndicate to buy one of Norm Booth's Dragons, for Cuneo to sail. She had been imported from the Danish yard of Pedersen and Thuessen, and had had little racing. The Queenslanders renamed her *Jock Robbie,* in memory of the past Commodore and life member of their club, John H. Robinson who had been a champion of the Olympic cause until he was lost overboard from his own motor yacht, *Floodtide,* on Moreton Bay in 1966.

Cuneo, an optometrist, is a perfectionist in the Tasker tradition who spares neither himself nor his crew in preparing his boat and perfecting handling techniques. From May 1967 until the trials on Botany Bay the following April, they sailed every weekend, both days, and two week nights as well. At the same time, Cuneo explained, they "re-organised the boat from the bottom up, applying the normal small-boat principles. We tried to arrange her to work like a machine, leaving us to concentrate on sailing her fast."

In the winter of 1967, the small but enthusiastic bunch of sailors sailing the Star Class on Pittwater, New South Wales, sent their champion David Forbes with Ron Toft as crew to the world championship in Copenhagen. They finished only thirty-seventh in a fleet of sixty-five but absorbed a lot of knowledge about the tuning intricacies of this twenty-two-foot-eight-inch veteran. The Star, designed in 1911, is now the oldest one-design yacht afloat, but remains one of the most difficult to tune. Elvstrom once pronounced that the Star teaches more about sails, tuning, and tactics than any other yacht. Forbes and Toft improved to twelfth in the Portuguese championship and seventh in the European championship later in their tour.

The New South Wales Finn Association sent two promising youngsters to the Pacific Finn Cup in Los Angeles and the Pre-Olympics at Acapulco, Tony James and Peter Burford. While they did not shine, although Burford's thirteenth in the Pre-Olympics was a fair result, both were to benefit from their experiences when they pushed Ron Jenyns hard in the trials the following year.

The 1968 trials rightly laid claim to being the greatest regatta ever staged for the Olympic classes in Australia with 164 entries. There were sixteen 5.5s, forty-nine Dragons, forty-six Flying Dutchmen, and thirty-seven Stars involved in sixty-nine races over twenty-nine days on Botany Bay. Value of the fleet was conservatively estimated at $800,000 and the regatta cost close to $20,000 to run.

But a few weeks before it began, the Australian Olympic Federation dismayed officials with an announcement that the yachting team would be reduced to eight yachtsmen plus a manager, which meant that one complete three-man crew would have to be eliminated. The AOF's decision was part of a wholesale slashing of numbers from the 302 it sent to Tokyo to about 170 for Mexico following criticism of the unwieldy nature of the team, misbehaviour of some competitors, and the inclusion of a number of competitors well below international standard.

None of these criticisms could be applied to the yachting team which had acquitted itself well and, on the basis of total performance as a team, was second only to the USA in the yachting at Japan.

Yachtsmen made angry protests to the AOF, pointing out that the heavy investment in new boats had begun four years before and at this late stage it was unfair to drop any class from the team. Other arguments were raised on the basis of the team's good performance in previous Olympics; the strength of yachting (with the claim that it was Australia's second biggest Olympic sport); that only one crew could be sent from each class; and that this crew would compete in all races as there was no elimination at the Olympics.

Against that storm cloud, the trials went on.

The hours of practice and slavery to their boat paid for Cuneo and his crew, Tom Anderson and John Ferguson. They easily won both the Prince Philip Cup and the Olympic trials in the Dragons and were ranked number one on the Australian Yachting Federation's priority list for the

AOF. The number two nomination was Ron Jenyns who won four of the seven heats in the Finn trials; James took two and Burford one. Jenyns was superior to these younger helmsmen in breezes over ten knots where his ability to extend his body rigidly from the boat, instead of falling into the more usual, relaxed slump, wore down the opposition. Burford's effort in finishing third to Jenyns and James was an exceptional one. He had trained alone on St Vincent Gulf, Adelaide, where there are no other Finns, pacing himself against the other centreboard craft.

Third on the nomination list was the Flying Dutchman, *Sidewinder*. Carl Ryves and Dick Sargeant won their trials against high pressure in the end from Jim Hardy and Max Whitnall in *Shiraz II*, with the outcome swinging on the final heat. Ryves and Sargeant had to beat *Shiraz II* in that heat to win and, after a match race all round the course, came home fourteenth. This was one place ahead of *Shiraz II*. Dave Forbes, with Dick Williamson crewing, won six of the seven Star Class heats. Besides his overseas experience of the year before, Forbes had been sharpened by the great number of races sailed by the Stars that season. It was somewhere around ninety.

Bill Northam's gold medal winner, *Barranjoey*, figured in a sensational finish to the 5.5 metre trials. Bill Solomons, skipper of the Sydney Harbour Eight-Metre *Saskia*, and a member of the 1962 *Gretel* squad, was to have sailed *Carabella*, a brand-new boat built especially for the trials by Kevin McCann to the latest Britton Chance design. But while they were preparing this unusual boat Solomons and owner McCann had a disagreement and Solomons walked off. With only a few days remaining to the trials, Solomons chartered *Barranjoey*, which had hardly raced since the 1964 Olympics. With Scott Kaufman and Mick York crewing, Solomons tied the series with Norm Booth who was sailing a new design by Olin Stephens, *Southern Cross III*. As he had a greater number of wins, the tie was broken in Solomons' favour.

But *Barranjoey* was still last on the list of nominations to the Australian Olympic Federation, possibly as a ploy by the AYF. After all they could hardly leave the gold medal winner of the previous Games out of the team. Tony Manford was nominated as manager and Jim Hardy as reserve. After further lobbying and argument, the AOF agreed to let eleven crewmen and a manager go to Mexico. Jim Hardy stepped down as reserve, and Tony Manford could sail if required. Then Mick York had to withdraw from *Barranjoey*'s crew for business reasons, so Jim went into the crew. Just before the Acapulco Olympic regatta, Bob Miller was unofficially seconded to the team as sailmaker and maintenance man, a reserve if necessary.

All the Australians sailed well at the Acapulco regatta. The team was more consistent than any other with not one of the five boats finishing worse than seventh in the final points lists. But they weren't good enough to win a medal. The difficulties of going straight from a southern hemisphere winter to the Olympics in September, without any hard racing beforehand, were later emphasised by all crews. Ron Jenyns was

A Dragon racing in a twenty-five-knot sea breeze on Cockburn Sound, the protected, perfectly fair racing water thirty miles from Perth

The Soling class boat *Silver Mist* in late afternoon light on Broken Bay. Owned by Lindsay Allsop, she was subsequently skippered by Ken Beashel in the 1971 world championship on Long Island Sound
RIGHT: The 5·5 metre *Pam* racing against a late afternoon sky on Broken Bay, New South Wales. Gordon Ingate sailed her to victory in this Australian championship and later took her to Norway to win the Scandinavian Gold Cup

5·5 metre yachts racing in the Australian Gold Cup championship on Sydney Harbour. Although each yacht in the 5·5 metre class is of a different design, the "fives" enjoy extremely close racing. In the 1964 Olympics, Bill Northam won Australia's first yachting Gold Medal with a "five"

132

Catamaran sailing is dangerous but spectacular work, as displayed by this Manta class cat on Cockburn Sound. At top she nosedives, digging in the leeward hull with the risk of tripping and capsizing, and the bottom photograph shows another Manta "flying a hull" RIGHT: A well-sailed Manta at about her ultimate speed in best trim

B
23
JOKER

Ocean racers at a regatta in Cockburn Sound, south of Fremantle, Western Australia

fourth in the Finns once more. "Again and again he showed he had the talent to climb through the fleet," wrote one observer, Jack Knights of England. "What he lacked was the professional application to avoid some quite careless mistakes."

John Cuneo's crew was fifth in the Dragons. The sea—"a strange lumpy sea on top of the ocean swell" from a hurricane influence in the area—baffled him. Ryves and Sargeant were fourth, only .7 of a point away from a bronze medal. Their downwind technique let them down, and it was important on the long, ocean swells. Rodney Pattison and Iain Macdonald-Smith took home Britain's first Olympic gold medal for twenty years. Their performance, after a disqualification in the first race forced them into patterns of extreme caution in the later ones, was the highlight of the regatta. It marked an end to the British attitude in sailing that it was unsporting to try too hard and that playing the game was the thing. Pattisson, a lieutenant in the Royal Navy, had been given the whole summer off with full pay to sail in European regattas beforehand. And the British support group, which included a meteorologist, was the strongest in the Games.

Dave Forbes and Dick Williamson finished sixth in the Star fleet which included three previous gold medal winners, among them Elvstrom. Hitting a mark in the fifth heat, when he was lying fifth, cost Forbes a higher overall placing. Bob Miller said of Forbes at Acapulco: "He is one of the few people who never blamed his equipment. He blamed himself when things went wrong and faced facts so that he was improving himself all the time."

Barranjoey, seventh in a fleet of fourteen, was outclassed by the newer short-keel 5.5 metres. Swedish youngsters, the Sundelin brothers (Jorgen, Ulf, and Peter) won easily. *Barranjoey* had her planking stove in by an out-of-control Mexican Navy workboat that charged into the moorings. But the temporary repair was effective and the boat was restored to mint condition for Bill Northam when she returned to Australia.

In November 1968, the International Yacht Racing Union selected a new, three-man keelboat class for the 1972 Olympics in place of the 5.5 metre.

The replacement was a fast but demanding twenty-six-foot-nine-inch one-design sloop, the Soling, designed by Jan Linge of Norway. The IYRU felt the cost of the 5.5s was getting out of hand and that the cost of a strict one-design class like the Soling, which could be mass-produced in fibreglass, was better suited to the Olympic concept. Australia was away to a flying start in this class, thanks to the astuteness of Phil Rudder who gained the local building rights from Linge long before the IYRU gave the blessing of Olympic status. Within two months of landing the building moulds in Sydney, Rudder had orders for fifty Solings. The first Australian championship for the class, in Easter 1969, drew thirty-eight entries. It was won by Carl Ryves and Dick Sargeant, with Alan Walker joining their crew.

The win earned Ryves and his crew a trip to Europe for the class's first world championship in Copenhagen that July. They made a promising start to their campaign with good results in regattas at Hanko in Norway and Marstrand, Sweden. But a collision put them out of the first heat of the worlds, and they finished fifteenth overall. Paul Elvstrom was the winner.

I was in Copenhagen for that series, arriving a little late while the first heat was in progress. I was shocked to see Ryves, Sargeant, and Walker busy on the quayside at Skovshoved Harbour, transferring fittings from a broken mast to their spare. They told me that about twenty minutes before the start, pre-occupied with tuning adjustments, they hadn't noticed the American, "Ding" Schoonmaker bearing on on starboard. Schoonmaker didn't see them either and the Americans speared the Australians' *Waltzing Matilda,* and dropped the mast over the side as cleanly as if it had been smitten by an axe. Elvstrom, passing by, shouted some words of comfort: "It could have been worse, it could have been me!" Carl, who has always placed more importance on the human element than the boat element in his sailing, accepted the mishap philosophically: "I'm not superstitious about these things," he said, and went out next day for a fourth. But as the series went on, it was obvious he didn't have the speed of the top Scandinavians, the Swedes and the Danes, who dominated this event.

That same northern hemisphere summer, three 5.5 metres campaigned around Scandinavia for the world championship and other events. While the class had lost Olympic status, there was still strong interest in Australia and the trip swung Australia's submission to have the world championship held the following year in Australia. While they didn't star in the world championship, *Pam,* owned and skippered by Gordon Ingate with Mick Morris and Ian Nathan in the crew, did lift Scandinavia's most prized yachting trophy, the Scandinavian Gold Cup. This solid gold chalice of unusual design (it looks something like a huge snail), encrusted with diamonds and rubies, arouses quite fierce national rivalry between the Scandinavian countries. It is sailed on a sudden-death knockout basis, each country allowed to enter only one yacht in a three-race elimination series. The winners go into the final and these three boats keep sailing until one earns three wins over the whole series. This system suited Ingate's aggressive tactics; the breezes tended to be fresh, and crew and boat were right at home in the short and confused seas at Hanko, Norway. They won the third qualifying race then took the next two to clinch the series from *Fram,* sailed by Crown Prince Harald of Norway, and *Nemesis* (Charlie Shunway, USA). The other two Australian fives on that trip were *Crest* (Carl Halvorsen) and *Kings Cross* (Frank Tolhurst).

For the 1970 world titles for the class off Broken Bay, Dave Forbes joined Kevin McCann to skipper *Carabella* to a fine win from America's *Nemesis,* sailed by flamboyant American jet-setter, Ted Turner. *Carabella,* disappointing in her early days, was dramatically improved by the addition of a separate spade rudder made possible by a rule change not

World Flying Dutchman champions Rodney Pattison and his crew Iain Macdonald-Smith will probably never forget this day off Largs Bay, Adelaide. With the wind gusting well over thirty knots and a wild sea, only a handful of boats survived. *Superdocious* was beating to windward here, but her crew have the sail eased right off to keep her on her feet long before the world championship. Jim Gannon, an old Ken Beashel crewman, was the for'ard hand. He had recently returned from the American west coast where he worked for and sailed with the San Diego sailmaker, Lowell North, 1968 Olympic gold medallist in Stars. The fleet was of good class, with entries from Norway (Crown Prince Harald), Sweden, and the Bahamas. And suddenly, Dave Forbes looked to be the man going places fastest in Australian yachting.

That same season, an even more important world championship was held in Australia, the Flying Dutchman, on wild and woolly St Vincent Gulf. This was the last appearance of that incomparable British team, Rodney Pattisson and Iain Macdonald-Smith. And they won again, once more under the pressure of an early failure. In the second race, they broke a rudder gudgeon on *Superdocious* while leading. Runner-up was another British crew, John Truett and Edward Leask, in *Hucklebuck IV*, and the Australian champion, *Invader*, manned by Craig Whitworth and Max Whitnall, was third. *Invader* suffered an initial setback, capsizing while holding the lead in the wild third heat when the wind touched forty knots in the gusts. *Invader* broke a shroud and the wheel winch used for varying its tension, and it took the crew some time to find the right settings again for this complex piece of mast-raking equipment. *Invader* eventually came good with a second and a win in the last two heats.

The 1970-71 season, with the Olympic trials only a season away, brought a surge of activity in all classes. The Dragons had their world championship in Hobart. The previous year, John Cuneo, with John Shaw and Ross Bradbury, took Greg Cavill's *Jennifer* to Majorca where they were runners-up in the Dragon Gold Cup world championship.

The world championship on the Derwent drew a truly international fleet. *Adios II*, with Norm Booth joined by Carl Ryves and Pod O'Donnell, won the Prince Philip Cup which preceded it. But in the championship, victory went to the Swedish Sundelin brothers, the 5.5 metre gold medallists. A retirement from the sixth heat, when a broken spreader threatened to bring down the mast, ended Booth's chances. He led all the way in the final heat. The Sundelins had to finish worse than fifth to miss the title but they brought their *Debutant* home second. Yet it still wasn't all over. *Maj Britt* (Axel Holm, Denmark) protested against *Debutant* over a crossing incident concerning another boat. But after a long hearing, this was dismissed.

So Norm Booth just missed out for the third time on winning a world title. After that, he gave yachting away for a time to concentrate on his new spare-time interest, farming. But this first-class helmsman is never out of the sport for long. He returned to the Dragons for the 1972 Olympic trials. Booth steers a boat well and will go to any lengths to obtain what he feels is winning equipment, from the ends of the earth if necessary, and his boats are always in immaculate shape.

The 1972 Olympic yachting events at Kiel, Germany, re-established the Australians among the world's best in the Olympic classes, following the years of doubt since Bill Northam's gold medal win in 1964.

FACING PAGE: *Firebrand* (Noel Brooke and Lawrence Baillieu) leaps a wave in world championship competition

FD
KA 170

Significantly, the two gold medals won by Australian crews went to those headed by Dave Forbes and John Cuneo, blooded at the previous Olympics. Both had campaigned earnestly on international circuits since Acapulco in 1968, and benefited tremendously from experience in Europe just before the 1972 Olympics. The Australian Yachting Federation gained permission from the Australian Olympic Federation to send the yachtsmen away before the main body of the Olympic team, in time to compete in European regattas. The team, managed by David Linacre, was the best prepared and organised Australia has had.

Dave Forbes, after finishing twenty-eighth in the Kiel Week regatta and tenth in the European championship in Sweden, virtually discarded all his equipment. He chartered a European Star with an American-made mast and boom, recut a mainsail himself and with crewman John Anderson made the whole boat mechanically perfect. By the time the Games started, they had the fastest Star in the fleet. The tricky winds literally sent one famous competitor round the bend, but they read them better than most and returned consistently high placings: 3-8-2-3-4-1-3.

John Cuneo re-thought his whole approach just before the Kiel Olympic regatta. He could only manage fourteenth in the Dragon Gold Cup and could not get his boat, *Wyuna*, going in the choppy Baltic seas. But he sorted out his tuning problems with the help of Olympic team reserve Mike Fletcher, the sailmaker and tuning specialist who also persuaded him to re-organise crewing techniques. Fletcher felt that Cuneo had been trying to do too much himself within the boat instead of concentrating on helming and making full use of his hands, John Shaw and Tom Anderson.

They began the Olympics sensationally, three wins in the first three races. Cuneo started brilliantly, the boat was fast, and he picked the wind shifts well. On the fourth race, he crashed to nineteenth and then a non-finish through lack of wind in the fifth race put Cuneo under pressure. But he stole a third placing in the sixth heat, and in the final heat finished fourth after pushing the American boat, the only competitor with a remote chance of beating him, back to twelth position and right out of the running.

The bright young stars of the Australian team, John Bertrand in the Finns, Mark Bethwaite and Tim Alexander in the Flying Dutchmen, were definite medal prospects that came undone in the difficult light winds and calms. Bertrand, twenty-five, who is assisting Bob Miller in the America's Cup challenger design, finished fourth. He was back in eleventh, seventeenth, and ninth in the opening races. A third and a seventh put him back in the running but then a cruel did-not-finish hit him badly in heat six. The time limit ran out after only four of the fleet of thirty-five had finished and Bertrand sat becalmed completely within a few yards of the line. Had he finished before the limit ran out, he would have won a silver medal. He was second in the final heat.

Bethwaite, son of Frank Bethwaite, the founder of the Northbridge Senior class, could not cope with the light winds. After an opening fourteenth placing, he placed consistently, 6-4-4-4 to be within reach of a medal. But a fourteenth in the sixth heat put him out of the major placings, and with a twenty-second in the last heat, he and Tim Alexander finished eighth. Britain's Rodney Pattisson won his second gold medal.

Australia will be looking to both Bertrand and Bethwaite for the same kind of deeper second-time-round approach that yielded Forbes and Cuneo their medals.

The other Australians were lost beyond mid-fleet. Bob Miller in the Solings had speed but could not pick his way through the shifts, and Gordon Ingate in the Tempests had a truly dreadful series. But the gold medal wins in the Dragons and Stars were enough to encourage all Australian Olympic class sailors to sail those lonely miles in preparation for the next Olympics in Canada in 1976.

Bill Northam

"Oh, the drums go bang and the cymbals clang . . ."

Bill Northam, gold medal winner at Tokyo Olympics

IT'S EASY TO UNDERESTIMATE Bill Northam as a yachtsman. We know that he's won an Olympic gold medal, Australia's first in yachting. And we know that while he had a great boat and a great crew in Pod O'Donnell and Dick Sargeant, he was solely responsible for organising it all to his own success. In his sixtieth year he steered the boat skilfully, with absolute concentration, to defeat the world's best. He must have been under tremendous psychological pressure as he sized up his competitors.

But that wisecracking old fellow in the green Australian Olympic team jacket, which still comes out of mothballs for prize-night presentation speeches, just seems too darn happy-go-lucky to have succeeded in the grim technology-ridden business of modern yacht racing.

Yet Bill, as yachting opponents have found, has a shrewd mind and hunger for success behind his comic mask and grin full of teeth.

He didn't begin to sail until he was in his late forties. But he brought to his sailing all the skills of management and psychology that he had picked up the hard way, on his way to the top of a big company and in surviving the hectic politics of the Sydney Town Hall where he became leader of the Civic Reform Group.

The subtleties of steering a yacht came easily to him. So he was encouraged, by his early success with *Gymea* ("A great old Sydney-Hobart job"), to heed the urgings of some old-timers in the Royal Sydney Yacht Squadron to buy an Eight Metre yacht and challenge for the Sayonara Cup. This trophy, then the most important symbol of big-yacht supremacy in Australia, was for interclub challenge and the Victorians had held it for twenty-three years. On a business trip to England, Bill bought *Saskia,* designed and built by William Fife, the famous Scot.

"Fife claimed she was the best he ever designed," Bill says. "She has a beautiful hull."

He took her to Melbourne and easily won the Cup in 1955, winning three races out of four from the defender, *Frances* (Ernie Digby) and another challenger, the Tasmanian *Erica J.* (Ted Domeney). The following year, *Saskia* defended the Cup against *Frances* and *Erica J.* off Sydney Heads, winning three of the four races by the biggest margins ever recorded in Sayonara Cup racing. *Saskia*'s supremacy virtually ended that racing apart from a final throw, in 1962, by Bruce MacGregor and David Petley from Victoria with *Brigitte* (formerly *Frances*). *Saskia*, then owned by Mr R. E. Jeffries and skippered by Bill Solomons, easily won in three straight races.

Bill Northam, in the meantime, had sold her and bought *Caprice of Huon* from Hobart. He won a lot of races with her; one of the big disappointments of his life was being becalmed in Storm Bay in the 1958 Sydney-Hobart race when he reckons he was in a winning position. He finished fourth.

He tired of ocean racing as he felt too much work fell on the owner. So he sold *Caprice of Huon* and had a fast, hard-chine forty-two-foot Sabre Class yacht built, called *Jazzer*. About that time, he helped talk Sir Frank Packer into building *Gretel* and was on the management committee of the *Gretel* syndicate. Then, in 1963, he made the decision to build *Barranjoey* for the 5.5 metre Olympic trials the following year. But this is the way Bill tells it:

"They were slinging off at me in the early stages until *Jazzer* got going and began giving the Fives an awful whacking. When I arrived back at the boatshed one day, they said, 'Why don't you come into class racing instead of racing an over-blown Vee-Ess?'"

Bill said, "I dunno, how long have you guys been in class racing?"

"Five years, that's how long it will take you," was their reply.

"That's interesting. There's an Olympic year next year. I think I'll get a boat and have a go at you fellows."

Then, according to Bill: "The first and biggest job was to sign on a designer. I knew that Otto Meik was bringing in an Ohlson boat for Jock Sturrock. Bill Luders, the American, was recognised as a successful designer of Fives and his boats appealed to me as all-weather performers. I made a trip to America especially to talk to him and he agreed to design the boat for me and to design it without runners. It was the first time this had been tried in the Fives and after Luders broke four masts himself, trying out the idea, he was finally satisfied with the no-runner rig which had come through a very heavy day's sailing in winds of up to forty knots.

"I knew I had a boat, designed by one of the best in the world. I'd lined up a good builder, Jeff Clist, in Balmain. Our sailmakers had not done much at the time with 5.5s and I went for Hood sails, from America, which were the best in the class.

"Now I had to get a crew, and they had to be world's best. The two I wanted, and who nobody else had, were Pod O'Donnell and Dick Sargeant. I'd watched them from the time they first went aboard *Gretel* and through the challenge match at Newport where they sailed on the foredeck together. They were a real team; they worked in unison and they were practical men who could mend sails and do all the engineering work on the boat; they knew about tuning and race tactics.

"But getting hold of them was a problem. They'd stayed overseas after the 1962 challenge and had just separated. One was on a cruise to Italy and the other in the States somewhere. I sent them about six pre-paid wires and never got an answer. I reckon they thought it was a joke when I said I was entering. But when I told them it was a Luders design, and I was going to use all-imported Hood sails, the replies came that they were on their way.

"They arrived back at Christmas, 1963, only a few weeks before the trials. I was in hospital at the time, getting a cartilage out of my knee, and couldn't even attend the launching. Cecil Boden, the naval architect, had watched the building of the boat from start to finish as I didn't want to run into any measurement difficulties. And she floated perfectly and measured in.

"We began training, spending hours a day with a stopwatch on all our manoeuvres and sail-changes until we could do them blindfolded. They used to make me do thirty blinkin' gybes straight off—and that was getting a few too many, I was getting pretty tired—just to make me used to pushing the tiller behind my back and pushing the boom over. You can easily make a mistake as you've got to work one hand one way and the other hand the other way. And they'd make me do it until I could hardly stand up. But that's the sort of training we did, and all in a few weeks.

"Dick Sargeant was for'ard with Pod on the sheet. Sarge was very strong and wiry, not too heavy, and a little temperamental which is a good thing . . . He did his onion every now and then, but he was always ready to go.

"When we began racing, I used a lot of psychology with these fellows. I used to call them 'rope-jerkers' and they'd get as wild as blazes and say 'we'll show the old coot we're rope jerkers!' I really drove them mad to the point where they worked better than anyone I had ever seen.

"In the trials at Lake Macquarie, a lot was made of my age. I was in my sixtieth year and no-one that old had ever won a gold medal at the Olympics.

"I won the Australian championship by just a few points. There were clearly only three of us battling it out—Sturrock, Booth, and myself. They'd had a lot of experience, particularly Sturrock, where I'd had only a few weeks. So they didn't take the beating too well.

"When it came to the Olympic trials, there was really an attempt to get me into trouble by various ones and we developed into different camps. But I used to get at Jock, too, to upset his concentration. He couldn't take his eyes off me.

"'By gee, you know,' I'd say, 'you're not holding me Joe, I'm going through yer. Get down and have a look,' and he would and was gone.

We were through. 'You're the bloke who's too old,' I'd say, 'and you've been to too many Olympics. You ought to get out!' Oh he loved me.

"We had a narrow win, but these things usually are close. Jock and Otto protested about the course and said they wanted to bring it up to the Australian Yachting Federation. Otto Meik went all round Australia by plane, talking to the delegates, but at the meeting in Sydney they endorsed my selection. I couldn't put my nose into Melbourne for a while; they wouldn't have a bar of me there, and Jock and I became bad friends. But that's all blown over now and I think I've been invited back to just about every club in Melbourne for prize nights.

"But it was a lively issue at the time and I left with a doubtful honour for Tokyo. The newspapers were hard, too. I remember the night we left. John Crosbie, the manager, and I left early to line things up over there. We were hanging about at Mascot, feeling a little foolish in our Panama hats and uniforms. And only my five grand-children came to see me off. An hour after we were flying, Crosbie showed me a newspaper. He hadn't been game to give it to me before. It said, 'Why did they send a no-hoper like Northam, the bloke's too old, he'll never see it through.'

"And that attitude was taken up by a lot of people. I played on it when we got to Enoshima, where the Olympic yachting was held. Different ones would come up to me and say, 'Are you the manager?' and I'd say, 'No, I'm the rubber-downer,' so they didn't know where they were. Tell them nothing, but get as many goats as you can because the more blokes you fight with, the more they'll be looking out for you on the water, trying to get you instead of sailing their boats.

"I had to fight for permission to get our crew to Japan early. I had collected all the weather reports for thirty years, but everyone told me the Enoshima water was very tricky. We arrived there ten days earlier than the other nations and I consider that made all the difference. We were first boat on the water, out before even the Japanese. So we were well broken in. Then a cyclone hit the place which kept the late-comers ashore for a week.

"We'd trained hard before we left Australia, too. I was always frightened I'd go in the legs, as you mostly do when you get old. I had to make sure they'd stand up to the jumping around in the slippery hull of *Barranjoey*. So for four months before we left, I was up at half past five, running and walking, every morning. The local shopkeepers used to cop it from their wives. 'Why don't you get out like that old bloke and run some of the weight off?' they'd say. The shopkeepers have put my prices up ever since. But we were all fit, and if you are physically fit, you are mentally fit. The Olympics are a big strain. You've got to be able to give it, and you've got to be able to take it.

"For the three or four weeks we were there, we did an awful lot of sailing; seven hours a day, and even when the cyclone was approaching and seas got really rough, the boys still made me do six hours a day. And it was very, very hot. I lost a stone and a half during the time I was in Japan. Just before the races, I went down with what I thought was pneumonia, and it could have been a bad dose of the 'flu. For three days I was a really sick bloke. They sent me down drugs which I couldn't take because of my ulcer.

"We won the first race and only lost the points lead once, after about the third race. Then I got it back again with a win. Our record was three firsts, a second, third, fourth, and a disqualification. The disqualification in the fifth race put us in an awkward position, and it was my lapse. We'd been covering Straulino, the Italian, for thirty minutes and rounding the mark I forgot all about him as we went for the spinnaker. And bang, he was up on me.

"By then, it was down to Don Macnamara, the American, and us. He had a good reputation as a skipper and two good fellows with him although they were not as good as mine. His Luders boat was almost identical to mine, the only difference being two portholes in the side of his. He wanted me to have a look at his boat before the races. When I asked about the portholes, he said, 'You'll see. You are not going to know what I'm doing but I'll be able to see what you're doing through these.'

"'Well,' I said, 'You've got 'em in the wrong place, Mac. You'd better put them in the bow if you want to follow what we're doing; they're no good on the side.'

A Flying Dutchman dips into a trough on St Vincent Gulf, with jib furled waiting for the starter's signal

"He never forgave me for that one. And going out to the starts, we'd get alongside and I'd sing 'Macnamara's Band,' and he'd get really mad. He's a very serious bloke. The two boys didn't go along with this and I said, 'It's alright boys, you just leave the brainwork to me and just do the rope jerking and I'll show you how this thing can be worked.' And there's no doubt about it, Macnamara spent most of his time watching me instead of what he was doing.

"I felt the pressure too, towards the end. When we started, I thought we could win a medal, but had no idea it would be a gold. Every race, when it became apparent we were going so well, the others were making it more difficult for me. I was getting to feel tired and develop aches. I'd find myself seizing up with the tension; I'd absolutely get the cramps and have to hand the tiller to Pod and just bobble around a bit to slacken off, and I'd be right.

"The last race ended in a most extraordinary way. It looked for a bit as if Macnamara could win it and beat us for the gold medal. We were leading, laying the windward end of the line in comfort, a quarter of a mile from the finish, abeam and to windward of Macnamara, and some other boats when we ran into this freak puff which put them all ahead. The boys had a look and said, 'Gee, you're unlucky. They've tacked and they're going to cross us. Don't look, just concentrate on your sailing, but we're gone.' But then I couldn't resist it. I had a look and there saw what I'll never forget. Macnamara was ahead of us alright, but to leeward of the Swede, Lars Thorn, who had won in Melbourne. And I thought, 'You've won yourself a gold medal. This bloke's gone a million. He's to leeward of the Swede who'll take him right into that flag at the leeward end of the line. You've won a medal. It doesn't matter where we come.' And we just came about and went for the line. And sure enough, Macnamara tacked, and tried to clear the Swede's bow, but he had no hope. They hit, and Macnamara was disqualified.

"How do you win a gold medal? You have to have perfection in every single thing—boat, rigging, sails, handling, and rules. We went to a series of lectures in Sydney by an acknowledged expert, Rolly Morgan, before we left. You've just got to be fit and not make one mistake on the course. And this is difficult through seven races. I made one, but there was a bit of a miracle going for us up there.

"You cannot afford any breakages. Every day we had a list of maintenance jobs and we'd do most of them straight after the race when all most of the guys want to do is get in and have a beer. My two fellows would stay on the boat.

"I'd say, 'Do you want a hand?' They'd say, 'No, we want to see the end of you!' 'All right, chuck us the smallest bag and I'll take that off with me.' And they threw the main at me every time. But every day they took everything to pieces, went up the mast, checked all the halyards, felt for 'tails' protruding from the rigging wire that could snag a spinnaker, tested all the sheaves. We never broke a stitch and we had four complete sets of rigging and four sets of sheets. We took a complete set of tools and swaging apparatus with us from Australia and were entirely self-sufficient. We were organised as close to perfection as you could be. And that's something Australians have yet to learn.

"I reckon it is better to do a lot of tough individual crew training before putting things into effect in a race. You can't train in a race. You have to go overseas and see what's being done with the boats of your class. I was able to do it, luckily, on my business trips and was up with the innovations of the time. Yet we had the most simply laid out of any boat in Japan. There was nothing complicated but everything was in a place where you didn't have to reach for it.

"We trained ourselves to sail on compasses. The crew would give me a course for the next leg three minutes before we got to the windward mark. On rounding, I'd set my course to the one they had given me and not budge, not move the boat around to set the spinnaker. They'd have to set the pole absolutely right. And being navigationally-minded, they did nine times out of ten. Time and time again we got through guys who were wriggling their boats around, trying to fill their spinnakers.

"We were the first to use twin wind tell-tale feathers with little counter-balanced wheels on an arm on top of the mast. This meant that you could see them whether you were sailing from leeward or windward of the mainsail. The thing we did have, that no-one else woke up to, was a speedometer. The boys wouldn't believe in it at first, but it was absolutely invaluable.

"If I saw a boat picking up on us, I'd ask them to give me the speedo reading. They'd tell me and I'd say, 'We're a quarter of a knot out, you've got to get it.' So they'd reluctantly trim the sheets, we'd find the quarter knot and away we'd go again. It settled a lot of arguments and in the end they'd use it to check on my steering.

"We housed it in a hole in the thwart carrying the track across the boat and would cover it up after the race. Someone once asked Pod and Dick what the hole was for and they said:

"'For a can. The old bloke can't do it any other way.'"

Strength and close attention to the wave pattern is needed to guide this Flying Dutchman through a heavy sea

Y
418

THE CATAMARANERS

MY FIRST REAL CONTACT with the catamaran men left a lasting and, I think, accurate idea about what this breakaway from the mainstream of sailing is all about. It was early in 1963 and I turned up one bleak morning at Blairgowrie, on Port Phillip Bay, to have a look at the twenty-five foot C-class cats trialling for the selection of a Little America's Cup challenger. I wandered over to one of the five contenders, *Matilda*, and was idly inspecting her unusual mainsheet hawse arrangement when a stranger thrust a power drill into my hands and said: "Quick, drill me a set of holes for those jib leads," and raced off. After I'd worked on the boat all morning, I found out that the excited one was Peter Hooks who, with Peter Joubert and Geoff Shaw, had designed the boat. She was running late for the racing that afternoon, and everyone was being roped in to help finish her off. And no one minded. It was just impossible not to be caught up by the enthusiasm of the effort.

In those days, the catamaran sailors were still regarded as eccentrics by the main body of yachtsmen although class racing was well established, in Victoria at least, and catamarans had been introduced to Australia in 1954 by boatbuilder Charlie Cunningham and his son, Lindsay. Through the 1960s and early 1970s, these prejudices were to be broken down by the successes of the catamaraners. They won the Little America's Cup (more accurately, the International Catamaran Challenge Trophy) in 1970 after three unsuccessful attempts; had an Australian design, the Australis, selected by the International Yacht Racing Union as its singlehanded one-design cat; and they gained general acceptance within clubs and State associations for their skills in tuning and boat-handling needed to win important events in these high-performance racing machines.

FACING PAGE: An Yvonne, slicing to windward, flies a hull despite efforts of the hard-swinging crew

Catamarans, with the slight resistance of their slender hulls and the power advantage of a crew trapezing from a point, eight, ten, or twelve feet to windward of the buried lee hull, are the fastest practical racing sailboats afloat. A C Class cat, the grand-daddy of them all, will hit along at a steady thirteen or fourteen knots in a good breeze and touch bursts of up to twenty-five knots in the puffs.

The drawback to yachtsmen who have begun their sailing in other classes is that the time it takes them to tack, pushing the resistance of two hulls instead of one through the eye of the wind, robs them of the fun of close tactical racing. There are still tactics. And for devotees, the thrills of high-speed sailing more than compensate. Australia's strong, steady breezes are ideal for cats which are disappointing in really light weather. And because their very speed quickly shows up tuning deficiencies—an out-of-tune boat falls miles, not yards, behind—the catamaran sailors are wholly subservient to the cause of boat speed. They have pioneered the real rig advances of the decade, the wing mast and the over-rotated rig.

Besides sailing skills, the catamaraners have brought fresh approaches to Australian yachting, such as high-pressure promotion. With a new type of sailboat, and most of their followers newcomers to sailing, they were not hamstrung by convention. So they happily rounded up commercial sponsors to finance their first challenge for the Little America's Cup in 1963. Sponsorship has become a very necessary part of Australian yachting, with commercial firms helping organise major regattas as well as contributing towards the expenses of overseas travel. But in those days, it had hardly been touched by the other classes and was considered "not quite nice." The Australian Catamaran Association produced its own magazine and directed a stream of publicity through newspapers and yachting magazines. Other classes took up these promotion measures.

In the early days, the cat men were a breed apart, concentrated in a few clubs. Sandringham and Blairgowrie were the main ones in Melbourne, where the hub of the movement was, and Woollahra was the club in Sydney. But gradually cats gathered strength and acceptance by the yachting community to the point where, in 1970, on being offered a separate committee within the structure of the Yachting Association of New South Wales, the cat men declined. They preferred to take their place instead on the centreboard sub-committee with delegates from the mass of the monohull classes. They, and everyone else, felt that was where they belonged.

It all began back in the 1950s when Charlie Cunningham became interested in catamarans. He was a boatbuilder who during the war years had designed the popular Gwen 12 sailing dinghy. He also had made a name for himself as a builder of rowing shells. Charlie Cunningham and his son, Lindsay, a talented engineer with a mania for experimenting with sailboat rigs, put together a couple of box-section plywood hulls which led to the Yvonne Class, a twenty-footer, which began racing in 1954 and which is still sailed keenly today in the southern States. It is one of the few cats that carries a spinnaker, a subject of wonder to catamaran sailors in America and Europe. After the Yvonne came the Quickcat, an ungainly-looking but simple to build sixteen-footer which has surprised its designers and critics alike by surviving strongly into the 1970s. There are 250 boats registered in Victoria alone and 90 in New South Wales.

Other classes followed. Peter Hooks designed the Attunga 20. The twelve-foot Kittycat by Jim Young was introduced from New Zealand. But the Cunningham designs dominated the early 1960s and they eventually had a dozen classes to their credit.

The yachting world first took real notice of the Australian cats in 1963 when Australia challenged Britain for the International Catamaran Challenge Trophy. The trophy, donated in 1961 by the Sea Cliff Yacht Club, New York, is for match-race competition on America's Cup lines between International C Class catamarans. Probably the most exciting sailboats in the world, they have restrictions loose enough for quite way-out experimentation. They are limited to a twenty-five foot overall length, fourteen-foot beam and 300 square feet of sail, including the spars.

They have become more and more complex until you virtually need an engineering degree, which Lindsay Cunningham has, to figure out the complexities of *Quest III* which eventually won the Little America's Cup for Australia, and the Cunninghams, in 1970. Their tall rigs, forty or more feet high, make them almost unmanageable in a fresh breeze. They cost a lot and are up to $10,000 if you paid a professional to build one. So they are impractical as class-racing boats, But they offer perhaps the greatest challenge of all to the experimenter and the boat-handler.

Back in 1962-63, the Australian Catamaran Association, under the forceful presidency of Frank Strange, a convert from yachts, was able to induce five of these spidery monsters to enter the trials. It rounded up all sorts of help. There were donations of materials as well as cash to help the builders of the triallists and to fly the winning crew to England. Frank Strange even succeeded in "biting" $200 from Sir Frank Packer on his return home from the 1962 America's Cup challenge. His way: "You missed the big one, help us bring home the little one." In the end, they raised more than enough to finance the challenge which involved sending two boats, two crews, and a manager to England at a cost of around $20,000. There was a surplus of nearly $6,000 left over for future challenges.

The two cats selected were the Cunninghams' first *Quest,* and *Matilda*. *Quest* reflected the rowing shell influence that has permeated many Cunningham designs. It had long slender hulls fining out to plumb, sharp, stems and sterns; decks rounded to shed the water and cut wind resistance, underwater sections rounded to dampen pitch. They'd "tank-tested" the hulls in a nearby irrigation ditch. In a way-out search for super lightness, the hulls were made of a honeycomb cardboard core covered in sailcloth which was then impregnated with polyester resin.

A pair of twenty-two-year-olds from the fishing and pilot service town of Queenscliff near Port Phillip Heads, John Munns and Graeme Anderson, won a round-robin, change-boat selection series at Blairgowrie. John Taylor and Peter Scarfe were sent as reserve crew with Max Press as manager. Earlier that year, Munns and Anderson, sailing an Yvonne, had set a new record of two hours and thirty-two minutes for the annual Williamstown-Geelong race. They averaged more than fifteen miles per hour and arrived before a hard, hot Port Phillip northerly at such a pace that they caught the finishing officials still lunching ashore.

In England, after some more races, *Quest* was finally selected but went down 4-0 to the formidable English defender, *Hellcat IIIS* (for special). It belonged to a breed of Hellcats, designed by Rod Macalpine-Downie, which had previously disposed of two American contestants. *Hellcat IIIS* was completely different to *Quest* with transom stern, raked overhanging bow, and a very tall rig. The Cunninghams, still convinced that their hull shape was right, took heed of the rig. The following year, they fitted a taller rig to *Quest*, narrowed her beam to twelve feet and Lindsay took her to America for the North American championship. Although she finished the series runner-up, through sailing mistakes by Cunningham, she proved herself faster than the winner, *Sealion*, which, the following year, went to England for another unsuccessful challenge.

The Australians challenged again for 1965. The hulls on *Quest* were badly crushed on the ship bringing them home from America and another *Quest* was built from the same mould. But it had plywood sides moulded into fibreglass underwater section which concentrated weight and stiffness where most needed. In America Lindsay had seen his first wing mast and on *Quest II* a similar streamlined aerofoil mast of plywood and aluminium, fifteen inches wide and four inches thick, tapering to a fine top was added. Still *Quest II* retained sloop rig.

There were trials, against five other boats, and more fund-raising. Max Press, the tireless publicity man, turned disaster into dollars for the challenge fund by selling a sequence of pictures to magazines. It showed *Waratah*, crewed by Max and Bob Brown, cartwheeling and capsizing while towing a water-skier in a promotion stunt.

Lindsay Cunningham himself took the helm of *Quest II*, with John Buzaglo crew. They won the right to go to England where they faced another Hellcat type, *Emma Hamilton*, sailed by the experienced catamaran skipper, Reg White, with John Osborn as crew. *Quest II* was the fastest boat, but *Emma Hamilton* was better sailed, her crew more at ease on the tricky, tidal Thorpe Bay course, and they had all the luck.

With the series tied at three races all, *Quest II* was leading by a minute with less than three miles to sail when she was overpowered by a black, smoky squall that Lindsay Cunningham estimated to be more than forty miles per hour. *Emma Hamilton* survived it but *Quest II*'s slimmer bows dug into two successive waves and the pressure on the thirty-seven-and-a-half-foot-high rig sent her into a fatal cartwheel. Lindsay, very dejected on his return home, defended the seaworthiness of the boat. He said he thought she had nose-dived because the forebeam was faired

FACING PAGE: The new international Tornado catamaran, a two-man twenty-footer, has a strong Australian fleet

KA 34

down instead of up, and as C cats were not meant to race in winds over thirty miles per hour, races should be called off when the wind exceeds that strength after the start.

For Australia's next challenge in 1967, the Cunninghams built *Quest III*, fuller and more buoyant in the ends than *Quest II*. But the main change was in the rig and here the Cunninghams made a mistake. Believing that saving weight of at least sixty pounds would more than outweigh the efficiency of the wing mast, they discarded it and used a conventional alloy spar to spread a una rig. But they placed a "sock" of cloth around the mast, extending two feet back into the sail to clean up the air flow. In early trials, *Quest III*, skippered by Bruce Proctor with Lindsay Rees as crew, proved faster to windward than *Quest II*, which was campaigned by Lindsay Cunningham with Graham Candy acting as crew. However, before the final trials, Proctor dropped out with appendicitis and Lindsay Cunningham also withdrew. Peter Bolton was brought in to take over *Quest III* and he and Lindsay Rees were selected to crew her in England. Another Hellcat type, *Lady Helmsman* skippered by Pete Schneidau with Bob Fisher as crew, won four of the five races and only lost the fifth by breaking a centreboard.

Quest III was not well tuned and Peter Bolton, although a good skipper, had insufficient experience with the boat. As before, the Thorpe Bay conditions told against the challengers. But the real deciding factor was *Lady Helmsman*'s very efficient wing mast developed by Austin Farrar after many hours in Southampton University's wind tunnel.

In 1968, the three-year-old *Lady Helmsman*, crewed by White and Osborn, beat the American challenger *Yankee Flier* (Greer Ellis/Bill Hooten) 4-2. Like *Lady H*, *Yankee Flier* carried a una-rigged wing mast. Then, just when the Little America's Cup looked like settling into the same rut as its famous namesake, the British, seemingly impregnable with their rig expertise behind the hometown advantage of the Thorpe Bay mudbanks, lost it. At their ninth match, it was taken from them by the Danes in their first challenge. *Opus III*, skippered by Gert Friedriksen with designer, Lief Wagner-Smitt, as crew, won four races to three over *Ocelot*, designed and built by Reg White who again had John Osborn as crew. *Ocelot* was an old boat, dusted off by Reg as a last resort and probably slower than *Opus III*. He used all the tricks in his deep bag against the Danes, right down to a last-ditch episode in the last race that brought his sportsmanship into question. White, a leg of the course behind, cut out two marks and tried to blanket *Opus III* in the very light wind, slowing her so that she would not be able to finish within the time limit.

Australia, rather tentatively, challenged the Danes for a match in 1970 and amid some surprise its challenge was accepted, ahead of Britain's, by the Skovshoved Sailing Club. It was suggested that the Danes were not altogether happy with the British tactics of that last race.

Meantime, the Cunninghams had devoted almost all their efforts into designing the most efficient wing-mast imaginable. They built their own wind tunnel, tested a variety of rigs on models, and then tried prototype wing masts in match racing with two A Class catamarans. Drawn into the action to sail *Quest III* and help with the experiments were Bruce Proctor and Graham Candy.

Quest III was rebuilt, the hulls remaining the same but the mainbeam shifted back eighteen inches, hulls and central fore and aft beam strengthened, and a radial mainsheet track fitted.

But the masterpiece was the new wing mast, forty-one feet high, three feet six inches wide and twelve inches thick, of light plywood with cedar and urethane foam formers every four inches and a half-inch foam skin covered with thin Terylene impregnated with aircraft dope, then covered with polyurethane paint and a light, glossy, plastic surface film. It had complicated sail shape controls with diamond stays leading to two of the full-width sail battens and other wires from these battens to a nine-foot long crossbar, the latter attached to the boom to vary the twist of the sail. Backstays were fitted to trolleys on the half-circle mainsheet track to automatically follow the rig around when it was rotated. It was terribly complicated and difficult to tune but easy for the crew to operate once it was set up.

For the 1970 challenge, Dunlop Australia Ltd donated $12,000 which ensured that two crews could be sent to Copenhagen. Jock Sturrock was appointed team-manager and Lindsay Cunningham technical adviser. The effort shaped up impressively, but there were doubts and misgivings through the final selection trials on Port Phillip Bay. Bad weather and a series of mishaps to other competitors cut through the opposition. Bill Hollier, who was a reserve for the so-close 1965 challenge, designed and built a new boat in Sydney. But his arrival at the trials was delayed by his breaking the wing mast while test-sailing in Sydney. *Quest II* had sunk, another triallist, *Warlord,* was overturned on the beach one night by a gale and smashed and *Rumdoodle II* filled up after a capsize in the first race of the trials and was torn apart by the seas during the tow to shore.

To compound the anxiety, *Quest III* and Hollier's boat, *Red Roo,* did not beat a B Class cat, the Cunningham-designed *Wild Cat* by as much as they should when she was tossed into a trial race as a yardstick. *Quest III* won all seven trial races, with *Red Roo* clearly next best and both were sent to Copenhagen. After a week of match-racing on the Oresund, *Quest III* was confirmed as challenger and she then had a week of tuning trials against *Red Roo*. The Danish defender was *Sleipner*, an advance on *Opus III* by Wagner-Smitt. Her rig was simpler and thirty pounds lighter than *Quest III*'s with the wing mast three feet shorter although bigger in area. It was made from styrene foam, strengthened with fibreglass and a thin plywood skin. Wagner-Smitt skippered her himself with Klaus Anton Neilson as crew.

The boat looked impressive but was launched only three weeks before the races and suffered from the lack of a tuning partner. Another Danish cat, *Dulcinea,* owned by Ib Pors-Nielsen and to have been sailed by Paul Elvstrom, broke her unstayed cantilevered wing mast—all mast, with an aircraft-like trailing flap instead of a sail—two weeks before the match and could not be repaired in time.

Quest III won the first three races by margins of one minute twenty-four seconds, two minutes thirty-six seconds, and twelve minutes, the biggest margin of the series. It looked all over with *Quest III* having to win only one more race, but the Danes were far from beaten. Paul Elvstrom took a hand. The sail was re-cut and the Danish crew was learning, and improving their boat, all the time. They won the fourth race in a twenty-knot wind, leading all the way, but narrowly until *Quest* broke a main-sheet wire on the last beat and dropped from two boat lengths behind to two minutes fifty-five seconds behind at the finish.

After a compulsory lay day, the Danes won the fifth race by default. It was blowing hard, with a heavy sea on the Oresund. On the way to the start, *Quest*'s mainsheet traveller jammed on the track, making her unmanoeuvrable, and threatening to capsize. The crew headed her carefully for home, intent on saving the rig, while *Sleipner* completed the course under mast alone but still in two and a quarter hours, averaging sixteen knots on one reaching leg.

By now it was obvious that the simpler *Sleipner* wanted a blow and *Quest III* lighter weather. But the sixth race began in a moderate ten to fifteen knot wind, neutral ground. Again, Wagner-Smitt outfoxed Proctor on the starting line and built his slight lead from here to a winning margin of one minute nineteen seconds although there was very little difference in boat speed. The score was three races all and the winner of the next would take the cup.

Graham Candy, writing in *Yachting*, re-lived the great tension of that deciding race: "On *Quest* we worked half the night, improving the operation of all the gear and altering the mainsheet system to enable the crew on the trapeze to vary the twist of the sail all the time to suit the wind strength. We were praying for light weather and had a long session back at our hotel with Lindsay Cunningham and our team manager Jock Sturrock on tactics and techniques.

"In the morning, there was not a breath of wind, in answer to our prayers, but the breeze slowly rose until by the start it was ten to fifteen knots again, with a slight chop, which gave neither boat an advantage. This time, Bruce made sure of the start and *Quest* crossed the line to windward of *Sleipner* and going fast. The rig was setting well although the light weather battens were too soft for the breeze, and Bruce covered fiercely all the way, rounding twenty seconds ahead at the windward mark. We fought off the Danes on the reach, although they were going faster, and won back our margin again on the broad reach and the beat. The whole race was really a close, hard tactical duel, with the Danes attacking all the time. At the end of the second close reach, they were only five seconds behind, but on the broad reach we were able to trim *Quest*'s rig more rapidly to the changing wind and we opened up a lead of forty seconds. Despite the additional covering tacks needed on the wind, we were able to increase our margin on the next three legs, and in a steadily freshening breeze, *Quest* forged ahead to cross the finishing line fifty-nine seconds in front of *Sleipner* and the Little America's Cup was ours. At last we had done it, rewarding hundreds of people throughout Australia who had fought for seven long years to win the Cup. It now rests in its new home at Sorrento Sailing Club in Victoria, but morally it belongs to Charlie Cunningham because he and Lindsay have done far more than anyone else in winning it for Australia."

Quest III, skippered by Bruce Proctor with Graeme Ainslie crewing this time, retained the Little America's Cup on Port Phillip Bay in 1972 with a perfect 4-0 score over the American challenger, *Weathercock*. *Quest III*, with her sophisticated and very adjustable rig, was a lot faster than *Weathercock*, sailed by two keen youngsters, Chuck Millican and Jack Evans. Ironically, Lindsay Cunningham was first influenced by the possibilities of aerofoil wing masts by a mast *Weathercock*'s designer, George Patterson, built in 1963.

In the 1972 challenge match at Sorrento, *Weathercock*'s lower-aspect wing-mast rig looked positively ancient against *Quest III*'s tall, clean, and perfectly controllable "mast-sail." Lindsay Cunningham went to enormous pains to make *Quest*'s sail adjustable in shape to meet all strengths of winds and all sailing angles, down to fashioning articulated battens which could be adjusted to varying camber from the boat while racing.

While most of the glamour attended the Little America's Cup challenges, the cat scene as a whole multiplied and diversified. The strength spread from Melbourne, to Sydney, and to the other State capitals and waterways like Lake Macquarie. Even Darwin took up catamaran sailing, almost exclusively, and two good boats were designed there by Neil Fowler, the fourteen-foot *Arrow* and the eleven-foot *Arafura Cadet*; both have won wide acceptance as classes down south.

An annual festival of championships, Cat Week, was begun in 1966 at Sorrento with 153 catamarans constituting the biggest catamaran regatta ever held anywhere. The classes were still mainly Cunningham although the Kitty Cats were there from New Zealand and the English-designed two-man twenty-foot Mantas, Artunga 15s, and an assortment of C cats raced.

The development of one-man eighteen-footers and two-man twenty-footers was spurred by the impending trials, held in 1967 by the International Yacht Racing Union, to select international one-design classes of this type. The IYRU catamaran sub-committee issued loose restrictions within which candidates for a series of trials could be designed. An A and B Class Association was formed in Australia to administer these divisions and set about financing an expedition to England for the trials.

The Cunninghams developed boats for both divisions, heavily based on their *Quest* shapes. One of their B division designs, *Mehitabel*, sailed by Sydney surgeon, Peter Blaxland, won representation but in the A division, a sleek newcomer designed and skippered by Graham Johnston from Botany Bay won selection, taking all five heats of the A Class

A Tornado zooms across the harbour with a minimum of fuss

"world" championship at Blairgowrie. It might be pointed out that the cats have always had a weakness for tagging "world" to any important championship. In one race, Johnston went around the course only seven seconds slower than *Quest III*.

In the IYRU trials that August at Sheppy in England, the B division winner was clearly *Tornado*, designed by England's Rodney March, victor in seven of the nine races. *Mehitabel*, with one win and a string of seconds, was next best. *Tornado* was subsequently selected as the international one-design, much to the disappointment and anger of Charlie Cunningham who still maintains that his B-classer is faster and stronger than the *Tornado*.

Graham Johnston's *A-Cat II* won the A division trials and later, IYRU recognition as its single-handed one-design. While clearly superior in all winds, she had very strong opposition with three other boats outstanding: the Danish *Catalina* (Leif Wagner-Smitt), *Bambi II* (Neil Coster, Britain) and *Unicorn* (John Mazotti, Britain). Johnston broke the full-length bottom batten in the first round of the first race and had to retire. In the second, Johnston was leading at the final leeward mark when he capsized in rounding. In race three with a shifting, dying breeze, he was only third, twenty-one minutes behind Wagner-Smitt. But Johnston would not accept defeat. He had his sail recut overnight, returned his rig, and won the remaining four races.

Two seasons earlier Johnston, a printing engineer, had never even sailed a boat and his success surprised everyone, including himself.

"I used to go down to Woollahra Sailing Club and watch the cats," he said, "mainly Cunningham Australis at that time, and got some idea of what made them go. I almost built a Manta but instead sailed for a season as crew on a Sheerwater with Harry Percival. The following winter, I was determined to build my own boat. I would have brought in an American A-Lion, but the duty was too high. Then Harold Stevenson and I decided to build our own single-handed cats. I had never done anything like designing a boat before and had never even attempted to draw a compound curve. But I drew this boat and made a three-foot model of it which I took around to all the experts. They told me it would be a 'nose-diver.' They added: 'It's no good because there is no buoyancy up the front.' The idea then was to prevent nose-diving by building fullness into the for'ard sections. But I believed, with a fine stern as well as a fine bow, you could use your body weight to make the stern dig in aft and rock the bow out when you had to. But no one agreed with me."

One who did agree with Graham was his brother, Kevin, who helped mould the prototype hulls in gaboon plywood. The hull weight of this fine-ended, streamlined, truly beautiful cat, is just under 100 pounds. Winning selection as an international class was just part of the story. The Johnstons have worked hard steadily ever since to give the class impetus, against a number of frustrations. At the end of the 1970-71 season there were about fifty boats in Australia with another sixty overseas. But at that time, with a more simple method of building designed to make the somewhat difficult construction much easier for amateurs, a surge of interest was expected.

Graham is still a keen Australis sailor. He piloted his *Woftam* (said to stand for "waste of time and money") to victory in the world Australis championship at Cat Week, 1971, on Botany Bay. "I enjoy one-man sailing and the 'hairiness' of sailing A Class," he says.

Cat Week has become an institution on the sailing calendar and has been held in Darwin, 2,875 road miles from Sydney. More than 200 boats will gather for the racing, with crews, their families and friends, for a week of sailing and socialising. The entry for the 1971 carnival, held on Botany Bay, reflected the gradual change in the composition of the cat fleet. Newer one-design classes like the Tornado, Australis, Stingray, Arrow, Paper Tiger, and Hobie Cat all drew substantial entries with a swing away from the open A and B classes. But two Cunningham open Bs, *Wild Cat* sailed by the Swinnerton brothers, Paul and Neville, and *Hunter* skippered by Bruce Proctor, cleaned up the Tornadoes who entered the Open B "world" championship. This was all much to the delight of Charlie Cunningham.

The Stingray is a "junior" B Class, eighteen feet long but with an eight-foot beam to permit road trailing without having to dismantle the boat. Designed by Jim Rae of Sydney, its main strength is at Manly Club. Darwin's Neil Fowler has a successful design, Black Witch, in this same category. The Paper Tiger is a one-man New Zealand design and the Hobie Cat, a fourteen-footer, was designed by American board-rider, Hobie Alter, as a surf cat.

The Tornado, destined for Olympic status in 1976, has forged quickly ahead in Australia with seventy boats in 1971. Its construction, with the amateur builder in mind, was initially of wood, using the stitch and glue method. Two sheets of 4.5 mm plywood are cut to shape and sewn together along the keel line with wire. The joint is fibreglassed. The sheets are then bent into a deck jig, the transom, centrecase, and deck beams fitted plus two ply bulkheads and a longitudinal styrene foam spacer at the bow. Fibreglass Tornado hulls have since been introduced and are built professionally in Sydney by the IYRU's licensed builder, Mark Hookham.

But amid the gleaming new shapes in fibreglass and compound curve plywood at Cat Week 1971, the venerable Quickcat was still the biggest single class, with thirty-three entries. Easy to build, strong traditions of class racing, cheap, who knows the reason for its continued popularity? More than 2,300 sets of Quickcat plans have been sold and an estimated 800 built in Australia up to 1971.

Into the seventies, with an estimated 2,400 cats sailing in all parts of Australia, the movement appears to be swinging away from the experimental open classes towards the newer one-designs, probably because by that time a complete selection of one-designs was available from trainer to potential Olympic class. And the catamaraners are no longer regarded as wild-eyed eccentrics. When I asked Bill Hollier why they had elected to join the Yachting Association of N.S.W. centreboard sub-committee instead of taking up the offer of a separate multihull committee, he replied:

"Well, why not? We're not freaks. We've all got the same problems." And he had me there.

Charles Cunningham, designer (with his son Lindsay) of seventeen catamarans

Charles Cunningham

". . . they think you are mad, but you are not."

CHARLES CUNNINGHAM, the father of catamaran sailing in Australia, is what is politely known as a controversial figure. He's excitable, outspoken to the point of being downright tiresome if you don't agree with his point of view. He feels, wrongly I believe, that he was "got at" over the International B Class trials. In all, he's a prickly old character but he knows about boats and providing that's the subject he'll talk for hours with friend or foe.

During the second World War he designed one of Australia's first plywood centreboarders, the Gwen 12, which endured as a popular class into the 1970s with more than 2,000 boats built. It was fast, seaworthy, and cheap enough for youngsters to build. Most important, in Cunningham's view, it was a strict one-design.

Then came the cats and with them he was fortunate in having the help of his son. Lindsay is a Bachelor of Engineering honours graduate who loves tinkering with the go-fast elements of rigs and Charlie says their design relationship is something like that of Gilbert and Sullivan: "I would get nowhere without Lindsay and he would get nowhere without me. I do most of the scheming and Lindsay works out all the stresses, weights, and measures." They have designed a total of seventeen cats from the earliest, the Yvonne and the Quickcat, to the Little America's Cup winner, *Quest III*.

During an early challenge for the Little America's Cup, I asked Charlie why he wanted to be in it. He said: "It helps put Australia on the international yachting scene and a little bit of the glamour of the America's Cup has rubbed off on it.

"These C Class boats have terrific speed. They are simply sailing machines. But the most important thing of the lot is that a boat costing \$1,400 to \$1,800 easily outsails these Twelve Metre boats they are spending half a million on. They're just money mines. As soon as you say that, they think you are mad but you're not. There it is."

Charles Cunningham was born at Geelong, Victoria, in 1903, to sea-going traditions. This is how he tells it:

"When I was four or five, I remember my father relating the adventures he and his father had out in Bass Strait, running a crayfish boat from King Island to Melbourne. They had no diesel motor but depended on sail alone. It was a hard life, but they were pioneers and they had to battle through. My father used to describe hull shapes and how different boats performed in different conditions and this gave me my first interest in boats and hull design.

"I never lost the love of the sea he inspired in me and, in 1915, I went to New Zealand where I took up an apprenticeship in shipwrighting and boatbuilding at Port Chalmers. When I came back to Australia, I saw there was not much future in boatbuilding. It was a seat out of the pants job, so I went into house-building until the Depression. I still had a love of boats and, during the Depression, I found time to build a few boats for people who wanted to try and make a living from fishing. I started up a travelling library around the Melbourne suburbs to help make ends meet, and quite a few sea-going books got mixed up with the fiction.

"Then the war came along. Not being good enough for national service, I went back into boatbuilding and worked at this until the end of the war. It was during the war that I designed the Gwen 12. I used to mess around with a piece of scrap plywood, twisting it and working out how I could get a decent hull shape with a nice clean entrance forward with one twist of a ply sheet.

"I branched out on my own as a small-time boatbuilder, got the Gwen 12 going, and then built about sixty plywood rowing skiffs. Some rowing clubs approached me to build them and later, all the public schools. I was one of the first, if not the first, to use plywood for rowing skiffs in Victoria. I tired of the rowing skiffs as the price had been cut on me by other builders and so I wandered back into sailing craft.

"About that time, 1951, catamarans became news. Lindsay and I were very interested in *Manu Kai*, considered the first catamaran to attract world-wide attention. She was designed by Woody Brown, an American aircraft engineer, helped by Rudy Choy, now a very big name in American catamarans.

"We thought we'd have a go at a cat, so we built a square-section plywood 'cigar,' eighteen feet long by roughly two feet deep in the middle, tapered at the ends. We linked them together, put a wide mast on it, and sailed it around the Albert Park Lake, and at Sorrento. We fiddled around and modified it to quite an extent by increasing the length to twenty feet at the deckline and putting a bit of fore and aft spring in the flat bottom.

"We took this boat, which we named *Yvonne*, into the annual South Channel race off Sorrento and in a very rough chop beat the fleet, including 6-metres, by more than an hour. We covered the fifteen-mile course in one hour twenty-seven minutes, amazing for that time.

"We further modified the *Yvonne* by adding a very deep forward section which made her knife through the seas. Lindsay re-drew the plan and it became the foundation design of the Australian Catamaran Association. We later added a spinnaker to increase the thrills. They had twenty-nine boats start in the national championship for the class in Adelaide, Christmas 1970, which shows you just can't keep a good boat down.

"Then some of the cat chaps asked us to turn out something smaller for those who wanted a less expensive boat. So we designed the sixteen-foot Quickcat, early in 1955. The Quickcat became very popular, although it met with a lot of hostility. They'd say you couldn't put it about, and it wouldn't go to windward, and all sorts of things. I'm amazed at how it has kept going. I think it still has the biggest numbers among the cats in Australia. We regarded it as almost a temporary design at the time. Then someone said they wanted a boat in fibreglass, so we designed the XY 16; like the Quickcat, a one-man boat but versatile enough to put a family aboard. Then came the little C cat in fibreglass and the Unicat in plywood, followed by the Austral 20 which became very popular at Woollahra and spread all over the place.

"We built a cruising cat, *Alouette,* mainly Lindsay's idea. She's still around, a thirty-five-footer with a swing keel, something like a blown-up Quickcat with a cabin. But we found that the addition of ballast slowed her down below cat performance although she does perform very well in hard weather. We should have persevered with that boat. In the main, I agree that catamarans or trimarans are more of a risk at sea than monohulls but have gained a reputation worse than they deserve through so many starry-eyed amateurs wandering into them that should not have been allowed to do so. They should have a survival cocoon built into them, with enough beer and biscuits to last for a few weeks, and a highly-competent crew on deck.

"The Little America's Cup thing came up in 1962 and we tested models for *Quest* in an irrigation channel near my home in Mordialloc. Basically, we've stuck with that shape, very slightly modified, through *Quest II* and *Quest III*. We placed a great deal of faith in the hulls and they have never let us down. The results of the 1963 challenge are pretty well known. You only have to look at the rig on *Quest* to see what went wrong. We were still very confident that *Quest* was a good boat; so much so that Lindsay took her to the North American championship. But over there, some mysterious things happened. One nasty little boat got in the road of *Quest* that shouldn't have been in the race, and in another race they were instructed to go to a certain mark and unfortunately there were two marks very similar and Lindsay went for the wrong one. Anyway, he came home convinced that he had the faster boat, very disgruntled and very unhappy about the result.

"He blows hot and cold on the big-time racing; he's too conscientious, worries and lets it get him down, although he is a brilliant sailor when he wants to be.

"Over there, Lindsay was impressed by a boat with a wide mast called *Sprinter*. We had rather pooh-poohed the wide masts and we'd tried a few ourselves. But he came back with the idea of trying a sloop-rigged wing-mast boat and the result was *Quest II*.

"So Lindsay decided to be in the competition, with a lot of other big names. John Munns sailed a boat he designed himself, *Joy C.*; Lock Crowther, the trimaran designer planned a boat called *Nemesis*; the old *Matilda* was dragged back into the fray and John Henry bought the

FACING PAGE: The Yvonne 20, the first catamaran designed by Charles and Lindsay Cunningham, is one of the few cats that carry a spinnaker

Y
10

squashed hulls of *Quest* and produced a very smart boat which ran very close to John Munns. But *Quest II* showed she was clearly superior. Lindsay sailed her very well. John Buzaglo, his crew, was very enthusiastic, and in England they had easily the faster boat. But the Thorpe Bay tidal conditions tricked Lindsay. Tactically, he might have done a bit better and some of the things Reg White did to him were rather cruel.

"Then there was that capsize when they had it won, more than half a leg of the course in front. What did I feel when that happened? Well, I am a fatalist, I always think the worst right up until the last minute; where if I do win, I'm the happiest person in the world. Quite the opposite.

"The 1967 challenge was a very poor turnout altogether. Frankly, we made a mistake, persevering with the pocket luff when we should not have done so. In England, we could have pulled the fat out of the fire if I'd had the support. I wasn't allowed to have enough say in that series. I was offered, while we were there, foam and all the facilities from a local factory to improve our rig on the spot. These pocket-luff sails are a real write-off because you've got to keep chasing the shape all the time. The pocket luff compresses the amount of batten inside the pocket unduly, transferring the fullness to a different part of the sail. When we set it up here, in Melbourne, it was good. But it slowly got worse to such a state in England that I wanted to fill the pocket with foam. But the boys wouldn't be in it, and I didn't have the power to make them be. I reckon if we had put some foam in and stiffened the leading edge of the rig, we'd have still been in the picture.

"The *Lady Helmsman* rig in 1967 convinced me the wing mast was superior, but it also brought home how much local conditions had to do with it. We were told that the English crew comprised 'a couple of mugs.' Bob Fisher had been around that course more than anyone else and although he was the for'ard hand, he was a for'ard hand-skipper. He used to refer to Schneidau as 'my skipper' as if he were his office boy, although Schneidau was a good sailor too. They convinced us there were no tactics in the course at Thorpe Bay. The more I saw of that place, the more I could see we were going to be very lucky to get it away from them.

"But then the Danes did it for us. Wagner-Smitt is a very smart man. He's a tanker designer and has wind tunnels and test tanks at his disposal. We were a bit lucky to get the challenge because previously the English had stated they'd give the Danes the challenge on the understanding that if they did win it, they'd give England the following challenge. Well, this fell to pieces. I believe it was because of Reg White's tactics in trying to blanket the Danes while the time limit ran out for the last race of their challenge. The Danes were furious.

"We had a good look at *Quest III* for the 1970 series. We decided against building another pair of hulls just the same as the old ones although we modified the bow slightly. We'd concentrate on the rig. We decided to have what had now become a conventional wing mast, roughly three feet six inches wide. I made up a wind tunnel with an old five horse motor driving an air screw. I made the tunnel itself from sheets of redwood veneers, rolled into the diameter with a correcting square in it of vanes spaced about four inches apart at Lindsay's direction, and a water tank on which the models floated. They were anchored and Lindsay put tensioning gauges all over the thing to measure the thrust and lift, push and shove. We'd turn on the motor and watch how the models performed in the tunnel, which was about twenty feet long. We tested seventeen different mast models: foils, pair of foils in tandem, wing mast with sloop rig, the lot, and number 17 was the mast that eventually went on to *Quest III*. Lindsay spent hours of spare time on this for nearly six months.

"We did have to sacrifice a certain amount in drag to get the overall efficiency in the shape of the sail. It had struts, stays, correctors, and various other controls, and it had to be just right. But Lindsay's ferret-like ability to make things work got it going. When he was a kid, he'd pick an old clock to pieces and it would go better for it afterwards. That's his style, he can make things work. And he made that rig work in Denmark.

"We had a lot of trouble with Bill Hollier who was quite sure he had the faster boat when we were preparing for Denmark. And it was a fast boat. We spent nine races convincing Bill and we nearly wore the rig out on Bill so that when it came to the real thing, Lindsay and the boys were scratching around all the time to keep it going. It's a highly-developed thing and it had to be perfect. Fighting as they were for lightness and strength, pieces would wear a little after one or two outings and would have to be replaced. That's how they came to pull out before the start of the fifth race. Bruce Proctor deemed it best to return to shore in the interest of the boat as, accidentally, some of the gear had been put back wrong. The mainsheet rollers were under an enormous strain, about 3,000 pounds on the track. They were very sensitive and if you put one back the wrong way around, they'd grip and jam.

"After they scored the three straight wins, I said clearly to the chaps here that they only had to be very careful and not break anything and they'd win. But even I got a bit apprehensive when it came to the last race.

"Wagner-Smitt is a very good skipper, more liable to take a chance than Bruce who is inclined to play safe, although he is a very, very good skipper too. So his performance looked much more impressive than Bruce's except once Bruce got the lead, he never let Wagner-Smitt through. Bruce had been a little too tentative on the starting line but when he lost his temper and really got a good start in the last race, that really decided it.

"*Sleipner* got to within five seconds but Bruce sacrificed a minute or more all around the course, overlaying marks slightly to make sure he did nothing silly on them and keeping between the other boat and the mark all the time. He ground the Dane right into the dust. Then he won by almost a minute because once he was satisfied he only had to reach the windward mark, he went for it. That is Bruce's type of sailing.

Known in the catamaran business as "boneyarding," an Arafura Cat is heading for the bottom

"Now I've retired. I've eased out of the C Class slightly although I was in the *Quest III* syndicate for the defence in 1972. I think that C Class development has almost reached the design ceiling and that future progress will be mainly in refining what we have, improving handling techniques and rigs.

"The B Class has been a big disappointment to me because we clearly and definitely have turned out the better boat. You can discount my own enthusiasm if you like, but all the evidence is there. We designed our boat in the belief that, like the *Tempest*, it would have to be very well built. Then this *Tornado* turns up. You get two pieces of ply, stitch them together, put your foot in between and just about lose it in the process, jam in some foam, and that's a boat, that's an Olympic class? Consequently, they've been breaking up. Three down here at Sandringham have just fallen to pieces. 'Sandy' conditions are pretty strong, it's the worst place they could try them out, and in some overseas countries where there are lots of light winds, the *Tornado* might get away with it. They've started building them in fibreglass which makes the boat heavier still and consequently slower. Our boat has had no structural troubles at all, and we have produced a faster boat.

"At the 1967 trials, the rig that Peter Blaxland had was his own, with only a twenty-eight foot mast (against the *Tornado's* thirty-one feet) and he had a special centrecase put in, which was a farcical thing and only added weight to his boat. And he didn't sail well. We made the mistake of fiddling around with the pocket luff on the *Quest B* and this helped the *Tornado*. And I believed there would be two years for this boat to be proved before an IYRU decision was made.

"The Swinnerton brothers came along with their *Quest B* and beat two C Class boats at the Catamaran Classic at Sandringham and beat Lindsay's una-rigged *Beta* by about three and one-half minutes. We switched her back to a sloop rig quick smart and found the difference.

"But, typical of Australians, they are knockers, and the *Quest B* has received little support."

The crew prepares for mark rounding in a Tornado catamaran race

America's Cup challenger *Gretel II* climbs angry seas during training off Sydney Heads

THE AMERICA'S CUPPERS

THE AMERICA'S CUP is a freakish event. The yachts that race for it, of the International Twelve Metre Class, the largest class still being raced, are so expensive to build and maintain that they are only brought out in preparation for America's Cup challenges. And in Australia, the privilege of racing aboard one has meant sacrificing more than eighteen months to two years of active competitive racing for the tedium of training alone or against a lesser pacemaking Twelve. The challenges themselves have become as much exercises in business administration, politics, and technology as they have yacht races, involving all the things most people go sailing to forget.

Why, then, have Australians clamoured to challenge the Americans for this most elusive of all yachting prizes? Simply because it's there, yachting's Mount Everest. The Americans have defended it successfully twenty-one times against challengers from England, Canada, Scotland, and Australia. When someone wins it from them, that could be the end of it. But until then, it remains the sport's ultimate challenge.

The Australian temperament was inevitably drawn towards it. There was a move as long ago as 1888 to build a challenger. Successful Sydney designer Walter Reeks travelled to America to view the 106-foot steel centreboard sloop, *Volunteer,* which had defended the trophy the year before, and to discuss conditions under which the races would be sailed. Reeks wanted to build a 90-footer which, under the Cup's deed of gift of those days, would have to be sailed from Sydney to America to compete. He came home optimistic about the project but apparently failed to enthuse any financial backers.

Then in 1959, Australia did take up the challenge. The America's Cup was put within her reach by the decision after the war of the New

York Yacht Club to modify the deed of gift so that the match could be sailed in Twelve Metres. These were sloops of around sixty-nine feet at that time (to become shorter as designs progressed, to sixty-two feet) compared with 135 feet for the superb J-class boat *Ranger*, last of the pre-war defenders in 1937.

In 1958, the first of the post-war challengers in Twelves was sailed with America's *Columbia* easily defeating Britain's *Sceptre*. Australian yachting at that time was beginning to flex its muscles with some success behind it in Olympic yachting and a rising standard in ocean racing. And, with Britain's challenge widely publicised, the America's Cup was a talking point around the yacht clubs.

Sir Frank Packer, Sydney newspaper proprietor, was thinking of building a big new yacht. He had owned from 1930 until 1942 the sixty-five foot cutter, *Morna,* scratch yacht in the Royal Sydney Yacht Squadron's fleet and winner of a number of important trophies. Over a convivial lunch with Squadron friends, Bill Northam and Richard Dickson, the suggestion was made that he build a Twelve Metre instead, and challenge for the America's Cup. When an American reporter asked him later what had led him into the America's Cup, Sir Frank replied: "Alcohol and delusions of grandeur." While there may have been some truth in both propositions, there was a deeper reason.

It was to keep Sir Frank at it, spending well over $2 million on the 1962, 1967, and 1970 America's Cup campaigns. And it was not really any great love of sailing. After 1962, he seldom set foot aboard his Twelve Metre yachts. He didn't resume active sailing as he thought he might in 1959, his health probably preventing it anyway, and he preferred the sharper thrills of watching his horses on the racecourse to the measured pace of yacht racing. As a sailor, he hardly ranked as an armchair admiral.

But the America's Cup was something else. Here was the gamble of a lifetime and Sir Frank has seldom been able to resist a long-shot, in business or on the racecourse. He's game and he's tough, the survivor of many power struggles in building his $50 million newspaper and television empire. Gravel voiced and big (six feet two inches), a former New South Wales amateur boxing champion, Sir Frank rules his empire with a fist that extends to raids on reporters' expense accounts ("Well, why didn't you take the bus?"). While he's a tough boss, he's fair, with surprising lapses into benevolence. He has helped a number of employees out of financial corners and among the many stories about him is one about bawling out a copy boy for being slovenly dressed, then giving him the money to buy a new suit.

In 1962 a reporter for the American magazine, *Sport Illustrated*, wrote prophetically: "With the arrival of Sir Frank Packer to try for the Cup on the traditional course off Newport, Rhode Island, next September, the sport is getting—if not a winner—a different sort of loser, a challenger of a novel sort. Sir Frank has the traditional qualities—the skills of a good sailor and the sure poise of a gentleman skipper. But there is also in him an unabashed vigour, a scrappy trace of the alley cat. Off Newport, he may win, or he may lose, but he will not necessarily do either graciously. If he tried and failed to take the America's Cup every September for twenty years, he would never evolve into a lovable old loser like Sir Tommy Lipton. Losing is not his cup of tea and, although he is gifted with massive charm, lovable is not the word for him."

Sir Frank and his advisers, Northam and Dickson, with Keith Martin, one of his executives at Consolidated Press, set about reducing the odds, although this in itself involved Sir Frank in a heavy personal gamble. They retained young naval architect, Alan Payne, already well known for his ocean-racing designs, and secured the American Twelve, *Vim*, for crew-training and as a yardstick for their new boat.

Payne, born in England in 1922, came to Australia with his parents at the age of seven. They lived near the harbour at Rose Bay and Payne became a keen sailor, studied naval architecture at Sydney Technical College and the University of New South Wales. From 1945 he devoted himself full time to yacht designing.

Vim was chartered from her owner, John Matthews, and shipped to Australia for about $90,000. She was an old boat but a very good one, built in 1939 to a design by Olin Stephens who had first entered the America's Cup lists in 1937 by helping Starling Burgess in the design of *Ranger*. In 1958 the American defender, *Columbia*, only just won the defence trials from *Vim*, sailed by Bus Mosbacher.

At that stage Sir Frank had personally gambled $200,000 on the challenge without knowing whether Payne could design a boat which was faster than *Vim*. Unless he could, the deal would be off. It was only after Payne had tested five-foot models of his design in the test tank of the Stevens Institute at Hoboken, New Jersey, and given assurances that he had a design faster than *Vim*, that the syndicate was expanded to raise the $500,000 estimated to be needed in building the challenger and in shipping her to Newport. The other major contributors were the Ampol Petroleum Company Limited, which had itself been contemplating building a challenger, and W. D. and H. O. Wills, the cigarette manufacturer. In building and rigging the yacht, sixty-eight firms donated services, material, and money.

The challenge, foreshadowed in October 1959 with an announcement by the retiring Governor-General and Commodore of the Squadron, Sir William Slim, was formally lodged in January 1960 to an incredulous and peeved reaction from British yachtsmen who were also planning a challenge for 1962. The Royal Thames Yacht Club asked the New York Yacht Club whether it would consider substituting a "Commonwealth Club" as challenger and the Duke of Edinburgh wrote to the Australian Yachting Federation suggesting that a co-ordinating committee for a Commonwealth challenger be formed. Royal Thames Commodore, Captain John Illingworth, flew to New York for talks with the NYYC which sidestepped the issue by stating it hoped Britain and Australia would find a satisfactory solution.

Sir Frank Packer answered Illingworth's proposals for a solution with a cable which revealed a lot of Sir Frank's personal style:

THANK YOU FOR YOUR CABLED MESSAGE STOP THIS MATTER HAS NOW LARGELY PASSED INTO THE HANDS OF THE ROYAL SYDNEY YACHT SQUADRON WHO ISSUED THE CHALLENGE BUT THE SYNDICATE'S VIEW IS THAT THIS IS AN INTERNATIONAL TROPHY AND WE MADE NO SECRET OF THE FACT THAT AUSTRALIA INTENDED TO CHALLENGE, THAT A SYNDICATE HAD BEEN FORMED, THAT THE "VIM" HAD BEEN CHARTERED, THAT WE INTENDED TO BUILD A BOAT AND TO CHALLENGE STOP IN PUTTING OURSELVES IN THIS POSITION WE HAVE INCURRED GREAT PERSONAL EXPENSE STOP IF FOR REASONS BEST KNOWN TO THEMSELVES THE ENGLISH CHALLENGERS DECIDED TO DELAY THEIR CHALLENGE THIS IN MY OPINION IS NO JUSTIFICATION FOR QUESTIONING AUSTRALIA'S CHALLENGE STOP FURTHERMORE I FEEL THAT A CHALLENGE FROM AUSTRALIA WILL ASSIST AND INTENSIFY GENERAL INTEREST IN THIS GREAT RACE . . . I SEE NO REASON FOR AUSTRALIA TO WITHDRAW FROM ITS RIGHT AND JUST POSITION AS THE VALID AND FIRST CHALLENGER FOR THE 1962 SERIES AND AS I SAID EARLIER IN THIS MESSAGE WE AT NO STAGE TRIED TO CLOAK HIDE OR CLOTHE OUR INTENTIONS WITH SECRECY STOP THIS MESSAGE IS PERHAPS NOT VERY HELPFUL TO YOU IN WHAT YOU ARE SEEKING TO ACHIEVE WHICH YOU DESCRIBE AS "TO FIND A SOLUTION SATISFACTORY TO BOTH AUSTRALIA AND ENGLAND" STOP AS FAR AS WE ARE CONCERNED THE PRESENT SITUATION OF BEING THE FIRST VALID CHALLENGER IS QUITE SATISFACTORY FOR AUSTRALIA AND CALLS FOR NO SOLUTION STOP AS YOU ARE AWARE, HIS ROYAL HIGHNESS PRINCE PHILIP IS PATRON OF ROYAL SYDNEY YACHT SQUADRON SO NO DOUBT OUR CHALLENGE WILL CARRY HIS BLESSING STOP AFTER ALL YOU HAVE HAD A LONG UNINTERRUPTED RUN STOP MAYBE WE WON'T DO ANY BETTER BUT EVERY NOW AND AGAIN YOU HAVE TO GIVE THE YOUNG FELLOW IN THE FAMILY HIS HEAD STOP YOU ARE AT LIBERTY TO PLACE THIS CABLE BEFORE THE NEW YORK YACHT CLUB IF YOU SO DESIRE STOP FRANK PACKER

British feelings were soothed by an NYYC announcement that it would accept a challenge from Royal Thames for 1963 or 1964 if it beat the Australians and should it be beaten, let Royal Thames tackle the winner first.

The new Twelve was built by the yard of Lars Halvorsen Sons Pty Ltd on the Parramatta River, launched on 28 February 1962, by Dame Pattie Menzies, wife of the then Prime Minister of Australia, and christened *Gretel* after Sir Frank Packer's late wife. Payne was studious, conscientious, and co-operative to a fault. Assistant Warwick Hood recalled later how Payne would come down from the top of *Gretel*'s mast on the slips in Sydney just to take a telephone call from a reporter.

While basically *Gretel* was in the tradition of the newest American Twelves, Payne had some thoughtful innovations. She had a very flat run aft to a wide counter, designed to carry her heeled length considerably beyond her measured waterline length in a seaway. Her rudder had a straight trailing edge, instead of the rounded shape which had been favoured for almost a century. And she had one real innovation in sail-handling equipment; a system for linking the pedestal winch drives to put the power of four men on to a single coffee grinder winch.

Meantime, from more than 200 applicants, 28 were selected for crew training first on *Vim* and then with the two boats. These were split into two crews, "white" and "black" under two skippers, Jock Sturrock and Archie Robertson, a Sydney skipper with a good record in the Dragon Class and other round-the-buoys boats.

With no previous experience for guidance, formidable problems of rigging and equipping the boat were slowly overcome. De Havilland Aircraft Corporation handled the novel job of making the ninety-four foot aluminium mast from three imported extrusions, two thirty-five feet long and one twenty-five feet which had to be pressed into an elliptical tapering shape and welded together. Then it made a spare. More than forty sails were made, from Dacron imported from America, by Joe Pearce and Peter Cole. Preparation time quickly ran out and with only six weeks' sailing in Australia, struggling at first to beat *Vim*, *Gretel* left for America very much an unknown quantity.

The Americans took the Australians lightly. Only one new Twelve, *Nefertiti,* designed by Ted Hood the sailmaker, was built although three others, *Columbia, Easterly,* and *Weatherly* were altered. *Weatherly*, designed by Phil Rhodes with keel-shape re-designed by Bill Luders, and Emil "Bus" Mosbacher at the helm, won through the eliminations.

The Australians spent two months sailing *Vim* and *Gretel* off Newport, learning all the time. *Gretel*'s mast was shifted nineteen inches forward to take the hard weather helm out of her, but weather helm was still a problem and the Australians still had much to learn when the gun went for the start of the first race on 15 September 1962.

Syndicate head, Sir Frank, had a lot to learn, too. He had tried to keep his crewmen on their toes by keeping them guessing. This led to a lot of internal unrest among the crews. Sir Frank delayed final selection until almost the eve of the first race and for this race, navigator Terry Hammond was left ashore and the cockpit stacked with skippers; Trygve Halvorsen and Archie Robertson sailing there with Magnus Halvorsen and Jock who had been finally selected as skipper. For the subsequent races, Hammond and Norman Wright, the Brisbane 18-footer champion, replaced Trygve Halvorsen and Robertson. The foredeck hands were Mick York, Dick Sargeant, Peter O'Donnell; amidships were Frank McNulty, Bruce Anderson, Brian Northam and Trevor Gowland.

Weatherly won the first race by three minutes forty-six seconds in a ten to eighteen knot breeze. The Aussies, who had won many friends in Newport and broken the predictable pattern of British-American challenges, drew a spectator fleet of more than 2,000 boats. The start was delayed for an hour while the Coastguard cleared them from the line. Both yachts were using American-made Hood mainsails but

Weatherly's mainsail was flatter and more effective as the breeze freshened. Repairing a broken runner tail caused *Gretel* to overlay the windward mark at the end of the second heat and contributed to *Weatherly*'s margin.

September 18 was *Gretel*'s history-making day. For the first time since 1934 when Tommy Sopwith's *Endeavour* beat Harold Vanderbilt's *Rainbow*, a challenger won a race.

The course was over a 24-mile equilateral triangle with a beat and two reaches. For the fresh westerly, eighteen knots gusting to twenty-five, *Gretel* hoisted a flat Hood mainsail, originally cut for *Vim* in 1958. *Weatherly* hit the starting line first, by half a boat-length, with *Gretel* four lengths to windward. Both were sailing about the same speed but *Gretel* had to tack to clear her wind from the backwind of *Weatherly*'s sails. This led to a short-tacking duel with eleven tacks in seven minutes, Sturrock tacking to keep his wind clear, Mosbacher to cover. *Gretel*'s linked winches and the muscle of her crew spun the big yacht across the tumbling seas a second or two faster each time, and *Gretel* closed to within a boat-length, and rounded the windward mark only twelve seconds behind. The first eight-mile reach was too close for spinnakers. There was no speed difference, although *Weatherly* was officially timed as having gained two seconds on this leg. *Gretel*'s spinnaker was up and drawing first after the gybe, and Sturrock immediately edged her out on to *Weatherly*'s weather quarter. Just as *Weatherly*'s spinnaker was filling, at last, *Gretel* surged up, surfing on the face of a big wave, gaining enough to blanket some of the wind from *Weatherly*'s sails. Then *Gretel* cracked another wave and shot into the lead. *Weatherly* hardened up to come across *Gretel*'s stern and as she did so, the spinnaker pole was let go too far forward, cracking against the forestay and buckling. The accident cost the defender time, but not the race, which *Gretel* won.

As they did throughout the series, *Gretel*'s crew signalled for a lay day. This drew some criticism, as the forecast for the following day was for similar fresh breezes, where *Gretel* seemed at her best. But every day meant opportunity for improvement to the challenger.

For the third race on 20 September, *Gretel*'s advisory committee (of syndicate members, the designer, reserve skipper, and builder) insisted on *Gretel* again using the flat-cut Hood main while Sturrock wanted to use the fuller sail of the first race because the breeze was light. It was under eight knots at the start, fading and freshening later to ten. *Gretel* reached the starting line first, at the opposite end to *Weatherly*, and as they first crossed, fifteen minutes after the start, *Gretel* held the lead. She tacked to cover but *Weatherly*, sailing faster, soon crept from under her lee and then forced *Gretel* to tack out of the backwind. *Weatherly*, fifty-eight seconds ahead at the windward mark, took off on the first run of the windward and return course on the end of the dying breeze. *Gretel* was left floundering in a calm and at the leeward mark was twenty-three minutes behind. The wind freshened slightly and *Gretel* picked up to finish eight minutes forty seconds behind *Weatherly*.

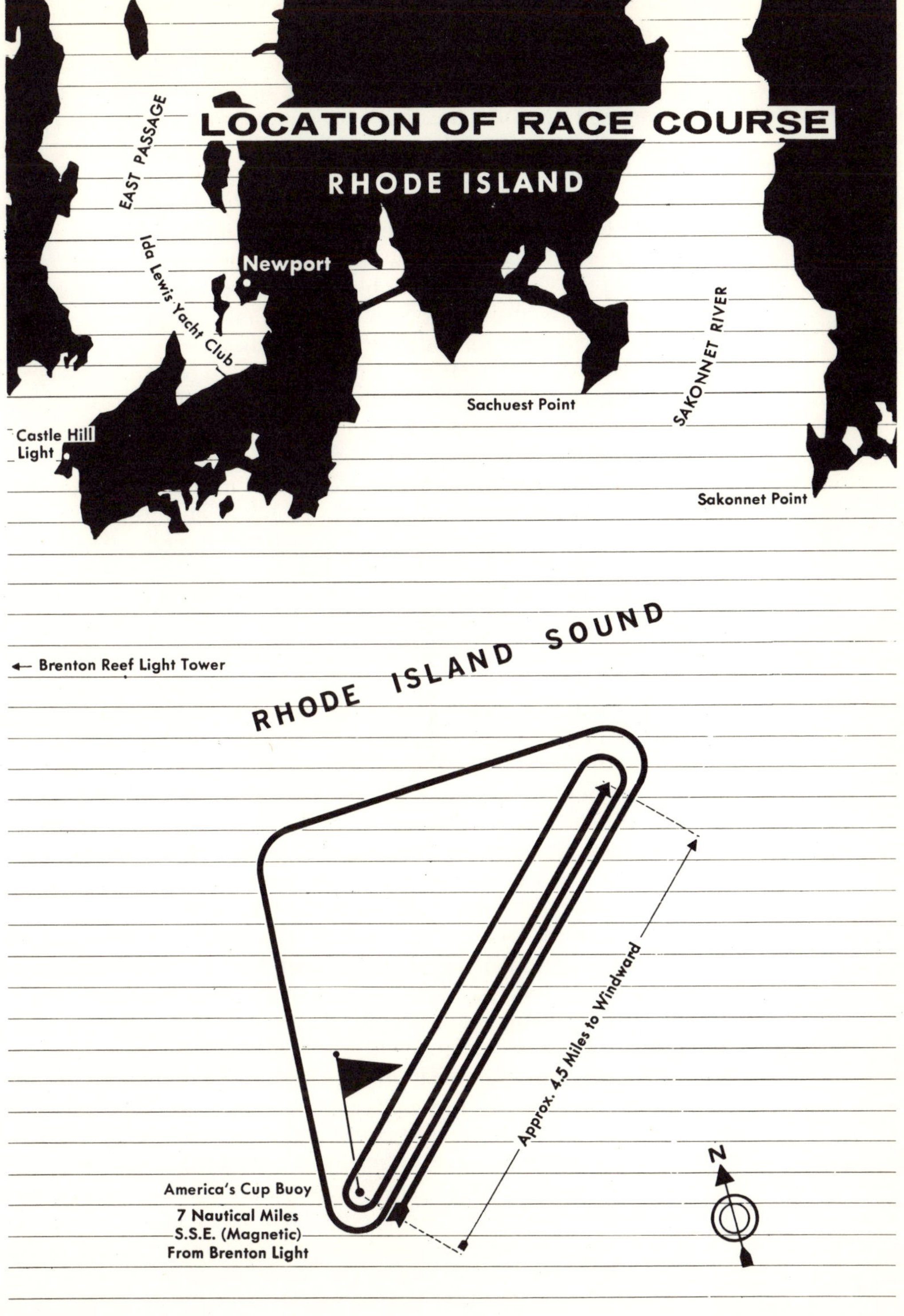
LOCATION OF RACE COURSE
RHODE ISLAND
EAST PASSAGE
Ida Lewis Yacht Club
Newport
SAKONNET RIVER
Sachuest Point
Castle Hill Light
Sakonnet Point
Brenton Reef Light Tower
RHODE ISLAND SOUND
Approx. 4.5 Miles to Windward
America's Cup Buoy
7 Nautical Miles
S.S.E. (Magnetic)
From Brenton Light
N

The fourth race, on 22 September over the triangle, was another very close one with *Weatherly* holding the advantage at the start. Beating into the six-knot wind, *Gretel*, forced to tack out of the defender's back-wind, went into another tacking duel. *Weatherly* was one minute twenty-six seconds ahead at the windward mark, by no means safe, and *Gretel* closed on the first reach under the spinnaker she had used in winning the second race, to within forty-five seconds. After the gybe, *Gretel* continued to gain. Then *Weatherly* changed to a genoa jib. *Gretel* followed suit. The reasons are disputed. Most accounts say the change was because of a wind shift. Some *Gretel* crewmen, however, believed the wily Mosbacher bluffed Sturrock into changing, leading him to change in anticipation of a shift that when it did come, wasn't pronounced enough to dictate the sail change.

Under genoas, *Weatherly* drew ahead. *Gretel* pulled away and re-set the spinnaker. *Weatherly*, further to windward, then set hers and, moving faster than *Gretel* which had to point higher to make the finishing line, slid across a mere twenty-six seconds in front.

The fifth race, over a windward and return course in a moderate wind of ten to fifteen knots, on 25 September, was an anti-climax. Both yachts hoisted flat mains, anticipating a stronger breeze. *Weatherly* pointed higher and sailed faster on the wind. Sturrock initiated another tacking duel but the wind wasn't fresh enough to give *Gretel*'s linked winches any advantage and *Weatherly* rounded the windward mark two minutes four seconds in front and eventually won by three minutes forty seconds.

The Australians came home believing they could win the America's Cup. The Americans—re-interpreting within six weeks of the challenge, the rules to forbid any future challenger from using US test tanks, sails, sail-cloth masts, winches, or fittings, apart from a few minor items—tacitly admitted they had let the Australians get away with too much.

Sir Frank, immediately after the British-American challenge in 1964, was keen to challenge again with *Gretel*. On *Gretel*'s return from America, the rig was moved another ten inches forward and, at Alan Payne's direction, three feet of her long, counter stern was lopped off. Shifting the rig forward had made it unnecessary for backstay anchorage and the weight saved of about 100 pounds or so could be put to better use in the keel as ballast. Then Payne announced, in November 1963, that he was retiring from yacht designing although he would offer his services if Australia again challenged for the America's Cup.

He said: "I am unable to make a worthwhile living out of yacht design in Australia because the scope is not here. I do not want to leave Australia and work overseas where I could make more money. Overseas firms of yacht designers manage to get by financially because they have about forty yachts of the same general type building each year against my two. New theories in performance, construction, the use of new materials and gear can be quickly assessed because of the big turnover in what I call design thinking."

Payne's remarks were just as true seven years later. Payne was tired out after that first America's Cup challenge. His business and health suffered. He had worked extraordinarily long hours and in the middle of it all contracted hepatitis. So he left yacht design to work as a design engineer for Russell Slade for whom he'd designed in 1961 the ocean-racer, *Janzoon II*, Australia's first big fibreglass yacht.

While Britain was preparing for the 1964 challenge, put back a year by the New York Yacht Club on the grounds that it was too difficult for owners and officials to race more often than every two years, other Australians caught the America's Cup fever. The Livingston brothers, John and Frank, head of a vast pastoral company, had the British design firm of Illingworth and Primrose working for more than two years on Twelve Metre designs.

The Livingstons were among the pioneers of Australian ocean racing. They were the first Australians to compete in the Transpac with *Kurrewa III* and with their sixty-five-foot cutter, *Kurrewa IV*, first to finish in four Sydney-Hobart races. While their interest in Twelves was well known, it came as a shock to Australian yachtsmen when the Livingstons announced, in September 1963, that they would build a boat for the 1964 British challenge. The brothers, who spent a lot of time in England during the Australian off-season, had recently been admitted as members of the Royal Yacht Squadron, Cowes. Britain at the time was desperate to find a second yacht to make a campaign of it with Tony Boyden's *Sovereign*. And the Livingstons were persuaded, "conned" might be a better word, into building a challenger as well, for Britain. As there was no time left to design and build a new yacht, they ordered an identical hull to the David Boyd designed *Sovereign*.

"The chance to get a separate design team and builder on the job, essential if we are to improve the breed, was lost," Illingworth lamented. "How I wish they had come to me with a firm request a few months earlier!"

The Livingstons' yacht was called *Kurrewa V*. They were happy to hand the whole thing over to the control of English 5.5 owner, Owen Aisher, who put Colonel Stug Perry at the helm. Hampered by poor sails, *Kurrewa V* was beaten by *Sovereign*, skippered by Peter Scott. *Sovereign* in turn went down to the American defender, *Constellation*, in four straight defeats with whacking margins: five minutes thirty-four seconds, twenty minutes twenty-four seconds, six minutes thirty-three seconds, and fifteen minutes forty seconds, on the new Olympic style 24.3 mile course. Olin Stephens designed *Constellation*, of which he said, "While showing some innovations from smaller classes, like sharp keel, scimitar-shaped rudder and vertically-bending boom, she could not claim originality." Bob Bavier skippered her, bringing her from behind in the trials to beat the Bill Luders designed *American Eagle*.

Meantime, Royal Melbourne Yacht Squadron Commodore, Otto Meik, announced early in 1964 that he planned to build a challenger. Otto, a close friend of Jock Sturrock, had soaked up the heady atmosphere of Newport in the 1962 challenge. He commissioned Warwick Hood, who was carrying on Payne's former business, to design the boat and sent Hood and Sturrock to America to study the form of the 1964 contestants. But after their return, Otto pulled out because of the time and money involved.

Sir Frank Packer had welcomed the news of Commodore Meik's plans. It could only be a good thing for yachting, he said, and help Australia's chances of winning the America's Cup. "The more experience Australian yachtsmen have in racing Twelve Metres, the better are Australia's chances of success," he said. Sir Frank said his syndicate would build in all probability a new Twelve Metre. The final decision was to be made after alterations to *Gretel* to improve her performance had been tank-tested against a new model to be designed by Alan Payne in conjunction with Trygve Halvorsen.

Jock Sturrock, unhappy at the way in which decisions on sail and crew selection had been taken from him in 1962 by the advisory committee of the *Gretel* syndicate, didn't want to sail for Sir Frank again. But after Otto Meik had dropped his plans, a strong group of yachting enthusiasts in Melbourne wanted to see Jock at the helm of another challenger. Among them was Fred Moylan, Vice-Commodore of the Royal Brighton Yacht Club, who got together a committee of yachtsmen which eventually led to the formation of the *Dame Pattie* syndicate.

The syndicate was headed by Emil Christensen who, as chairman of the big food company, Petersville, had plenty of administrative experience but didn't know much about yachting. The operation was built around Jock, who was given all the power he wanted; he had responsibility for selecting the crew and for setting up and running the boat. They set out to raise $500,000. Jock believed at the time that stories of the high cost of the 1962 challenge were put about to frighten off others, but in the end, the *Dame Pattie* syndicate was under-capitalised. Shareholdings could be taken in the *Dame Pattie* syndicate in two ways: fourteen companies each contributed $20,000 which was tax deductible as this purchased them advertising and public relations rights from the syndicate, a practice which drew criticism from the Americans who were unable to secure tax deductions on America's Cup yachts. Individual donation from yachtsmen was the second way to syndicate membership and goods and services were subscribed at less than cost. Warwick Hood designed the boat with Bill Barnett, the builder.

Sir Frank Packer and Russell Slade financed a programme to uprate the towing tank at Sydney University, built during the second World War, so that it could be used for yacht models. A senior lecturer in mechanical engineering, Mr R. F. Halliday, was sent to America for a month to study operation of the tank of the Stevens Institute and Sir Frank had his own engineers from Consolidated Press make the carriage for conveying the models along the tank. By January 1965 they were satisfied the Sydney University tank was equal to and, in some ways, better than the Stevens tank, and both design teams were using it—*Gretel* models by day, *Dame Pattie* models at night. So one of the major obstacles raised by the

New York Yacht Club's tougher line on the rules had been overcome. Only one real obstacle remained: making sails that would match the superb big-yacht sails of Ted Hood, the American.

The problem in sailmaking was in weaving the sail-cloth stable enough not to stretch out of shape under the enormous loads imposed by the powerful Twelve Metre yachts. At the time all cloth for sailmaking in Australia was imported and even against the top overseas brands, Ted Hood had gained an edge by weaving his own cloth in such a manner that stretch was reduced to the point where the sail cutters could make the correct allowances for it.

Two Australian textile firms took up the challenge and in the end both produced satisfactory cloths with Bradford Cotton Mills Ltd succeeding in making a good heavyweight cloth suitable for Twelve Metre mainsails and genoas. The other firm, Silk and Textile Printers, had the consolation of having its lighter weight cloths accepted by Australian sailmakers for general use and so all Australian yachtsmen benefited through having cheaper cloth for their sails.

The sail-cloth barrier was one reason behind Sir Frank Packer's unfortunate decision to alter *Gretel* instead of building a new yacht. He reasoned that *Gretel* would be allowed to use again her Hood sails of 1962 and the Royal Sydney Yacht Squadron eventually obtained a ruling from the New York Yacht Club that sails, spars, and winches used by the challenger in 1962 could be used by her in 1967.

New *Dame Pattie,* from its launching on 22 August 1966, proved herself completely superior to revamped *Gretel* which in the end, for the last few trial races, cast off her ageing Hood sail for a Bradford KAdron cloth mainsail. *Gretel* suffered from an astonishing decision by Sir Frank on selection of helmsman which in turn led to crew dissension and a minor mutiny. He began by following his policy of the previous challenge; having two crews work up in a competitive way under two different skippers. For six months, crews headed by Gordon Ingate and Eric Strain alternated on *Gretel* and *Vim* off Sydney Heads. Then out of the blue, Sir Frank appointed Archie Robertson, who had joined the campaign at a late stage as a pacemaker, as *Gretel*'s helmsman for the first series of trial races against *Dame Pattie* in January 1967.

After being beaten in the first two races off Sydney Heads, by one minute fifty-six seconds in a fifteen to eighteen knot breeze and eight minutes forty seconds in a ten to twelve knot breeze, Robertson handed over the helm to Tryg Halvorsen who officially won the third race. But in this, *Dame Pattie*'s mast crumpled and fell over the side when she was two hundred and fifty yards from the finish and between four and four and a half minutes ahead. Sir Frank took advantage of the break in the trials to request the Squadron to postpone the remaining selection trials from 25 February to 25 March, enabling another massive alteration to counter her obvious tendency to pitch in a seaway. In the initial alteration the stern sections had been veed, now the bow sections were made finer as well.

But in the seven races of the preliminary trials, *Dame Pattie* was again easily the faster yacht to windward, although she did lose ground downwind to *Gretel*. The only race *Gretel* won was the sixth where, in a strong sou'wester of more than twenty knots and a bad sea, *Dame Pattie* split the stitching in a genoa going to the finishing line and *Gretel* passed by. After three races of this series, the ring-a-rosies on *Gretel* continued with Halvorsen replaced at the helm by Gordon Ingate.

The final trials were to have been held in America but Sir Frank called for more off Sydney to evaluate still another modification to *Gretel*. Against the protests of the *Dame Pattie* syndicate, who said this would make it difficult for them to catch a favourable shipping schedule, the Squadron announced that three more races would be held on 5, 6, and 7 May. For these trials, Warwick Hood added a "bustle" to *Dame Pattie*'s afterbody, designed to improve the water flow from the deep mid-ship sections by carrying their lines further aft. Hood had got wind of similar design devices in the new American boats. While her successes against *Gretel* had inspired raptures about *Dame Pattie*, Hood maintained she was no more than a highly-advanced Twelve Metre design, not revolutionary or radical. He offered the syndicate a faster design once the *Dame* confirmed her class. With his first boat, he had remained on the cautious side, but now he felt he had found some startling new lines for development in the tank. There was still time to build another hull, but the syndicate did not have the money.

The final *Gretel* alteration, by Alan Payne, was the addition of an even bigger bustle, with the increased measured waterline length reducing sail area within the push-pull formula to the point where a ten-man crew was carried instead of the usual eleven. Ballast was added and the lead keel streamlined. A last move within the *Gretel* crew to have Eric Strain brought back failed and one of the leaders of the "mutiny" was dropped from the afterguard.

Dame Pattie walked away with these last three races, winning by margins of three minutes twelve seconds, nine minutes thirty-one seconds, and twenty-four minutes eleven seconds, although in this remarkable last race, the *Dame* gained her margin by moving into a new breeze pattern. By now it was May and the breezes were tending light. This suited the *Dame*, at her best in winds of under ten knots, and *Gretel*'s reduced sail area could not have helped her.

Sir Frank's decision after the trials not to take *Gretel* to America was no surprise. He sportingly offered *Gretel* and all her equipment to the *Dame Pattie* syndicate. They did take some of the sails and other spare gear, but elected to hire the American Twelve, *Nefertiti*, as trial horse.

So *Dame Pattie* went to America in an aura of confidence that came close to over-confidence. Sturrock had certainly steered her a lot better than any of the *Gretel* jockeys and the boat was fast, how fast could not be fairly assessed because of the way the *Gretel* campaign had been mismanaged. Jock had a good crew around him with his old mate Norm Booth, and Norman Wright from *Gretel* 1962 in the cockpit and the peerless Pod O'Donnell running the foredeck. The crew, overshadowed at first by *Gretel*'s more experienced campaigners, had become their equals as the trials went on. But in Newport, with *Nefertiti* not a satisfactory partner, they lost some of their edge through lack of competitive training while the young American crew-men became battle hardened through keen trials racing between four defence candidates.

While Hood's *Dame Pattie* was a good Twelve representing an advance on *Constellation,* the Stephens-designed American defender, *Intrepid,* was more than a step ahead. Her keel was shorter, bustle more pronounced and, perhaps the most important innovation, she had two rudders. The forward one, at the base of the keel, provided extra lift to reduce leeway half a degree, in the calculations of Olin Stephens. Her rig was advanced with the wind mechanism and grinder hands below deck, enabling a very low main boom to be carried.

There was the usual psychological warfare just before the challenge. Warwick Hood protested, justifiably, about some of the lax measurement procedures of New York Yacht Club Measurer, Bob Blumenstock, and claimed, among other things, that the flotation test had been made to check the waterline with some of the racing gear missing. *Intrepid* had to go through the test again and her skipper, Bus Mosbacher, was irritated. Bus's tiger-tooth smile came even closer to a snarl when he found that some of the *Dame Pattie* crew, aboard *Intrepid*'s tender in the search for calm water, had eaten lunches belonging to the American crew. He was really hostile, although an uneasy peace was negotiated over iced coffee at a meeting called by the Sydney journalist, Lou d'Alpuget, in the Newport Creamery. Bus's real friendship with Jock was fully renewed during a visit Mosbacher made to Australia in 1970 when Jock was able to explain that those sandwiches had been handed around by Mosbacher's wife, Pat.

Well, the scene was edgy, with tighter than usual security surrounding the *Intrepid*'s dock, and other minor irritations.

But after the somewhat hysterical build-up, the racing was an anticlimax. Not a disaster, but *Intrepid* showed in the first ten minutes of the first race that she had a slight edge in every vital department: hull, sails, rig, equipment, crew, and helmsman. Over the series, this meant that the *Intrepid,* on a 24.3-mile course, was on an average just two per cent faster than *Dame Pattie.* And that was enough. In the immediate letdown, recriminations flew against and between helmsman, designer, and sailmaker. But none of them deserved to be flayed. *Intrepid*'s keel-tab combination helped give her an ability to go higher to windward, and this just had to make Mosbacher look better than Sturrock. Joe Pearce's sails from KAdron cloth were slightly fuller than the American sails, maybe too powerful for the hull which was more tender than *Intrepid*'s. But they looked good except in the first race where a main, made only three weeks before, collapsed into luff-to-leech shudders because it didn't match the mast bend.

Intrepid won the first race by five minutes fifty-eight seconds although

Sturrock made his best start of the series, leading over the line by ten seconds. In the eighteen knot breeze, *Intrepid* was able to easily go through to windward, helped by the tab and *Dame Pattie*'s mainsail trouble. *Dame Pattie* looked more promising in the second race, the seven knot wind suiting her, and five minutes after start Sturrock squeezed up under *Intrepid*'s lee bow, forcing Mosbacher to tack to clear his wind. *Dame Pattie* tacked too soon to cover and *Intrepid* slipped away to the lead, gaining through a seven-tack duel which ended in Sturrock trying to throw a false tack which Mosbacher didn't swallow. *Intrepid* won by three minutes thirty-six seconds.

Dame Pattie was no match for *Intrepid* in the fresher, twelve to sixteen knot breeze of race three with *Intrepid* climbing to 200 yards of *Dame Pattie*'s weather beam within fifteen minutes of the start. *Pattie* staggered badly on the wind, taking so much water into the cockpit that three men had to pump most of the way. *Intrepid*'s winning margin was four minutes forty-one seconds. And she won the fourth race, in the ten to twelve knot breeze for which *Dame Pattie* had been expressly designed, by three minutes thirty-five seconds, gaining more than a minute on each windward beat.

Sir Frank Packer, who had watched most of the races with Alan Payne, quickly lodged another challenge through the Royal Sydney Yacht Squadron, for 1970. He engaged Alan Payne full-time, a designer's dream commission, to draw him a new boat, supervise its building, crew training, and all the other details. From start to finish, this was the happiest arrangement in management for any of the Australian challenges. Payne had the experience, and quiet but authoritative presence to command the respect of Sir Frank and crewmen alike. There were to be no more mutinies. But there was still plenty of drama to come.

At the time, Warwick Hood was also negotiating with a second syndicate that did not announce its intention to challenge until July 1968. This syndicate was headed by Norman B. Rydge Junior of Sydney, a well-known offshore owner-skipper and included former members of the *Dame Pattie* syndicate, Fred Moylan, John Birrell, and Sir Reginald Ansett. They, and Australian yachtsmen in general, were shocked to learn that Sir Frank had gained from the Squadron "exclusive right" to the 1970 challenge. The Squadron, rejecting the All States Syndicate's proposal, said that as no other offer to build a Twelve was received within the period that new challenges had to be made, thirty days after the last race of the previous challenge, the Squadron had challenged on the basis of Sir Frank Packer's undertaking to provide a yacht and had agreed to consult Sir Frank if any other syndicate sought the right to challenge.

When the All States Syndicate's offer was referred to Sir Frank he said, according to the Squadron, with a quote that makes strange reading alongside his earlier one welcoming the competition from Otto Meik's proposed boat: "His syndicate's earnest belief after careful consideration was that two potential challengers would not be in the best interests of the Australian effort."

The Squadron added in its official statement: "After a full consideration of the above, and the present situation in respect of time, resources and progress made at this juncture, the Committee of the Royal Sydney Yacht Squadron is unable to consider the offer to contest the right to be selected as the Squadron's challenger."

A furore followed. A group of Squadron members called a special general meeting to try and upset the Committee's ruling. Sir Frank took the wind out of their sails by "offering" to withdraw his challenge if the Squadron endorsed the All States boat. While a strong case was put for the obvious benefits of having competition between two yachts to select the best possible challenger, a motion to this effect was defeated by seventy-four votes to forty-eight. The majority view was that if the motion were carried, it would amount to a vote of no confidence in the Committee which was bound by its undertaking to Sir Frank, at least morally.

So the All States Syndicate dropped out. *Dame Pattie* lay forgotten on a mooring outside her builder's shed until Vancouver yachtsman, George O'Brien, bought her and shipped her to Canada. The All States Syndicate had planned to use her as a trial horse.

From October 1968 crew training began, first on *Vim* and then on *Gretel* and *Vim*, with two crews alternating under the leadership of Jim Hardy and Martin Visser. Payne, conscious that an Australian challenger had never reached the windward mark first in the America's Cup, had them practising starts and the initial stages of the beat to windward. *Gretel II* was built amid the usual secrecy by Billy Barnett and launched, later than hoped, on 12 February 1970.

Innovator Payne surprised them again. His boat was unlike any other launched that season by the Americans or the French who, for the first time, were to sail their challenger off Newport in an elimination series against the Australians for the right to meet the US defender. Other challenges, by British and Greek Clubs, had been dropped.

Gretel II was short and stubby, at sixty-two feet overall three feet shorter than *Dame Pattie*. Her forefoot swept straight down to the leading edge of her keel from the knuckle in the bow. The midship section was conventional for Twelves, deep and slack-bilged. But aft, she was "way out," with very full sections and a deep, convex-curved bustle. As she floated, with her broad reversed transom stern and bow-down attitude, deliberately induced to reduce freeboard for'ard, she looked like a duck with her tail in the air, not right to the eyes of anyone who hadn't seen her beautifully-clean underwater shape with streamlined lead keel, thin at the top and bulbous underneath, fairing into the hull. Some individual Payne touches were added: she was steered by two small wheels, one on either side of the wide cockpit, instead of the usual one big wheel.

There was no stringing the crew along this time. Twelve of the sixteen for America were named soon after *Gretel II* began sailing; Jim Hardy was appointed captain, Martin Visser vice-captain and Bill Fesq navigator. While Visser had kept Hardy hopping in the practice races,

12
US 22

FACING PAGE: *Intrepid* leads around the final mark. ABOVE: Representatives of the media aboard the Coastguard cutter *Point Turner*, one of the press boats. BELOW: Sir Frank Packer views the start of a race in the 1970 challenge from the stern of *Pearl Necklace*

especially on the starting line, Hardy's placid but strong character seemed better suited for leadership through the long and difficult campaign ahead.

As *Gretel II* was late in launching, a terrible rush followed to tune her in time for shipping to America on 4 June. And an unfavourable schedule meant she had to spend a long time aboard ship, cutting to a minimum the time available for practice in Newport. At first she didn't fare too well against old *Gretel*. The promise was there. She left a minimal wake that spoke of underwater efficiency and in bursts was really fast. Payne had fitted her with a bendy mast and there was a good deal of trouble in matching the sails to it. Right up into the last days in Australia, *Gretel II* was struggling to beat *Gretel* and she left quietly for America, form unknown.

For the first time in 1970, the America's Cup was preceded by a Davis Cup style elimination between the challengers before the real thing, and *Gretel II* faced formidable competition from *France*. She culminated a $3 million campaign by Baron Bich, the ball-pen millionaire. Bich bought or chartered the best Twelves he could lay his hands on: *Constellation, Sovereign,* and *Kurrewa V*. Then he had young American designer, Britton Chance, plan a yacht incorporating the latest US ideas before the French designer, Andre Mauric, drew *France*. The French Twelves were manned by crews of young sailors doing their national service. *France* was a force.

Gretel II had less than ten days left for sailing off Newport before meeting her. Fortunately a new mast, complete with vortex generators (rows of metal studs to control the flow of air around the mast), suited the boat and sails perfectly, and she quickly snapped into top gear.

But *France* was obviously fast, her crew (or crews, as there were three of them) moved with the snappiest precision of all in Newport that summer while the Australians had been too busy tuning their boat to do much training together aboard her. But the French sails were not as good as those cut by Peter Cole, in turn equal to the best American sails and certainly the best ever seen on a Twelve Metre challenger. And the Australians were helped by the extraordinary attitude of Baron Bich who put the Sir Frank Packer of earlier challenges in the shade with the rapidity with which he sacked and reinstated helmsmen.

One of his helmsmen, Pierre "Poppy" Delfour departed from the French camp, "never to return" just before the racing, after a disagreement with the Baron. Louis Noverraz, the Swiss 6 and 5.5 metre veteran sailed *France* in the first race. A wonderful light-air helmsman, he made a tactical mistake at the last mark which let Hardy in and earned Noverraz the sack from the Baron.

During the two-day break which followed, Delfour returned. He steered *France* in the second race with a completely new crew, except for two winch-men. *France* had downwind speed, twice gaining the lead from *Gretel II*, but *Gretel II* was faster to windward and won by one and a half minutes. Delfour was sacked. Noverraz returned with most of his crew for the third race, but *Gretel II* led all the way in an eight to seventeen

*Gretel II*s mast with its exotic titanium top

knot breeze after pushing *France* across the line before the start. *Gretel II* won by two minutes twenty-four seconds, but amid some drama. Dave Forbes fell overboard during a spinnaker set but hung on to the main-sheet and was hauled back aboard. The tack fitting for the genoa parted, 100 yards from the finish, and the sail shot to the top of the forestay.

For the fourth race, Baron Bich made a Newport joke come true, taking the helm himself for an embarrassing result. He mistimed the start so badly that *France* was a minute late. Then he got lost in a thick fog. *Gretel II,* with Bill Fesq accurately plotting her course, picked her way around the marks to finish. But *France* became hopelessly lost and in the interest of safety, Baron Bich lowered sail and called up his radar-guided tender.

In a spectacular outburst the following day, he claimed he had been "dishonoured" and that the international race committee controlling the elimination had endangered his boat and the spectators. He also claimed Jim Hardy was lucky. But later when he had calmed down and when one of the challenge races was called off in fog less thick than the one which halted him, there was sympathy for his point of view. And the Baron, once he was defeated, placed his boats and sails at the disposal of the Australians for comparative training. With this unhappy experience behind him he has, like Sir Frank, learned the hard way and his challenge for 1974 should be better for it.

Meantime *Intrepid*, re-designed by Britton Chance, beat the latest Stephens' boat, *Valiant*. Some Americans believed this helped prove a theory that the newest Twelves were slower than the old. Australia, from being underdogs before beating *France,* were suddenly being given a chance.

The challenge match itself was closer than the 4-1 score indicates, and the most acrimonious since 1895 when Lord Dunraven alleged the American defender had cheated by taking on extra ballast after her water-line length was measured.

The system under which the New York Yacht Club runs the America's Cup was the real cause of the dispute reverberating around the world. For, unlike other international yachting events where there is machinery for appeal to higher authority, the New York Yacht Club until the 1970 challenge controlled the racing with an absolute authority. Its race committee also heard the protests and there was no appeal. Its measurer's decision was final. The system had never been under such hostile fire before, probably because the racing had seldom been close enough for protest-lodging situations to occur. But in 1970 for the first time in years there was a real yacht race and the NYYC race committee suddenly became acutely aware of how vulnerable it was. For no matter how fair they were, and no one will disbelieve race committee chairman E. Devereaux Barker's assertion: "We are honourable men," they could never appear to be impartial. "It's like protesting to your mother-in-law about your wife," was Sir Frank Packer's comment.

The good thing about the 1970 row is that it has led to the NYYC deciding to appoint an international jury to hear the protests from the 1974 challenge and an authority from the International Yacht Racing Union to decide the disputes. The Australians may have lost some old American friends by continuing to dispute the second-race protest decision long after the event. But at least they have ensured a better system of justice for future challenges.

Alan Payne and Charley Morgan, builder of the Florida defence triallist, *Heritage,* were upset when they arrived in Newport to find Stephens and Chance were on to a small device, which they did not know about, to fiddle the waterline length with the approval of the measurer. Fairing strips and metal flaps extending from the hull on to the rudder on either side had the effect of lengthening the waterline on *Intrepid* by fifteen inches. Payne said he didn't feel these fairing strips made a great deal of difference to *Intrepid*'s speed but was concerned that the NYYC measurer, Bob Blumenstock, had interpreted the rule too freely by deciding the flaps were not part of the hull. Following his complaint, a quarter-inch slot was cut into the metal fairing strips at the waterline. Also on complaint by Payne, *Intrepid*'s toilet was floored and enclosed as it was required to be under the Rule.

Came the first race, and the first protest, before the start. It occurred in the pre-start manoeuvres and made no difference to the result although it must have affected *Gretel II*'s starting tactics for the remaining races. The Australians arrived in Newport believing that before the start, there was no proper course as defined in the rules and the starboard tack yacht could steer whichever way she liked—the port tack yacht had to keep clear. This meant the yacht on starboard could hunt the port tack yacht up and down the line to unsettle it. The situation had arisen many times when Visser and Hardy were sailing against each other off Sydney Heads and Rolly Morgan, acknowledged as one of Australia's leading rules expert, had given them the opinion that the starboard tack yacht was almighty before the start. So when *Intrepid* headed up from the leeward end of the line, on port tack, Hardy reached down towards her on starboard, hoping to force the American helmsman, Bill Ficker, to tack. When Ficker pulled away, Hardy pulled away, and when Ficker headed upwind slightly, Hardy followed suit. But Ficker kept going on port to the point where Hardy had to tack to keep clear. Both yachts hoisted protest flags. *Gretel II* protested under the fundamental Rule 36: "A port tack yacht shall keep clear of a starboard-tack yacht." *Intrepid* protested against *Gretel II* under Rule 34 which says that the right of way yacht shall not alter course to prevent the other yacht keeping clear.

The New York Yacht Club Race Committee dismissed both protests, finding neither yacht had infringed a rule. In its finding, it said that at the time when the two yachts were approximately two boat-lengths apart, *Gretel II* came under Rule 34 since it would no longer have been possible for *Intrepid* to take further evasive action. The two boat-lengths interpretation does not appear in the rule book and was disputed by the Australians who felt that *Intrepid* could have kept clear by tacking.

SYDNEY

Gretel II on the slips at Newport. The crew is rubbing her underwater surface to ensure minimum friction resistance

The Australians had a woeful time in that first race. An over-full, too-light headsail was selected for the first windward beat in an eighteen to twenty knot wind and lumpy sea. *Intrepid* got the better of the start, to windward of *Gretel II*, and led around the first mark by one minute three seconds. Then as *Gretel II*'s crew went for the spinnaker, the sheet came unclipped from the clew and the sail wrapped itself around the forestay, taking six minutes to clear. And if that wasn't disaster enough, Paul Salmon was swept off the foredeck after *Gretel II* gybed around the wing mark of the Olympic course to begin the second reach. It took two passes to fish him out while *Intrepid* raced away for an unbeatable lead, winning by five minutes fifty-two seconds.

Next day was a lay day, the day after the race was cancelled through lack of wind, and on 18 September, abandoned through fog. But on this day, the Australians cracked the American invincibility by leading around the windward mark by one minute fifty-four seconds. Martin Visser took the helm for the start in a nine-knot wind and out-manoeuvred Ficker. Poor spinnaker trimming cost *Gretel* time on the reaches and *Intrepid* was through her soon after gybe to lead around the leeward mark by forty-six seconds. By this time, the fog was closing in. *Gretel II* closed the gap again and was within 100 yards of *Intrepid* when the race was abandoned, two-thirds of the way up the second windward leg. The Australians had no quarrel with this decision and another lay day followed before the historic second race was finally decided.

By now it was clear that the lighter the breeze, the better *Gretel II* was. *Intrepid* seemed at her best in winds above the average ten to twelve knot range, and *Gretel II* in anything below that, with no difference in between. On 20 September, the most controversial race in recent America's Cup history started in a six to eight knot breeze. At the time few of us aboard the Coastguard Cutter, *Point Turner*, one of the press boats permitted on the "inside" of the course for photographers and radio men, realised there had been a collision on the starting line. Our view, and that of the bulk of the spectator fleet, was obscured by the committee boat *Incredible*. Here is a description of the start I wrote at the time and before knowing there had been a collision:

"After the two boats had tailed each other from the ten-minute warning gun, at two and a half minutes to go, Visser feinted a gybe to begin another circle on *Intrepid*'s tail but instead rounded up to a position square between *Intrepid* and the committee boat marking the heavily-favoured starboard end of the starting line. Visser was trying to stop Ficker starting in his favourite position—to windward of the opposition—by either forcing him above the committee boat or to pass astern of *Gretel II*. Both boats stalled out at a minute to go with *Intrepid* still out on *Gretel II*'s weather quarter and about 100 yards away, eyeing off the situation. At twenty-five seconds to go, *Intrepid* hardened on sheets and drove for the gap between *Gretel II* and the committee boat. *Gretel II* sheeted in too. I did think then that *Intrepid* had reached in (although the race committee found as fact that she had been close hauled) and that *Gretel II* did not have enough speed to 'close the door' and luff *Intrepid* the wrong side of the committee boat."

They collided, with a crash that was to be heard around the world. Two feet of *Gretel II's* stem went speeding off aboard *Intrepid* while the rest of her floundered eight lengths astern. A classic yacht race followed with *Gretel II* winning back the big distance she had lost after accelerating faster through a series of short tacks. She was forty-two seconds behind at the windward mark, lost a minute on the reaches, but again closed going to windward to round one minute twelve seconds behind. On the square run *Gretel II* slowly but surely overhauled *Intrepid*. Dave Forbes, who had proven himself adept at keeping spinnakers alive and filling in light winds, was at the helm. *Gretel II*, more buoyant and alive in the sloppy sea than *Intrepid*, surged up on her with every little wave, went past, bobbed ahead to a fifty second lead at the leeward mark and then a one minute seven second winning margin.

The Australian crew's jubilation was tempered by the knowledge that they had to survive a protest hearing next morning. They protested under rules which say that a windward yacht shall keep clear of a leeward yacht and that a yacht clear astern shall keep clear of a yacht clear ahead. *Intrepid* protested under Rule 42.1 (e) which says in part that after the starting signal, a leeward yacht shall not deprive a windward yacht of room to pass to leeward of the starting mark by sailing above a close-hauled course. *Intrepid*'s crew convinced the race committee that *Gretel II* had continued to luff after the starting signal until she was above close-hauled and had she fulfilled her obligation to fall off to a close-hauled course, *Intrepid* would have had room to pass between *Gretel II* and the committee boat.

Martin Visser and Jim Hardy maintained that *Gretel II* had never gone above close-hauled. Martin said the jib had been freed off to allow the main to keep the boat, moving very slowly in the light air, on course. This had caused the jib to collapse in the top, giving the impression that *Gretel II* was above close-hauled. Then just before the collision, the air flow around *Intrepid*'s sails pulled *Gretel II*'s jib back, leaving *Gretel II*'s head to drag around to starboard under the pressure of the main alone, and into collision with *Intrepid*.

The committee believed Bill Ficker's evidence that he came in close-hauled. Under Rule 42.1 (e) it didn't matter whether or not he was reaching but by finding he was close-hauled, their next assumption had to be that *Gretel II* was above close-hauled as the yachts approached the line on a converging angle. The point the Australians should have argued more forcefully at the time was that there was enough room for *Intrepid* to have passed inside the committee boat without colliding with *Gretel II*.

"Our preparation for the protest meeting was inadequate," Visser told me later, "I didn't put anything like the homework into the subject that I should have. We had had a long, tiring day on the water and went to bed at 10.30 that night. I had been lulled by the belief that there was enough doubt to have re-run the race.

"Since there was more room than *Intrepid* needed to clear *Gretel II* and the starters' boat, the argument whether *Gretel II* was sailing above close-hauled or not is of no consequence. Jim Hardy and myself both hold the view that had *Intrepid* hardened up at the moment she was able to, and this was a while before she actually did, she would have cleared us comfortably. Especially with the speed she enjoyed, we would not have been able to get close enough to bother her. Instead, Bill Ficker kept coming at us, without ever moving one fraction of an inch off his course, until the time of impact."

Visser charged the race committee with being lax in their procedures for hearing the protest, claiming Ficker had taken over telling his witnesses' stories, instead of just questioning them. Race committee chairman, Dev. Barker, announced the committee's decision to a stunned press conference. During questioning which followed, a reporter asked if there had been agreement on the facts. A ringing "No" came from Visser, standing at the back of the crowded Newport Armory, traditionally the press headquarters for the series. Visser, at the insistence of reporters, was called up to state his side of the story. One questioner took the line that Visser didn't know the rules. To that he replied that two years after he had first learned to handle a sailboat in Holland where he was born, he raced a local one-design under the International Yacht Racing Union Rules in 1931 and he has competed under them ever since.

He added: "Being keenly interested in the legal aspects of sailing, I consequently became part of various protest committees in Australia and overseas. For a number of years now, I have acted as chairman of the Royal Prince Alfred Yacht Club's protest committee."

Visser was a reserve for the Dutch Olympic team of 1948 before coming to settle in Australia with his parents. He is a boat-builder and designer and worked full-time as Payne's assistant before the 1970 challenge. On the water, he's aggressive. Ashore, he's inclined to be outspoken. He had his say in Newport.

The Australians twice sought to have the protest re-opened on the grounds of new evidence, claiming that *Intrepid*'s overlap was established when *Gretel II* was less than two boat lengths from the committee boat and that consequently *Intrepid* had breached Rule 42.3(a). The New York Yacht Club committee replied that this mark-rounding rule did not apply at starts where 42.1(e) governed and dismissed the request as neither introducing new evidence nor arguments on the rules not previously considered.

At the second attempt, the Australians quoted a supporting opinion for a 42.3(a) protest they had gained from English rules authority G. Sambrooke Sturgess. The race committee replied by quoting Section 22 of the Race Conditions:

"The decisions of the Race Committee of the New York Yacht Club in all matters pertaining to the Racing Rules shall be final, and there shall be no appeal therefrom."

By now, the racing had gone on with *Intrepid* scoring another win to load the scales heavily in favour of the Americans. But had the result hinged finally on that protest decision, Sir Frank Packer might have taken the matter to the New York Supreme Court to challenge the validity of the protest committee's procedures. Ficker won the start of the third race. Visser, unsettled by collision of race two and the protest, was never to shape up well again on a starting line. *Intrepid* held a narrow lead until the start of the square run. With *Gretel II* fifty-three seconds behind, there were real hopes in the Australian camp that *Gretel II* would repeat her fast-running performance of the second race and pass *Intrepid*. But in the freshening breeze, eighteen knots by this time, *Intrepid* was harder to catch and *Gretel II*'s navigator, Bill Fesq, took the blame for a tactical error which caused *Gretel II* to cover 200 yards of extra distance. He misjudged the most favourable angle at which to gybe for the mark in a thick haze which made it difficult to see. *Gretel II* rounded one minute sixteen seconds behind instead of the thirty seconds she otherwise could have been. This was just too far away for *Gretel II* to begin a tacking duel, which in the rising sea and wind could have had *Intrepid* in trouble and *Intrepid* won by one minute eighteen seconds.

Needing only one more win to wrap up the Cup, *Intrepid* won the start of the fourth race in a ten to twelve knot wind, but *Gretel II* chased closely all day. By now, her crew had mastered the art of sail trim downwind and she no longer lost ground on the reaches. She was twenty-nine seconds behind at the windward mark, twenty-four at the wing mark, but lost on the second reach when the wind veered, heading the yachts. *Intrepid* had a special headsail Ted Hood had devised for such a situation. It was this spanker (cross between a spinnaker and a genoa jib) which pulled *Intrepid* away to a forty second lead at the leeward mark. *Intrepid* consolidated her lead on the second beat, gaining, as the leading boat always does, by being first to reach some shifts in the wind. On rounding, *Intrepid*'s precise young crew goofed and wine-glassed the spinnaker. But they recovered and at the leeward mark, *Intrepid* was one minute two seconds ahead, the America's Cup almost won. But then Ficker and his tactician, Steve Van Dyck, made a bad tactical blunder. They failed to cover *Gretel II* in this switching, fading breeze. After a couple of early tacks in which *Gretel II* tried to clear her wind which *Intrepid* followed, the wind freed twenty degrees, leaving *Intrepid* laying above the finishing line with *Gretel II* fifteen boat lengths to windward but 100 yards behind. At that point, *Intrepid* should have taken the insurance of a short tack across to cover *Gretel II*. But with the finishing line, and an end to the drawn-out series, beckoning, *Intrepid* held on. As they sailed for the finish, the breeze dropped to the range, under eight knots, where *Gretel II* was superior and she began to overhaul the heavier *Intrepid*, dying in the left-over slop. Ficker tried then to put in a short covering tack, but it was too late, and he tacked back for the line when he realised he couldn't cross *Gretel II*'s bows.

The breeze swung back towards its original heading and both boats fell below the finishing line. *Intrepid* tacked first, within 200 yards of the line. "Go *Gretel*, Go *Gretel*," the chant arose from the massed spectator fleet. She crossed *Intrepid* by about two boat lengths. There was some argument in *Gretel II*'s tensed crew. But against urgings that they should tack and cover *Intrepid*, Hardy and Visser held on until they could cross the finishing line on their next tack. They reasoned, correctly, that to tack directly on to *Intrepid*'s beam would give her the chance to regain the lead through forcing a lee-bow situation. By standing on and trimming for all possible speed, *Gretel II* was able to tack smoothly in the dying wind to fetch the line. *Intrepid* had to put in an extra tack to reach the line and finished one minute two seconds behind.

The fifth race was from the start the most exciting of the whole series with *Gretel II*, steered by Jim Hardy this time, starting to windward and dead level with *Intrepid*. After two and a half minutes, with *Intrepid* slipping into the turbulent wind from *Gretel II*'s sails, Ficker tacked to clear his wind. *Gretel II* crossed in front, but so close that Hardy had to stand on for a time to ensure he retained clear wind when he tacked. Then *Intrepid* gained a favourable lift in the shifty wind and when the yachts converged again, *Intrepid* was close enough to force *Gretel II* on to starboard tack. They split tacks again and when they next crossed, *Gretel II*, after lifting on a favourable shift, was again clearly ahead. Hardy tacked to close-cover and *Intrepid*, after tacking to clear her wind picked up a favourable lift to regain a narrow lead. Finally both boats after fourteen tacks were laying for the windward mark, bow to bow. But another slight shift in the capricious wind put *Gretel II* just below the mark, forcing Hardy to tack under the stern of *Intrepid*, which laid the mark, and back again. These two extra tacks forced *Gretel II* forty-four seconds behind at the windward mark. After two tense downwind reaches, *Gretel II* was only thirty-nine seconds behind at the leeward mark and the cat-and-mouse windward battle was on again.

Gretel II closed to within biscuit-toss of *Intrepid* and only superb covering tactics by Ficker kept *Intrepid* ahead through a short-tacking duel of eleven tacks. Finally, the delicate situation was reached where *Gretel II* had clear wind and was to leeward of *Intrepid*, but prevented from tacking back on to starboard, and towards the mark, without breaching the rule for tacking too close. *Intrepid* was just far enough to windward to keep her sails out of the disturbed air on the windward sides of *Gretel II*'s sails. Hardy alternately squeezed high and pulled away to gain speed, trying to wriggle off the hook that Ficker had baited. But Ficker matched every nuance and finally carried *Gretel II* right past the layline to the mark. Then, with *Gretel II* safely tucked away, *Intrepid* tacked, freed sheets and raced back for the mark at full speed on a close reach. She had turned a dead-even situation into a fifty-one second advantage around the mark.

Downwind, *Gretel II* closed the gap. Her crew, their sail-handling now perfect, changed to a smaller spinnaker, hoisting it inside the bigger one without spilling an ounce of wind. She began to close rapidly. Her crew had realised that with a major shift in the wind, there could be no windward beat to the finish, and no chance of passing *Intrepid* unless they could beat her to that leeward mark. They almost made it, rounding only twenty seconds behind, but that was enough for *Intrepid*. She was able to lay straight back for the finishing line. Hardy, who never gives up, tried all the moves available to him—easing first out to windward, and then off to leeward to pick up speed and hope that the wind would shift back again. But Ficker took no chances this time, covered every move, and won by one minute forty-four seconds.

Australia's finest challenge had come to an end. All the elements of success had been there but one, and that was experience in first-class match racing. *Intrepid*'s crew had sailed thirty-three matches, before the series began, to *Gretel II*'s four, against *France*. *Gretel II* was an outstanding boat, equal to if not better than *Intrepid*. Peter Cole's sails matched Ted Hood's. The crew, after their first-race horrors, welded into a good combination considering they were a mixture of two crews and had very limited time to mould themselves into a single team aboard the new boat. They learned quickly, as they went along. Hardy steered well, remaining ice cool as the pressures mounted. There were some tactical lapses, but the Americans suffered them too.

Emerging from the fog of race three, *Intrepid* leads *Gretel II*. A miscalculation of the downwind tacking angle cost *Gretel II* some time here

Sir Frank Packer, the lessons of the previous challenges well absorbed, was a true leader. Through the preparations in Australia he let Payne, Hardy, and Visser make almost all the decisions on campaigning the boat. And in Newport, he backed their decisions. Although he made suggestions himself, they were usually sound ones. The only time I was aware of his putting any pressure on Payne and Hardy was one lay day when *Gretel II* took an interminable time calibrating her instruments in smooth water while Baron Bich was out on the course, waiting for a trial race.

"He was a good leader in victory and defeat," said Martin Visser. "Whether spirits were high or low, he used to come in at night time and try to get everybody in the right frame of mind for the next race."

On the morning of the fourth race, which would be the last if they lost, he asked Jim Hardy and Martin Visser to see him at his hotel. They discussed the tactics for the day and just before they left the room, Sir Frank turned around and said: "I know you boys will do all you can to win but if you have to lose it, don't be worried about it, don't have it on your mind. I knew this was on the cards before I started."

Gretel II's challenge showed the America's Cup will be won some day from its chapel-like chamber within the New York Yacht Club.

Jim Hardy, Olympian, America's Cupper, always seeking more competition

Jim Hardy

"I see myself as a plodder."

GENTLEMAN JIM IS THE nickname and it fits this big fellow with the big heart. I don't think I've ever heard Jim Hardy say an unkind word about anybody; that is until the 1970 America's Cup challenge where he did say some unkind things (although in a nice way) about the New York Yacht Club Race Committee.

But that benign exterior surrounds the uncompromising mind of a winner. Bob Miller, who has raced against him a good deal in Flying Dutchmen and Solings, says: "He's a good competitor, very hard and very tough. Never try to cross him on the wrong tack. Even though he's nice 'Gentleman Jim' he'll nail you if given the opportunity."

Jim does spend a lot of time working on his boats, ensuring all the gear is just right and leaving nothing to chance. And, during a series, where other helmsmen are inclined to tail off under the pressure, Jim improves.

He has had many successes in sailing. His greatest was winning the world 505 championship, beating the great Dane, Paul Elvstrom, into second place in Adelaide in 1966. He's also been close to greatness a number of other times. After the last race of the 1970 America's Cup, on the long tow back to Newport, Jim told his crew: "I don't know of any Australian yachtsman who has run more seconds than I have. And this is another one, a pretty important one, but just another second place."

Jim was disconsolate after that race. He told the press conference:

"I do feel considerable disappointment in a personal feeling that I have let Sir Frank Packer down, let Alan Payne down, and third and not the least important, my own crew. We were provided with a boat equal to *Intrepid*. Bill Ficker has outwitted me and gone on to win the series. I will always think that I have let the side down a bit. But I certainly haven't felt that it was not worth while. It's been a marvellous series, full credit to the winner." Jim's self-criticism should not have been that harsh. I know of no other yachtsman better suited temperamentally to the great pressure of America's Cup racing. The bigger the occasion, the better he likes it and he's unbelievably calm in a crisis.

Jim Hardy just had to be a yachtsman. Born in 1934 in South Australia to a yachting family, Jim began sailing when he was ten at the Brighton and Seacliff Yacht Club in a leaky old twelve-foot Cadet Dinghy, called *Mermaid*. His father, Tom M. Hardy, a master yachtsman and owner of the yawl, *Nerida*, later to win the Sydney-Hobart race in 1950 under the ownership of Colin Haselgrove, was killed in a plane crash when Jim was only five years old. But he left behind a houseful of yachting books.

"My interest in America's Cup yachting," says Jim, "goes back to reading such books of my late father as *The Lawson History of the America's Cup*. I adored the plates of the old yachts."

Jim's two older brothers were sailing, his mother, Eileen, was keen on the sport, and although no pressure was put on him to take it up, he inevitably did so. "When I took to sailing, I'm afraid I became quite fanatical about it," he said. He wasn't long satisfied with sailing *Mermaid* off a thirty per cent handicap and craved his own boat. So he built his own. The Cadet, with its traditional clinker planking, is not an easy boat for anyone to build, but the thirteen-year-old Jim Hardy figured it was the only way he'd get a boat of his own. He called her *Nocroo* and built another for Fred Neil, *Noctoo*, which won the Stonehaven Cup, the Australian championship for Cadets. Jim never won a Stonehaven Cup although he was runner-up once. But he was inspired by his opponents, especially Tony Manford from Perth. "Manford was the perfect goal. I'll never forget the kick I got out of beating him in the invitation race in Adelaide in 1948."

When he reached the Cadet age limit, nineteen, Jim built himself a Twelve Square Metre Sharpie, *T. M. Hardy*, and with this and two other boats was a top competitor in the class from 1952 to 1960. His second-place complex began here. He was runner-up to Rolly Tasker twice and John Cuneo three times before finally beating Cuneo for the Australian championship in Perth in 1959. He was the only South Australian to show a glimmer of interest in the 1956 Olympic trials but was again second, going down to Tasker.

In 1960 he bought a Finn for the Olympic trials. "I was again the only one in South Australia, but I took it on because I wanted to go for something better all the time." Jim finished seventh.

Then he sailed 505s for two seasons, winning the South Australian championship. Sailing took a back seat in 1961 and 1962 while he passed his final accountancy exams. Then his brother, Tom, asked Jim to move to Sydney to take over the New South Wales branch of the family wine merchant business. So Jim became resident director and manager, New South Wales, of Thomas Hardy and Sons.

He quickly became involved with Sydney sailing, taking on the Flying Dutchman class. He won the State championship in 1963 and the Australian in 1964 with Andy White, who had crewed for Rolly Tasker, on the trapeze. But they were second, again, to John Dawe and Ian Winter in the 1964 Olympic trials. Jim earned a trip to Japan as reserve, wryly noting that the other two reserves, Ron Jenyns and Tony Manford, had also won national championships that year before being beaten in the Olympic trials.

"Tokyo was good for me," said Jim, "I learned a lot just from watching the way other people went about their sailing."

On his return he continued sailing FDs until the world championship in Adelaide induced him back to the 505s. And he and Max Whitnall won it. Bob Miller, who made the sails for their *Black Bottle*, said: "One of Jim's idiosyncrasies is that he always tries to have the other thing. If all the competitors have such-and-such a boat and sails and masts, Jim has the exact opposite. He likes to be different. I think he figures that if he does well with these things, the others will be straight away at a disadvantage. And this worked for him in the 505s. He was probably the only one in the championship that had our sails."

In 1966, straight after the 505 world championship, Gordon Ingate introduced Jim to Twelve Metre sailing by inviting him to join his crew for the 1966–67 campaign against *Dame Pattie*. Although he missed out on a trip to Newport with *Gretel,* Jim went in the winter of 1967 to England where, with Max Whitnall crewing, he sailed into third place in the first world championship for the Tempest Class—the new Olympic two-man keelboat destined to make its first Games appearance at Kiel in 1972. On the way home, he went to Newport and saw the 1967 America's Cup. The childhood pictures from the old books came to life against the gossip in the Black Pearl and Dorians, hangouts for the Twelve Metre crews.

Jim came back to the FDs for the 1968 Olympic trials on Botany Bay, with Max Whitnall, for another second, to Carl Ryves. But he won a place as team reserve and finally sailed at Acapulco in *Barranjoey* when Mick York had to drop out. After that he went straight into the America's Cup campaign for 1970.

"I love the Twelve Metres," says Jim. "I went into it with my eyes open and having the 1967 campaign under my belt was a tremendous help. Campaigning for the America's Cup is like training for the marathon. There seems no end to it. And I could never have done it without the help and understanding of my wife, Anne." The Hardys have two boys, David and Richard.

The Hardy calm withstood the rush of preparing *Gretel II* for Newport, and then through the elimination series, which after an uncertain beginning resulted in a rout for *France*.

"Mechanically the French crew were better than ours and understandably," Hardy said. "They were national servicemen who were good yachtsmen and who had been sailing full time on the French Twelves. They were very slick, while we had been so busy overcoming *Gretel*'s tuning problems that we hadn't even put up a spinnaker staysail when we arrived in America. In the first race, when we made a spinnaker change, or a headsail change, the French would finish a similar change before we could, even though they started after us.

"To me, Louis Noverraz was the most impressive of the French helmsmen. I had watched him at the Acapulco Olympics and had a close view of him winning the silver medal in the 5·5s. There was no question that he was a good operator. But he really did get tired on that first day which became a very long race in light winds. We fooled him to gain the lead around the last mark. The time before on that same mark, we tried to round close to the mark and sail past *France* to windward, and couldn't. As we approached the last time, I told Dave Forbes I wanted both rudders hooked together to make her more manoeuvrable and I warned the crew I was going to give the appearance to Noverraz that we were going to try and establish an inside overlap to encourage him to squeeze his boat towards the buoy. He did just that and stopped dead. We sailed straight through his lee.

"I don't think Baron Bich had cause for complaint over the last race when he became lost in the fog and had to retire. His boat was inadequately prepared for fog while ours was prepared. Bill Fesq pleaded with Alan Payne to have some provision designed into *Gretel II* for plotting in fog. Alan took some convincing but re-designed the layout aft to accommodate Bill virtually for this one exercise. Well, *France* didn't have that. She had on board that day Eric Tabarly, classed by Fesq as one of the world's greatest yachtsmen, who was quite capable of navigating *France*. But the Baron had overlooked giving him the necessary equipment to do it.

"After we beat the French, and defeated *France* again four more times in unofficial races, I felt at last that I had personally earned the right to sail in the America's Cup, that I wasn't just handed a silver spoon, given a yacht, and told to take part in the America's Cup. And this was a tremendous feeling.

"But as we went into the first race with *Intrepid*, everyone had the jitters and it turned out to be a very grim day all round. The biggest single reason we went so badly that day was that we had never before made the twelve-mile tow out to the America's Cup course. The races against *France* had been closer to land. But the Americans had raced twenty-eight times on the Cup course during their trials and twenty-eight times had been towed out.

"So we went out on a very grey, rough day, and I think most of the crew were feeling sea-sick; everyone was quiet. Because of our delicate halyard lock system, which is hard to engage with the boat rolling, we towed out with the main up. And that made it even more of a rough old journey. And my choice of the eight ounce headsail to start that race was bad; it was just too full for the conditions. There was that brush with *Intrepid* before the start. We were a little too early for the start itself, having to pull away, giving *Intrepid* an advantage. It was a nasty day to steer the boat with a big slop from the spectator fleet on top of the heavy seas. Then the spinnaker tied in a knot. Then Paul Salmon fell in. It was more like McHale's Navy than an America's Cup challenge. But we were not too despondent afterwards. The boat had shown promise and on the last beat we took some time out of *Intrepid*.

"For the next race, which was called off in the fog, Martin Visser started the boat and made a great start before handing the helm over to me. This came about as a result of a confession session we had among the afterguard. Alan Payne dropped the thought that Martin should start the boat as he had been a little more aggressive than me in the starts off Sydney Heads. Martin felt he was much better than I at starting. I said I had won a lot more races than Martin but he replied: 'You've become very clever as a defensive starter. I always had the offensive.' My job was to win the America's Cup and I thought: 'He's got more confidence than me,' so I agreed to the idea. While we had sailed on in fog against *France*, I think that race against *Intrepid* was rightly called off, because there was a pretty pronounced wind shift at the time which would have reduced the race to a follow-the-leader soldier's course."

Then came the second race, a brilliant victory turned into bitter defeat. Jim's feelings at the time are summed up by his comment published in the American magazine, *Sail*:

"I will never until my dying day be able to understand how a windward yacht can come charging in at an angle, bounce off a leeward yacht, get a two-minute advantage, lose the race because the other boat sailed a better race, and then be awarded it on a protest. *Intrepid* was not close-hauled as she came down on us at a big angle, and even if we were slightly high—and it would have been just for a second—doubt had to exist as to who was right. The very worst thing that I thought could happen to us was that we would have to sail the race again. I couldn't in my wildest dreams see how he could sustain a 42·1(e) against us. I said to Martin 'If they get out of this one, I'll get out of sailing.' "

After that controversy had run its course, I spoke to Jim again about that famous protest. He said in a calmer, but still insistent, vein: "There's always two sides to an argument and my feeling in this last America's Cup is that while we might not have been right all the time, there was a sufficient element of doubt to give us a fairer go. I think the Americans tried very hard to be just, but they didn't try at all to make it appear if it was just. I thought they acted with integrity but we had some case for appeal as far as the overlap situation was concerned.

"And there's a new consideration to our argument that *Gretel* was close-hauled. A Twelve Metre, in very light conditions with calm water, can build up to a hull speed of say seven knots in a five-knot wind. Once they are doing that, the apparent wind comes way forward of the true wind to the point where the boat seems to be sailing off the wind. Under the same conditions a Twelve travelling very slowly, as we were going up to the line, can sail a lot higher into the wind as the apparent wind is not affected so much by the boat's speed.

"For the speed we were doing, there was definitely some case for us still being close-hauled and I think there was some case for *Intrepid* saying she was nearly close-hauled, for she was doing twice our speed—about five knots to our two and a half. I think Bill Ficker probably still feels in his heart that he was close-hauled. He said at the protest meeting that was as high as he sailed all day. When he built up that speed as he approached the starting line, he couldn't go much higher. We could because we weren't going any speed at all. But we couldn't get this argument over at the time.

"I feel in my heart we really did win two races and we lost three races. And that's enough to lose the Davis Cup. We lost the America's Cup 2-3.

"I think that right up until the moment of impact, what Martin Visser was doing was right. Photos taken at the point of impact show our jib lifting, but that could have been caused by the blanketing effect of *Intrepid*'s sails on the windward side which left a terrific velocity of wind around the leeward side of the jib.

"The windward boat had to prove it was in the right and the *Intrepid* syndicate did the job at the protest hearing. My confidence that we would win the protest was at first shaken when a member of the committee disagreed with my contention that Bill Ficker's diagram of the incident was wrong. Ficker drew the yachts sailing on parallel courses when they had actually approached the line with a difference of forty-five degrees in their courses. I took a couple of photographs from the table to emphasise the difference in courses and then this member of the committee said: 'That's not right. It all depends on the position of the blimp' (from which the photos were taken). Then I knew we were for it.

"By the third race, our downwind speed, so lacking against the French and in the early Cup races, had improved to the point where it was more than equal to *Intrepid*'s. Basically, the problem was too many chiefs and not enough Indians. Dave Forbes was in charge of sail trim. Martin Visser was my assistant and tactician, and Bill Fesq was the navigator. Yet the four of us always seemed to put our oar into sail trim on top of the spinnaker trimmers themselves and the foredeck. It wasn't until I told John Bertrand that I was giving him the entire say with the spinnaker trim, pole position, and everything about it, that we began to improve. He's an honours engineer and really lifted his game to that challenge. John got more of a feel for it and the rest of us put our minds more to steering the yacht. We improved dramatically every race in that department but we sadly needed the twenty-eight races that *Intrepid* had during the US trials.

"In the third race, on the run, we got within twenty seconds of *Intrepid*

Gretel II crewmen. From left: Paul Salmon, Dave Forbes, Bill Fesq, and Martin Visser. Salmon fell overboard in race one but proved an excellent forward hand; Dave Forbes steered on many downwind legs; Bill Fesq navigated; and Martin Visser took most of the starts and was at the helm during the sensational collision but then made a mistake in figuring the best angle to gybe for the mark. We just lost track of it in the haze.

"A mistake by Bill Ficker gave us the fourth race. I made an observation of the wind direction at the windward mark the second time around and on the last leg I said to Bill Fesq that even though *Intrepid* was laying the finishing line I reckoned the breeze could still be blowing from its original direction near the line. So we made one more tack out and sure enough, as we went up the leg, the breeze went back towards its original heading. By that time, when Ficker had to come back towards us, he couldn't cross us. It was bad on his part to have ever let us make that extra tack without covering us. And it was after that I got the feeling I could beat Ficker."

Jim blamed himself for some tactical errors in the last race: "Martin Visser gave me the right answer when I asked him shortly after the start of one of our covering moves, and that was for me to apply a beam cover rather than a tight cover on *Intrepid*. Martin was afraid that under close cover, *Intrepid* would tack and go out to sea where Ficker might pick up a lift. We tacked on to a lift and at the same time gave Ficker dirty wind which forced him to tack from a lift to a knock. He went off on this knock for a while and sailed into more breeze, tacked back, lifted and sailed past us. I thought my manoeuvre was right, partly because I'd been abused for not covering sufficiently, from all quarters, and I took complete charge of that race. I almost said to myself, 'Well look, Martin, I'm going to crack the decisions today' because in earlier races, after the protest one, Martin had been flattened a bit and to me had made a couple of decisions that weren't right."

Jim refuted criticism I had made that on the second beat there was a chance, when the boats looked bow to bow, for *Gretel II* to have driven off to leeward, to a lee-bow position. He and Martin Visser said that although *Gretel II* was accelerating faster through a tack, the point was soon reached where there was no difference in speed and *Intrepid* was pointing fractionally higher. Jim added: "If we had tried to pull away and gone through to leeward, he would have just pulled away and gone over us. *Intrepid* was definitely faster than us the moment she cracked her sheets, I think because of her longer waterline length and bigger mainsail.

"Finally, he was too close for us to tack again and he took us out past the layline. The only thing to do was become passive about it because the farther you go beyond the layline, the more chance you have in a way because you both reach back and you don't really fall into his wind shadow. On the run, we probably didn't change to that smaller spinnaker early enough, but we had run so well in previous races with the medium one. The shift at the end robbed us of any chance on the last leg. One thing that annoyed me a bit about the America's Cup was that the committee in at least three of the races should have moved the windward mark, as they were allowed to, by fifteen degrees to compensate for the wind shifting after the start. They had time to do it within the sailing instructions, when we reached the wing mark. The wind had already shifted enough in that final race to make this necessary. It shifted more later. In that last race, with one better tactical move up that first leg we could have led around the first mark and I think we would have won.

"I'd like to have one more go for the America's Cup and, if I was invited again, with the Sir Frank Packer syndicate, with Alan Payne and basically the same sort of team as we had in 1970—the same as Bus Mosbacher did through the 1958 *Vim* crew, 1962 *Weatherly* crew, and 1967 *Intrepid* crew; all had the same sort of bones in crew structure.

This heavy block on an adjustable track takes the massive wire from the genoa sheets of *Gretel II*

"Sir Frank did all you could ask of a syndicate head and in Newport said to me the time had come when the boat was entirely in my control—choice of everything about it, I had all the say. Alan Payne was our leader through the whole campaign; he's a terrific guy and there were never any worries there.

"Martin Visser probably wanted to steer the boat, and I wanted to steer the boat; well, we finally resolved that and I'd want Martin to go again, as his experience is important and the advantages of Martin knowing the whole scene is worth a lot. You'd need a newcomer to have a lot of good points to overtake Martin Visser. I think this experience business is very important and for this reason I think to go with Martin and basically the same team is the right way to do it, although you'd need to bolster that team a bit here and there. To come with a new group and expect them to absorb all the various new experiences they have to face in Newport, plus win the Cup on top of that, is too much. We lost on the human beings, not the technology."

Jim has sympathy for the view that Australian yachtsmen should get more international competition but has some criticism of the lethargic attitude towards seeking out good competition at home:

"I don't think Australian yachtsmen travel around enough in their own country. I get quite disappointed when regattas are held in other areas of Australia and a lot of yachtsmen don't make the effort to go. Carl Ryves would have won a medal in Acapulco if he had towed his boat to Melbourne or Adelaide to sail in a series against unfamiliar faces. A lot of yachtsmen talk about getting the benefit of overseas experience and forget the local scene where, if they sailed on a lot of different venues in Australia, their adaptability to strange conditions would improve immeasurably. A common criticism is that we don't get enough light weather experience. It's there to be had, if you move around. This is what they do in Europe, but some of our top yachtsmen are a bit lethargic."

Gretel II trails *Intrepid* and both yachts are followed by an American tender. In the earlier races, *Intrepid* was faster reaching, but towards the end of the series *Gretel II* was as fast on all points of sailing

Who were the yachtsmen who had influenced Jim most in his career?

"Tony Manford for a start, for his terrific evenness of temperament which filters right through his sailing. This probably helps him keep the same crew together. One of his Dragon crew has been with him since Cadet Dinghies, in 1948.

"Rolly Tasker, when he puts his mind to it, is the most complete yachtsman I have ever sailed against.

"John Cuneo, for the immense amount of preparation he puts into sailing. He just could not help but do well. I would say that every hour he sails on the water would be backed by weeks of effort ashore. Unless you are well prepared, you just cannot beat the Cuneo machine, and I'm an admirer, not a critic.

"Colin Ryrie had extraordinary determination on the water. If the same sort of enthusiasm had gone right through his sailing, he would have been unbeatable. [Ryrie was killed in a speedboating accident in 1972.]

"Ron Jenyns is not unlike Cuneo, and a great Finn sailor. But I don't think he has the same overall yachting ability as Cuneo.

"Paul Elvstrom. I think the thing that impressed me most of all was his extraordinary clearness of mind. He knew what he should be doing in order to progress and did it.

"Craig Whitworth, another member of the Cuneo-Jenyns Queensland group, dedicated to preparation. It's more perseverance than flair with them.

"Carl Ryves, just the opposite, with the most natural flair for yachting.

"Martin Visser, tenacious, particularly on a starting line.

"There are others against whom I have not raced, but whose association has had a considerable influence on my career.

"Colin Haselgrove, South Australia's leading keelboat yachtsman for the last forty years. When my father was killed, Colin, a close personal friend of my father, was our next door neighbour at Seacliff and a director of our company. He took over as my yachting guide, philosopher, and friend. His continual encouragement has meant a great deal to me.

"Gordon Ingate, whom I must thank for introducing me to Twelve Metres. I find his insatiable enthusiasm for the sport of yachting quite infectious.

"Bill Northam, his absolute and astute management and drive for success has been most stimulating.

"Graham Drane, Victoria's dual Olympic Dragon skipper, exerts an unending mental pressure on his opposition. His self-examination of why he wins or loses a yacht race is absolutely ruthless.

"Trygve Halvorsen has a boundless wealth of seamanship and a relentless attention to detailed maintenance.

"And there is Bus Mosbacher. I keenly followed his Twelve Metre sailing from his first attempt with *Vim* in 1958 and I watched him in action at the helm of *Intrepid* in 1967. He is a very complete yachtsman but I think his real strength, which sets him apart from the pure technical

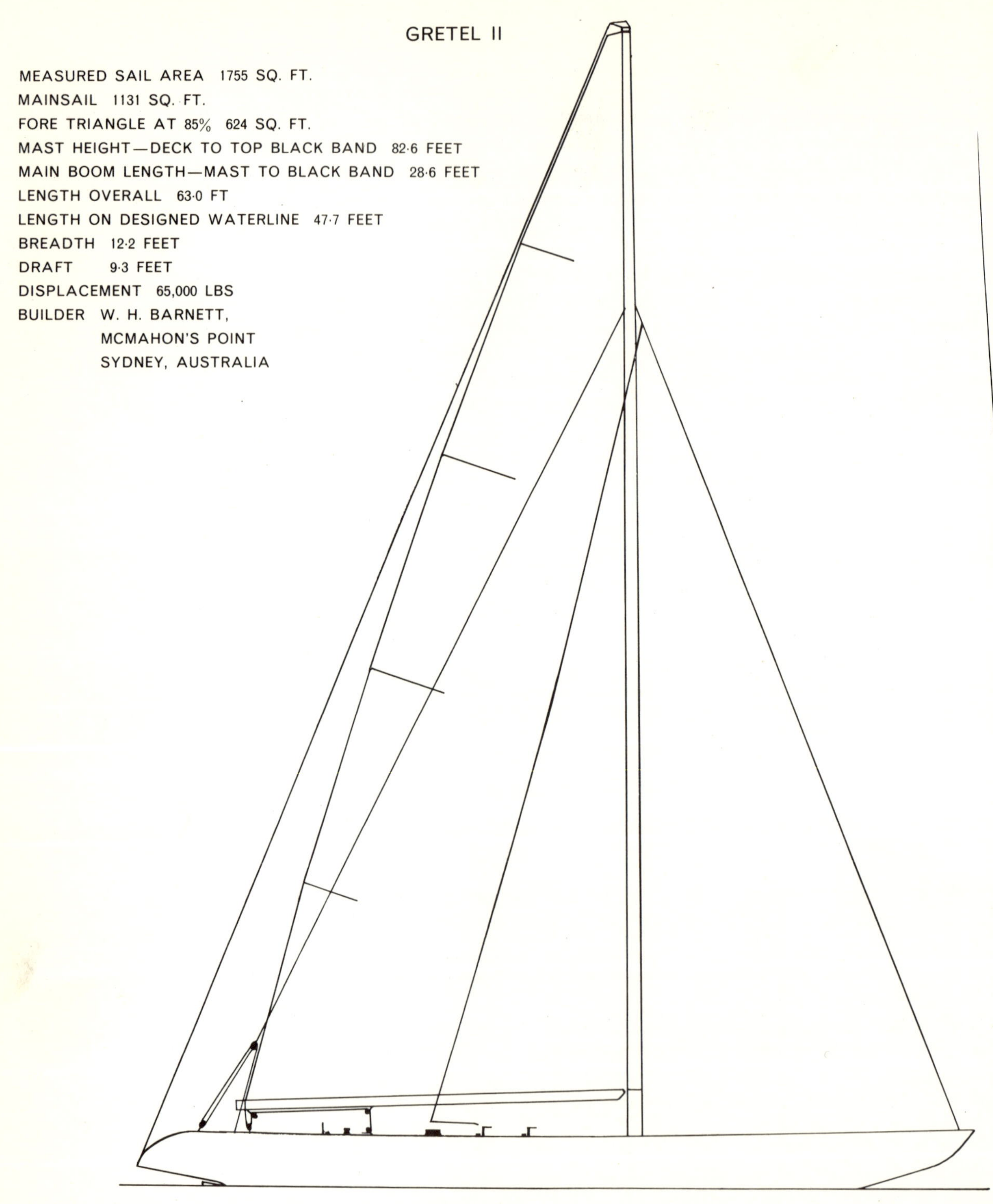
GRETEL II
MEASURED SAIL AREA 1755 SQ. FT.
MAINSAIL 1131 SQ. FT.
FORE TRIANGLE AT 85% 624 SQ. FT.
MAST HEIGHT—DECK TO TOP BLACK BAND 82·6 FEET
MAIN BOOM LENGTH—MAST TO BLACK BAND 28·6 FEET
LENGTH OVERALL 63·0 FT
LENGTH ON DESIGNED WATERLINE 47·7 FEET
BREADTH 12·2 FEET
DRAFT 9·3 FEET
DISPLACEMENT 65,000 LBS
BUILDER W. H. BARNETT,
MCMAHON'S POINT
SYDNEY, AUSTRALIA

wizards like Lowell North, is on the human side. He has the ability to get the best out of people.

"Peter Mander. I watched this New Zealander win a race in his gold medal winning series of the 1956 Melbourne Olympic Games in 12 Square Metre Sharpies. His singleness of purpose and ingenious originality of boat and gear made an everlasting impression at that time and also during the 1964 Olympics in Tokyo.

"The late Ossie O'Grady. The most sagacious yachtsman I have ever met."

But what of Jim Hardy himself?

"I see myself as a plodder. I have won some championships but I appreciate attributes I see in these other blokes that I don't always see in myself. I can beat the naturals if I have a bit of time to wear them down. Finally, through lack of attention to gear, the mast of the natural will fall out of the boat and you'll go by and win the race.

"I see the Twelve Metres as one of the best roles of my yachting career as it is so much a marathon thing. The mental attitude of Twelve Metre sailing is far more like rowing than sailing. I rowed at school, and we used to train every night for just one big race, the Head of the River. Training for the America's Cup is the same; it's a oncer, but you hope all the time you can have another crack at it if you fail."